QUIET RESISTANCE

QUIET RESISTANCE

LIVING WITH DISABILITY IN A
PALESTINIAN REFUGEE CAMP AND OTHER
TALES OF TENACITY

ALICE MERRILL

Matador
9 Priory Business Park,
Wistow Road, Kibworth Beauchamp,
Leicestershire. LE8 0RX
Tel: 0116 279 2299
Email: books@troubador.co.uk
Web: www.troubador.co.uk/matador
Twitter: @matadorbooks

ISBN 978 1788036 801

British Library Cataloguing in Publication Data.
A catalogue record for this book is available from the British Library.

Printed and bound in the UK by TJ International, Padstow, Cornwall
Typeset in 11pt Adobe Garamond Pro by Troubador Publishing Ltd, Leicester, UK

Matador is an imprint of Troubador Publishing Ltd

*To Sam
who believed I
could do anything.*

CONTENTS

INTRODUCTION

When I tell people I went to Palestine for three months to work in a refugee camp, one of the first questions I usually get asked is, "Did you go with an organisation?" Well no, I did not. I went independently, considered by some to be somewhat foolhardy, brave, mad or all three. To me it seemed perfectly reasonable as I know a number of people who have travelled around on their own having had a safe and enriching experience. Also, it was not my first time in Palestine so I knew what to expect from the Israeli authorities and IOF (Israeli Occupation Force) and I also knew how hospitable and friendly the Palestinians are, so I had no fears, only some apprehension about my ability to cope with living out of my comfort zone.

Perhaps some people thought I was too old to go off gallivanting to a 'dangerous' country, full of 'terrorists', when I should be content with my gardening and other homely pursuits. To me, this was my 'gap year', which did not exist when I was young, but now, recently retired from forty-four years of nursing I was ready to do what I really wanted to do.

Why did I want to go?

It started back in 2013 when I went on a Holy Land pilgrimage with a group from a local parish. To go to the Holy Land was a long-held ambition of mine and this opportunity presented itself as if it were meant to be. It was going to be a once-in-a-lifetime trip. Once before, in 2000, I had come close to achieving this dream, when I was doing a theological course at Sussex University and a trip was planned. I had managed to get the time off work and. my husband agreed to let me go but then it was cancelled due to the Second Intifada.

So, this was my chance. I am a widow, had enough money and my sons are independent. That pilgrimage was the start of my commitment to Palestine. My expectations were focused on the religious aspect – following in the footsteps of Jesus, but what changed me were not the dead stones of the many churches we prayed in but the 'living stones', the Palestinians who live their lives under the brutal Israeli occupation.

It is impossible, I would say, to visit the Holy Land and not be appalled by what you see and hear there. My first sight of 'the wall' was shocking. I knew about it, of course, but to stand beside it and look up at the sinister, grey watchtower looming above, knowing there were eyes watching our every move was incomprehensible to someone who takes freedom for granted.

That was the beginning of my education. When I returned, I knew I had to go back again but this time to do something useful. I searched the internet for opportunities and found JAI (Joint Advocacy Initiative) which is the umbrella organisation incorporating the YMCA, YWCA and the olive tree programme – Keep Hope Alive. They run ten-day programmes twice a year for olive-tree planting and olive picking for farmers who are particularly at risk of losing their land to Israel, combined with a full political programme.

The trip was so inspiring that I went again the same year for the olive harvest in October and again met like-minded people from all over the world, and gained invaluable knowledge and first-hand experience of life under occupation. My conviction that Palestine is suffering the greatest injustice in history, in which Britain has played and continues to play a leading role, was reinforced by each visit. My task was to disseminate the information when I got home, as that is where the work begins: to challenge other people's indifference and apathy, to bring the facts home, through one's own eye-witness accounts and increase the growing public movement for justice for Palestine.

There are many ways in which one can become an advocate and activist for Palestine. One important way is to lobby your local MP and MEP. Unfortunately, our present Conservative government is very pro-Israel and the majority of Conservative MPs are Friends of Israel. This country has very lucrative arms deals with Israel and strong ties with the US which bankrolls Israel with billions of dollars a year so it seems like a hopeless task, but giving up is not an option. A change of government or overwhelming public opinion could bring about very positive changes but it is people like us who are going to influence that change. At the annual mass lobby of Parliament for Palestine it was heartening to hear so many speakers from all parties express their concern, support and solidarity for Palestine and the actions they are taking to encourage more MPs to listen and judge for themselves how they can work for justice.

Very slowly the tide is turning. With the effect of the BDS (Boycott, Divestment, Sanctions) campaign that has seen the economy of Israel affected and its apartheid policies revealed, some progress has been made towards changing world opinion of Israel and recognising the State of Palestine. The Gaza assault in 2014 had a massive impact on world opinion but it has been quickly forgotten by most, and more than a year on the rebuilding programme has not been allowed to progress. Gazans are surviving in the ruins of their houses, water is scarce and predictions by world authorities state that it will be uninhabitable by 2020. Time is running out for the Palestinians. They will never give up their land and their belief in their Right to Return, but they need the help of the international community to bring pressure on their own governments.

After all my trips, I have written articles for the local parish magazine and given talks but since my three months in the refugee camp I find myself giving talks regularly to different groups through which I can spread the word and also raise some money to donate to the Olive Tree Campaign, MAP and Noor Women's Empowerment. The strongest message comes through eye-witness accounts which is why I am writing this account of my time in Al Azza camp. In my life books have had probably the greatest impact on me, in terms of understanding other people's lives. The written page is always my preferred medium so it seemed right that I should put pen to paper and attempt to tell my story of three months in Al Azza, caring for Echlas, the remarkable forty- three-year-old woman, disabled from birth, living an independent life under extreme conditions.

CHAPTER ONE

EARLY DAYS

20th January 2015

As the taxi slowed down to enter Al Azza refugee camp, I could sense the two young Moslem girls, my fellow passengers in the shared taxi, recoil in dismay at the grey concrete walls closing around us, blocking out the sunlight, seeing rubbish strewn around on the rough, pitted street, young children playing about amongst it. My thoughts were similar to what I guessed theirs were but I put on a brave, cheerful face, as if I was completely used to these surroundings, paid the driver and then I was on my own.

In time, I would feel at home here but that first impression has always stayed with me. The reaction of the two Palestinian girls I found surprising but later I learned that unless they lived in one, most Palestinians have not set foot in a refugee camp and have little idea of the conditions. After all, why would they visit a camp unless they had a reason to?

The houses do not have addresses as there are no street names or numbers so although Echlas had given me directions to find her house, in my confusion at finding myself in this alien environment I went towards a large four-storeyed building with a hardboard door but as I was working out how to get in a group of small boys surrounded me. They talked excitedly in Arabic, gesticulating towards the opposite alley.

"Echlas?" I said, assuming that everyone knew the whereabouts of their neighbours in this small community.

"Aiwa, Aiwa," they said and taking my case, led me to a green metal door which one of them firmly banged on. It was almost immediately opened by a young woman who spoke English, to my relief, and indeed was English, to my surprise. We thanked the boys as they stood looking in until we closed the door, no doubt interested to see another foreigner come to live in their camp.

Christina introduced herself and I immediately felt relaxed and relieved that there was another helper already here. My two Skype sessions with Echlas had led me to believe that she had no one looking after her at present but that one of her family would show me the ropes and I would be on my own until the next volunteer arrived. There had also been mention of a male helper. It transpired that Christina had answered an urgent appeal from Echlas and had come almost immediately as she was already in the country. It suited her as it gave her accommodation and food, and she had experience of caring when she nursed her father during his last months.

Following Christina into the gloomy interior, after the bright sunlight outside, I meet Echlas. She is sitting in a wheelchair, an electric fire next to her, a laptop in front of her on a table and I am not sure whether it is acceptable to give her a kiss or a hug but settle for a touch of her hand and a big smile. I tell her I am so pleased to see her and cannot quite believe I am really here; it has happened so fast since I first decided to come here for three months.

Christina fetches a plate and a fork and tells me to help myself from the large pot of food on the table. It is almost 4pm so I am not sure whether this is a late lunch or an early dinner but decide I should eat something as I have no idea when the next meal will be. Christina tells me it was cooked by a friend of Echlas' yesterday and she made enough for a dozen people so it will keep us going for the next few days. I am not overjoyed by this information, as inspecting the contents of the pot it does not look very appetising, being a mix of stodgy rice and vegetables, but actually tastes reasonable.

As I eat I am looking around and chatting to Christina at the same time. I notice she is wearing a pair of Mickey Mouse pyjama bottoms with black boots and a thick jumper. I wonder if this is home wear or if she goes out like this. I learn that she travels around as long as her money lasts and then goes back to England to earn some more to continue her nomadic way of life. She has just been in

Italy picking olives and then came to Palestine with no clear idea of what she could do here so the position with Echlas is giving her time to think out her plans. Her three-month visa runs out in March and she wants to see more of the West Bank and some of Israel before she leaves so I calculate we have about four weeks together. This makes me feel more comfortable knowing that Christina will be here to share the job of caring for Echlas until I have got used to being here.

The house is much larger than I had imagined. The room we are sitting in is the living room/dining room and all the other rooms lead off it. It is comfortably furnished with three couches and two armchairs, a coffee table and carpets on the tiled floors. On the painted walls are beautifully worked embroidery pictures, which I later learn are the work of Echlas' late Mother. There are two imposing black and white portraits of men in suits and *keffiyehs*, which on closer inspection are drawn, although they look like photographs. Echlas tells me they are her father and grandfather. The room seems gloomy despite the fluorescent strip lighting, common in all homes here, as there are no windows, apart from a long frosted one high up in the kitchen and a half-glazed door to the garden. Later on I realise why the house is built in this way; to keep the heat out in the summer and for security.

Echlas is a good-looking woman; thick black hair cut in a fringed bob, plump, freshcomplexioned face and a welcoming smile. I cannot completely ascertain her disabilities while she is sitting in the chair but I can see that she is able to feed herself with her left hand while her right hand seems to be immobile. Her English is fluent and I find it easy to understand. We talk about my journey, how my stay in Jerusalem was last night with Lauren, an American priest I met while olive picking last year, and about the plan for the rest of the day and who is coming for lessons.

Christina takes me to my room at the end of a wide corridor. There is a narrow single bed against one wall, a pile of Bedouin mattresses on the floor against another wall, a huge wardrobe, a small formica-topped table and a small armchair. It all looks worn and shabby and the carpet looks none too clean but at least I have my own room for now. Christina sleeps with Echlas at present but I wonder when it will be my turn and if Christina and I will share this room. I had seen another room next to Echlas' and just caught a glimpse of a comfortable-looking double bed and a window looking out onto the garden and wondered who that was for.

During the evening, various people come and go for Arabic language lessons with Echlas. She has a lesson room next to the kitchen so we move her and two heaters in there, answer the door, make tea, chat with the students, then huddle around the remaining electric heater. There is a trail of cables and extension leads for the various heaters and it all looks very unsafe but as I quickly learn there is no concept of health and safety here, a liberating but slightly unnerving situation until I get used to assessing the risk for myself.

The first two girls who arrive are having a lesson together as they are friends. They are German: one works for Joint Advocacy Initiative and the other cares for the daughter of a Dutch woman and her Palestinian husband who own a café in Beit Sahour, where a lot of internationals hang out. It is so interesting talking to them and finding out what they do and finding common links from when I was here before. I had been to the Singer Café and met Crystal and hope to have time this trip to visit again. Two young men arrive next. They also have a joint lesson. They are due to leave soon but have progressed very well in their Arabic. One is Scottish and the other Belgian and have both been working on an NGO research project and living in a flat with some other internationals in Beit Sahour. The last student is a thirty something Swedish man working at the newly established Natural History Museum of Bethlehem.

In the middle of all these comings and goings, Echlas' nephew from Hebron turns up. I was not aware that we were expecting him but Christina explains that he is here for some peace and quiet to do some studying for an exam he has tomorrow as it is too noisy in his own home. He will be staying in the garden room tonight and leaving early in the morning to go to Ramallah to take the exam. He is a very jolly, friendly young man, shakes hands with us and makes himself at home, making tea for us all then unloading some presents for Echlas – 200 cigarettes, chocolates and biscuits – and then buries his nose in his smartphone. There are hugs and laughter and chat between him and Echlas; he is obviously very fond of her and then he shuts himself up in the bedroom to work.

Echlas is now ready for bed so under Christina's instructions I do what I am told and we lift her into bed, undress her, give her a bedpan, then position her using the draw sheet to pull her up or to the side or down a bit until she is comfortable. Her accoutrements follow: her table, computer, ashtray, cigarettes and phone, all positioned so she can reach them. The last thing is to warm up her wheat bags in the temperamental microwave, and place them on her constantly cold legs.

It is now 10.30p.m. and I am thinking about my bed but I know Echlas sleeps late so feel I cannot just go off and leave Christina lying on her bed playing on her phone. I go and get a plastic garden chair and my iPad, book and diary to keep me occupied while Echlas is absorbed in her laptop. Frequently I get up and light a cigarette for Echlas and I wonder how Christina copes with this smoking, especially sleeping in the same room, but she smokes as well so perhaps it does not affect her. The wheat bags need heating up again, there are drinks and snacks to fetch from the kitchen and the time goes quickly; before I realise, it is midnight.

"Do you mind if I go to bed?" I ask, my eyes drooping with fatigue.

"No, of course not," reply Echlas and Christina looking up from their screens, and off I go to the sanctuary of my own space after a long and bewildering day.

Before I go to sleep I write in my diary, "not sure how I am going to cope with this. I am so out of my comfort zone. All the things I take for granted – a comfortable bed, warmth, a bedside light, a shower, toilet seat, dishwasher, kettle – are not available. But today is only the first day; I must give it time. From what I have heard so far, most people are reluctant to go home when the time comes. I am aware of the smell of smoke on my clothes and in my hair but I am too tired to grapple with the peculiarities of the bathroom tonight. I slide down onto the bumpy mattress, cover myself with the assortment of blankets and quilts necessary to keep warm and drift off into a deep sleep.

It's 5am when I am awoken by the call to prayer. The mosque is at the entrance to the camp but it sounds at this moment as if it is just outside my window. I listen to the unfamiliar Arabic words meaning nothing to me except "Alluha *Akbar*" which I remember from living in Saudi Arabia many years ago. The memories of that time come flooding into my mind as I listen to the immam, but that was a very different, oppressive and restrictive culture that was both a good and bad experience but one I am glad to have had. Unfortunately, it gave me a warped sense of Islam but since visiting Palestine my view has changed and I have come to respect and admire the religion.

The house is quiet so I drift off again but then another sound startles me awake. It is the sound of someone shouting at intervals, just one word, but very loud, and I learn later that it is the bread man who is trundling his wares around the camp on an ancient wooden cart, announcing his presence. At this moment I wish he was somewhere else but gradually his voice gets fainter as he completes his rounds in the camp and moves on to disturb some other late sleepers.

It is 9.45am and I am sitting on my bed wearing a cashmere jumper, a vest, a hoody, a fleece gilet and I still feel cold. From what I can see of the outside it looks sunny so may be warmer outside but the key to the back door is in Echlas' room and so is the lighter for the gas ring so I cannot even make a cup of tea. I wonder what time they will wake up? I make a shopping list: – lighter, kettle (we are using a broke-handled saucepan) and chocolate. This is definitely a time for comfort food.

I hear the sound of a door opening. "At last", I think, "they are awake". I go and help Christina with the bedpan and take note of how she puts Echlas on it. There is so much to learn and Echlas has so much patience but I suppose she is used to constantly reminding her helpers and teaching them as they are mostly here for only three months, the maximum time for an Israeli visa.

Echlas' room is next to the front door so the window looks out onto the narrow alley which divides her house from her neighbours'. The window is high up and the only way to look out is to stand on the bed but at least it is a source of light and air and gossip. On the wall adjacent there is a larger window behind the two beds but this looks out on a concrete wall. Apart from the beds there is a wardrobe and a shelf unit where Echlas' clothes and personal items are kept with some space for towels and bed linen and the volunteers' things. The room has been decorated by volunteers in the past and shows an imaginative and skilful hand with its frieze of grape vines around the door and windows. Above the volunteers' bed there is a tree painted on the wall adorned with cut-outs of people. These are Echlas' volunteers through the years whom she has drawn and coloured, bringing out the characteristics which, for her, defines them. Echlas remembers them all: their names, the year they were with her and what they were like.

On the floor between the two beds is a defunct electric blanket which serves as a mat so the volunteer avoids the shock of standing on a cold tiled floor in the middle of the night. I wonder why there is not a carpet on the floor as in the lounge but then realise that the bed has to be moved frequently to accommodate the wheelchair so it would not be practical.

After several cigarettes and a few tiny cups of strong Arabic coffee, Echlas is ready to face the day so we prepare her for going out. This is quite a lengthy process involving dressing her bottom half in pants and trousers and socks, then lifting her out into the electric wheelchair, adjusting her to a comfortable position, fastening the safety strap, dressing her top half, adding side cushions, foot blocks, a table, and finally washing her face and hands and helping her to clean her teeth.

It is a finely tuned process and when one is familiar with it can be carried out smoothly and efficiently but with a novice like me assisting it seems to take a long time.

We quickly get ourselves ready while Echlas smokes another cig and then we are outside and it feels so good to be in the fresh air and see the blue sky. I am excited at the prospect of seeing the camp again after the hazy impression I got on my arrival, and going into the town of Bethlehem, seeing some familiar places. Echlas is able to manipulate her electric wheelchair with her right hand but Christina walks alongside with her hand on Echlas' elbow to give her more power. The traffic seems pretty crazy to me with a lot of horn blowing and a distinct lack of a highway code but I rationalise that a wheelchair commands respect and consideration in any country, so step out with confidence.

Negotiating the potholes and irregularities of the camp road we arrive at a busy junction, where it is my job to stop the traffic to allow Echlas and Christina to cross. As the cars are slowing for the traffic lights the first half of the road is easy but the second half has faster traffic coming from two directions, so I hesitantly put a hand up and to my relief the oncoming car slows to let us across. Echlas has to travel in the road as the kerbs are too high for a wheelchair to get up and there is a certain amount of tooting but it seems to be more out of habit than aggression. We go uphill past Bethlehem University, which I remember visiting on my first visit to Palestine. It is a Catholic university, founded by the De La Salle brothers, and takes both Christians and Moslems. Since the Christian population is declining, 70% of students are Moslems and many of them girls. I was very impressed by the ethos of the university, particularly their *sumad* (steadfastness) in the Second Intifada when Israeli troops shot at the buildings and killed students, and their refusal to give up even when Israel closed them down. The tutors continued their classes underground and the students were determined that they would get their qualifications, despite the risk they ran by disobeying the Israeli authorities. One very moving story concerns a girl from Gaza who was suddenly prevented from travelling to Bethlehem by the IOF but the university arranged for her to continue her studies by correspondence. Eventually she achieved her degree and the Vice Chancellor travelled to Gaza where a special graduation ceremony was arranged just for her. The university calls itself a 'Beacon of Hope' and it certainly felt a very positive, joyful place when I visited. I am pleased that I am so near Bethlehem University. The thought is irrational but it makes me feel anchored to be so close to an establishment that I have so much respect for. Perhaps it is because I am a Catholic that I feel such an affinity to it.

The wheelchair struggles slowly up the hill but then we reach the summit and it is downhill at some speed until we hit the shops. There is so much to look at, so many people and such traffic that I find it takes all my concentration to keep up with Echlas and Christina. The small streets have cars parked on either side; there are no restrictions so it is a free for all. The wheelchair makes slow progress through the pedestrians and cars which all take ownership of the road, giving me some time to take in my surroundings. At the start of the *souk* the shouts of the vendors compete with each other, all offering bargains; some have even recorded their message and it plays repeatedly over a loudspeaker. The smell of fresh herbs and vegetables mingles with the appetising aroma of cooking falafel and the strong coffee sold by the street vendors from large brass coffee pots. Most of the vendors are men except for the elderly women sitting on the ground with their piles of home-grown produce in front of them which they bring in from the nearby villages to sell. They are dressed in the traditional embroidered long black dresses of Palestine, their brown faces weathered and wrinkled by time and the hot sun. Echlas buys from them whenever possible as she knows this is Palestinian food and not Israeli. Next to them tables are piled high with mountains of luscious strawberries – no plastic punnets here. They are scooped into a bag and weighed, which unfortunately does mean they can be a little squashed by the time they get home. Gaza is famous for its strawberry crop but since the Israelis stopped exports from Gaza these are likely to be from land stolen from Palestine. Bright, shiny red and yellow peppers, huge green cabbages and giant cauliflowers, bunches of unidentifiable leafy greens, purple aubergines, oranges, lemons, garlic, onions, potatoes, – *souk* shopping is a leisurely affair with pleasantries being exchanged over the vegetables and careful selection of the choicest items being made by the women to take home and cook for their families. The meat is sold in another part of the market, thankfully, as whole carcasses of fly covered animals is not a pleasant sight. Meat is relatively expensive here, although chickens are plentiful and cheaper, but the dietary staples seem to be rice, *freekeh*, bread, vegetables, eggs, *maftoul*, yogurt and spices. Echlas is a vegetarian so I am hoping to learn how to cook Palestinian vegetarian meals. We pass a man selling fish and I stop and look but cannot identify any of it. Echlas does eat fish sometimes and she said we will have it one day but his fish is expensive, being fresh.

We come to a shop selling all sorts of homewares where Echlas stops to look so I go inside and buy a kettle – my first purchase here in Bethlehem. I hope that Echlas is not offended but really that saucepan is dangerous and this kettle has a whistle so we will not waste gas. The road through the *souk* goes downhill and gets very rough underfoot. Echlas turns her wheelchair around so it is going backwards as she feels safer doing this. Once we are on even ground again she turns around. I would love to linger here and explore the *souk* but I am sure there will be opportunities when I am on my own. Now we have to get down to Manger Square to meet Echlas' relative for lunch. This is familiar territory for me and I half expect to bump into someone I know from my previous visits. Echlas' cousin is already sitting at a table outside the Peace restaurant so we join her and she and Echlas chatter away in Arabic while I people watch and Christina studies her iPhone. It is relaxing sitting here in the sun, feeling hot on my face, in January. We order some food and drinks. I have a burger, not something I would normally have and not what I had anticipated eating in Palestine, but it is a familiar item on the menu and I am so hungry. A large lorry pulls up right in front of our table, belching out exhaust fumes, so I glare at the driver and his mate and they turn the engine off. They both get out and start taking down the Christmas decorations which still adorn the square, and putting them in the lorry. Then I hear a Liverpudlian accent. "I recognise that accent," I say to one of the men. He stops and we start chatting. He tells us he works for a UK company called The Christmas Decorators and they work all over the world. He has been to footballers' homes and celebrities' homes, including Steven Spielberg's, but he said Bethlehem was the most friendly and hospitable place he has been and they had the best time here. His mates are busy dismantling the enormous Christmas tree in the square and it is interesting to see that it is made from a metal cone-shaped frame and covered with Astroturf-type material. I had imagined that the tree in Manger Square would be a typical fir tree but they are not native to Palestine, although the Israelis have introduced them onto the land to obliterate traces of razed Palestinian villages to deny their very existence. I wondered about the expense of employing a foreign company and why the Palestinians, who are so resourceful and innovative, could not do this themselves.

As the sun disappears behind the buildings in the square the temperature drops and it is time to move. We say goodbye to the cousin and take the easier route home along Star Street. It is less steep for the wheelchair and there is less traffic, most of the time. The aptly named Star Street (it is decorated with stars suspended from wires crossing the narrow street) winds its way up through the old, picturesque three-storey houses but most of the shops are shuttered and it is impossible to tell whether they are just closed for the winter or whether it is a permanent closure. I guess the second, unfortunately, as it seems unlikely that many tourists would venture this far off the main street through the *souk*. This is the road taken by the Patriarch when he comes from Jerusalem to the Church of the Nativity at Easter. Then it is thronged with crowds of people, noise and music but now all we see are a few locals and fewer cars. Business in the West Bank has suffered greatly for years since tourists are put off visiting by the deliberately generated perception from Israel that it is a dangerous place to visit. Nothing could be further from the truth. Those tourists who do come are mainly in organised groups and are herded about by their guides into the shops chosen by them. They are taken to the Church of the Nativity, maybe the Milk Grotto and the Shepherds' Fields in Beit Sahour and then whisked back to their Israeli hotels in Jerusalem.

It is a fairly long walk home but it is all new to me, this route, so I am taking mental notes in order to remember the way when I am out on my own. We take a different path into the camp, up a very steep, rough slope where the chair stops and shudders in protest so we give it a push and it just makes it to the top. The alleyways this side are so narrow there is just room for the wheelchair to pass through. Children of varying ages are playing in the alleys, running about playing 'it', a small group of boys are playing marbles, some girls playing hand-clapping games, just as we used to at school. They smile at us and say "*Marhaban*, what is your name?" They all know Echlas and are endlessly fascinated by her wheelchair, especially the boys who seem to have an innate affinity to anything with wheels.

The front door is difficult. Three turns to the right with the key opens one half, then large bolts to the top and bottom open the other half to enable the wheelchair to get in. The bottom bolt is so stiff I cannot budge it but Christina manages. The top bolt is wedged with a piece of card when we close it again and the bottom bolt needs a few vigorous kicks with the heel of a boot to close it. I make a mental note to source some WD40. Echlas has got cold on the way back as her body is immobile, so I immediately put her wheat bags in the microwave to warm up. Christina puts the new kettle on and we are all delighted by the whistle and the speed with which the water boils. Ashtray, cigarettes and lighter are retrieved from Christina's bag and the heaters turned on to warm Echlas up.

Echlas has been in the wheelchair for a long time today so she is more than ready for a change of position and probably needs to use the bedpan so we prepare her room to get the wheelchair in on the wall side of her bed, ready for transfer. There is a definite routine for this and Christina guides the process as she firstly removes the table, then the side pad, the back cushion and lastly the safety belt. She takes up position behind the chair and grasps Echlas' trousers at the waistband, while I move the foot rest out of the way and securely place my arms under her thighs and on the count of three lift her out of the chair and onto the bed. Echlas is not a big woman – she weighs about 8st, I would think – but she is a dead weight so I fear for our backs. This type of manual handling is absolutely contrary to the latest NHS guidelines although when I started nursing we did a lot of lifting of patients as it was the norm, the legacy of which was nurses with 'bad backs'. Luckily I was not one of them and having nursed pilgrims on the way to Lourdes in the train, under very difficult circumstances, I was used to improvising and taking calculated risks.

Having safely got Echlas onto the bed we undress her, leaving her T-shirt on, and give her a bedpan. It surprises me how long she can go without having a pee but one of her strategies is to take her diuretic in the early evening rather than in the morning as most people would. That done, we sit her up, put the back rest up and once she is adjusted in the bed, which can involve a lot of pulling in various directions with the drawer sheet to get her balanced right, we cover her up, put her bed table in place, her box with the mouse mat, her PC, ashtray, phone, pillow behind her back and wheat bags on the legs. She is now set for the evening. I enjoy driving her chair down the corridor but it is not easy to manoeuvre in a confined space so it can shoot off at top speed and crash into furniture unless one is very gentle with the controls, as I learn on that first attempt. Having safely got the chair into position I plug it into the charger for the next day's outing.

Christina and I tidy up, putting clothes in the wash or back in the wardrobe for another day and put the room to rights. Now we can relax for a while but I really need a shower, so gathering up my toiletries and towel I venture into the cold bathroom. The hot water comes from an immersion boiler on the wall, which has to be switched on about half an hour in advance. In the bathroom, more of a wet room really, there is a toilet without a seat, a shower, a sink which looks unused as there is another one outside the bathroom where we wash our hands, and a large, bed-like piece of furniture covered in blue plastic. Christina told me to use the bucket for a shower as the water comes out of the showerhead so slowly and feebly as to be totally ineffective, so I fill the bucket with water and pour it over my shivering body with a small cup. It is wonderful to feel the warm water as it cascades over my head washing the smell of smoke away, at least temporarily. Feeling clean, refreshed and warmer lifts my mood and although it is too soon to say I feel settled, I feel more optimistic. The most difficult thing to cope with is the uncertainty, not knowing what to expect from day to day. I seem to be bumbling along in the dark, groping my way through the day, just following others and unable to make my own decisions about anything, even what I will eat. Many people must have this experience in life on a much greater scale I tell myself, so I can cope with this and it will get better. This period of adjustment is bound to be unsettling but once I know the daily routine, I can anticipate and plan. Fortunately, at this stage I did not know that there was no daily routine and planning with Echlas was always subject to last-minute changes.

Today is Friday, both a Moslem and Jewish holy day, so not a good day to go to Jerusalem, something I will bear in mind for the future should I ever go there. I know Echlas cannot go there as Palestinians can only enter the holy city with a permit granted by the Israeli authorities. Bethlehem and Jerusalem are only 7km apart, twenty minutes by car, but most children here have never been to Al-Quds (the Arabic name) and the adults twenty or more years ago, if ever. Permits are granted to those who work in Jerusalem and for the holy days but the Israeli tactic is to grant a permit to only one member of a family, knowing they will not go on their own to celebrate.

Last night I took my hot water bottle to bed but I was still cold and kept waking up. At 7am I got up and refilled it and slept again until 9am. It is a slow start today. Now I have my own lighter I make tea and have some pitta bread with butter, which I bought as I love the butter here, and a banana. When Echlas wakes up she has grapefruit juice with a few cigarettes, then a sliced banana and coffee with more cigarettes. I have learned how to make Arabic coffee. We have three sizes of pot so if it is just for Echlas I choose the smallest, nearly filling it with cold water, heating it until small bubbles appear, then add one rounded dessertspoonful of coffee and stir gently until it comes to the boil. This takes judgement and swift reactions. The coffee must boil three times without boiling over, which makes an awful mess of the cooker. Removing the pot at the right moment is key. Coffee made, I cover the pot with a saucer and take it into Echlas on a tray with one of her plastic cups. Ordinary cups or glasses are too heavy for Echlas to hold so she has disposable plastic cups, filled to halfway. The smell of the coffee is so enticing but it looks so dark and bitter.

Echlas is staying in bed as she has a couple of Skype lessons to do so we will get her out later. I see on my iPad that the King of Saudi Arabia has died. I wonder what that will mean for the Kingdom. When I lived there, there was much speculation as to the turmoil that may ensue after his death – civil unrest, divisions within the family etc – but we shall see. I now have a SIM card, though no phone to put it in but I think Echlas mentioned that she would be getting a new phone so I can have her old one. Again, we shall see.

The cleaning lady (CL) arrives, a short, dumpy lady in a black *thoub* and *hijab* which she promptly removes on entering the house, revealing her very ordinary trousers and jumper underneath. I make more coffee and she and Echlas sit and chat for a while. I had expressed my interest in the garden to Echlas and suggested I might tidy it up and also sow some seeds that I had brought with me as a present. There had not been any time for that so far so Echlas sends the CL out into the garden to sweep the leaves. The garden is a small enclosed space with a large lemon tree casting much of it in shade, some vigorous looking pelargoniums and a couple of other shrubby type plants which I could not identify. There are plenty of weeds in the poor looking soil and leaves on the tiled areas, but with some TLC it could look quite attractive and it is somewhere to be outside when the sun is out.

I am washing up in the kitchen when I hear a shriek from the garden. I hurry out there to find the CL sitting on the ground cradling her left arm and crying in pain. Christina and I struggle to get her up on her feet and help her into Echlas' room to sit down and try to ascertain what has happened. It seems she slipped on the mud on the small slope going down from the terrace and fell on her arm which is now extremely painful, apparent even without translation. I attempt to examine it. She can move her fingers but her wrist is excruciatingly painful to touch. I persuade her to take two paracetamol while Christina looks for a crepe bandage and something cold from the freezer to apply to it. As Christina gently lays a bag of ice cubes onto the wrist the CL cries out in pain so Echlas decides she will have to go to the hospital. She phones Mohammed, her regular taxi driver, explaining what has happened. I ask if one of us should go with her, anticipating an interesting visit to the local DGH (District General Hospital), but Echlas says no need as her son will meet her there. The CL phones her son to arrange this and then the taxi arrives. I feel guilty, because if I had not mentioned the garden she would not have been out there to slip over. Echlas reassures me by pointing out that her shoes were to blame, being old and worn, which makes me feel worse thinking how little money she has and now she is going to be out of action for a good six weeks if the wrist is broken.

I had no idea that my nursing skills would so quickly be put to the test after my retirement but as long as I face nothing more challenging I can cope.

Now that we no longer have to stay in for the CL Echlas decides we should go out for a walk so we get her up, the reverse of the 'putting her to bed routine' but washing her hands and face and cleaning her teeth as well. Christina wants some time on her own to Skype some friends so Echlas and I go out on our own. This is good for both of us, to get used to each other. We go to a quieter, more affluent part of Bethlehem, across the road from the camp. The streets are wide and there are large detached houses with gardens and trees. It is pleasant to be out of the grey, claustrophobic walls of the camp and be able to see across to the hills. It would be a lovely view were it not for the ugly blot on the landscape which is the Israeli settlement of Har Homa. How Palestinians can see that every day and not seethe with anger I do not know. Perhaps they do but just do not show it. We pass a children's playground where families are enjoying the feeling of freedom out in the open space. It is a landscaped area on a slope with swings and roundabouts for the children and grassy banks and flat terraces to play football or sit and have a barbecue. There are so few open spaces like this so it can get crowded and it is not always as peaceful as it is today as the soldiers have been known to tear gas it.

We go as far as we can, then the road peters out into a track so Echlas can go no further but she tells me to go on a bit along the track to get a better view of the settlement. I walk further on between tall grasses and wild flowers, where butterflies flutter, and would rather not see the settlement at all but there it is, impossible to ignore, gleaming white, like a fortress on top of the opposite hill, a huge, forbidding township, so near I could walk across to it, built on Palestinian land. I feel such outrage that this can be allowed to happen and nothing is being done to stop it. It makes me feel angry, sad, despairing. I want to do something to stop this, to make this vile ugliness disappear. It is heartbreaking but sentiment will not help. I resolve to continue working for Palestinian freedom and whatever discomforts I may suffer can be nothing compared to what Palestinians suffer every day.

On our way back Echlas wants to stop for a cigarette but also insists I must be able to sit down so we find a suitable wall for me to perch on. As Echlas smokes she tells me about the house behind us. It is modern and built in an unconventional style with a high blank wall facing the road and an electronic gate at the entrance to the drive curving out of sight so there is no glimpse of the interior. It does look mysterious and Echlas thinks it looks like a castle. A car approaches and the gate goes up and we watch in surprise as the car speeds away up the drive.

Echlas and I look at each other.

"I have never seen anyone go in or out," says Echlas. "This is the first time. Did you see who was in the car?"

"It was a woman, but I only got a glimpse of her."

We speculate about who she is. I reckon she is an Israeli spy, infiltrating the local community. Echlas thinks she is an agent of the Palestinian Authority and perhaps this is a 'safe house'.

We hear the car again. The gate goes up and out it comes. It stops and the driver winds down the window. Perhaps she is going to ask us to move from the garden wall where I am perching so I get up prepared to move away.

"Hello," she says, "can I help you?" in perfect English which is odd since Echlas is Palestinian but perhaps she thinks we are both foreigners.

Echlas answers, "No, we are just having a rest on our walk."

The woman is very polite and with a wave of her arm replies, "Please, do go in and sit down, you are most welcome. And enjoy your walk." And then she is gone.

We look at each other in surprise.

"Why did she speak in English?" is my first question.

"She probably thinks I am foreign. It happens quite a lot when I am with volunteers and then I surprise them by speaking in Arabic, but I do not want her to know I am Palestinian," says Echlas.

"But why? She seemed very nice and why does it matter?"

"We don't know who she is and it is better she thinks I am foreign."

I do not pursue this as I instinctively know that I have a lot to learn about this country and the people, and I accept that Echlas has her reasons. It could be that she feels guilty about smoking in the street as this is not something that Palestinian women do.

I can see Christina walking towards us so we go to meet her and tell her about the mysterious woman but I can see Christina is not impressed. We walk back past the camp and continue on through a busy Bethlehem – Hebron road and down a hill and then up to the outskirts of Beit Jala, a small town to the north of Bethlehem. This is where the pizza restaurant is and although it is only 5pm I am really hungry and ready to eat almost anything.

Christina goes inside and brings a man out with her who lifts a heavy concrete block from the pavement and places it against the kerb so that Echlas can drive up into the restaurant. There are few places she can go as Palestine does not cater for wheelchairs but she knows the accessible places and the owners get to know her and go out of their way to help her.

He also gets an electric heater which he places on the table in front of her as she has got very cold again. I can see the pizza oven from my seat so I know they are freshly made as is the orange juice that I drink. We are the only people in the restaurant, perhaps because it is early, but I have the feeling that it is never busy and wonder how it manages to keep going. We notice the clever use of old video cases, used like bricks to make walls, and the decorative paper sculptures hanging from the ceiling.

The man who cooks the pizza is the owner and this is all his work so we congratulate him. He brings an extra paper napkin holder so that Echlas can have her plate on this, making it high enough for her to eat from. We fold the pizza so that Echlas can hold it in her good hand. It is delicious and we eat it all. The restaurant is warm and cosy but finally we have to face the cold walk home. It is now windy as well as dark so even more risky on the roads but we make it home and I surprise myself by thinking of it as 'home'. As soon as we enter the scruffy, narrow streets of the camp and see some familiar faces amongst the children, I know I am home.

Echlas says I can go out in the morning as she and Christina will sleep late and then she will have a shower for which her niece will be here as it is a major undertaking. It is too short notice to make plans with Susan and Michaela, friends who are in Jerusalem and Bethlehem, but I will use the time to take a walk to the *souk* and buy a few food items that Echlas does not provide. I eventually go off to my lumpy bed when I think I have sat on the plastic chair in Echlas' room long enough.

Today is Saturday. I go out quietly at 9am, confident I know my bearings well enough now to get down to Manger Square and back. It is liberating to be out on my own. I cross the busy road opposite the camp, walk up John Paul ll Street, past the university and down to the *souk*. It is full of life with vendors shouting their wares, displays of brightly coloured produce, families with children, young men, beautiful girls, some with *hijabs*, others dressed up in high heels and full make-up, in fact a typical Saturday morning almost anywhere in the world. I am dazzled by the array of clothes, scarves, bedding, household goods hanging up outside shops and spilling out onto the pavement. There is a tiny shop selling just spices. I stop to look and breathe in the wonderful aroma emanating from the different coloured heaps in their huge metal drums. The smell of freshly ground coffee is enticing but I cannot see any cafés around here. Boys pushing shopping trolleys piled high with goods weave in and out of the pedestrians, bringing in more to sell, probably working for their fathers. Street vendors sell freshly cooked sweetcorn, a popular snack here, and another sells yellow beans, steaming and pungent.

Some people call out "Welcome!" as I pass and I smile at their friendliness but later cynically realise they are probably trying to entice me into their shop. I do not see any other 'foreigners' here so I must stand out with my light hair. It surprises me that Palestinians are so welcoming to British people considering our shameful colonial history, the Balfour Declaration which gave away half of Palestine to the Jewish people and our continuing complicity with the US and Israel to deny the State of Palestine. The people I have met on my previous visits were all politically aware and fully conversant with their history which is so much part of their present. Perhaps this makes them more tolerant, being so knowledgeable and therefore without bigotry. They also have little media influence as far as I can see, having seen newspapers only in Jerusalem.

I am quicker on my own despite lingering to take in the sights and sounds of the *souk* and reach Manger Square earlier than anticipated. I decide to take a taxi down to Beit Sahour and visit Singer Café.

Beit Sahour is a small town to the south of Bethlehem and, together with Beit Jala, has the largest Christian population in the West Bank. I had stayed here twice previously in a hotel when I was olive-tree planting and olive picking, and felt an affection for the place. I am not absolutely sure where Singer Café is but hope I will recognise some landmarks when we get to Beit Sahour. There is never a shortage of taxis in Manger Square so I approach the first one, asking before I get in how much. He says twenty shekels and also says he knows where the Singer is but as we get to the town centre it is apparent he has no idea of its whereabouts as he begins asking passers-by. Between us we eventually find it in a side street just off the main road and I take note of its location for future reference.

Singer Café is a hang-out place for both Palestinians and internationals. It is unique in its style and function in this area although there are similar meeting places in Jerusalem and probably Ramallah. It is owned by a Palestinian and his Dutch wife Crystal who I had heard so much about on my first trip but did not actually meet as she was pregnant and so out of action as far as olive-tree planting was concerned. I did meet her at the olive picking as she was with us for much of the time, along with her very sweet and adaptable baby, Louise.

I go up the steep stone steps where old Singer sewing machines decorate the wall niches and into the intimate space of the café. There is no one here I recognise but the bar keeper greets me warmly and I order an Americano and a cookie as I missed breakfast. There is a smoking and a non-smoking area which is strange for me to see but so many Palestinians smoke and who can blame them when their life expectancy is so unknown. They could be shot tomorrow. There are books to borrow and notices about cultural events and walks. I see another example of imaginative upcycling in the toilet: two old wooden tennis rackets have been made into mirrors. I sit and cannot help hearing a conversation between three internationals sitting at the next table. They are talking about the hotel business and one hotel in particular that has great potential but needs upgrading. I am intrigued by this as my perception of Bethlehem, from what I have been told, is that tourists are not staying here. They are being brought in on day trips by their Israeli guides from Jerusalem where they stay in Israeli hotels but I have seen coaches outside some of the big hotels in Bethlehem so the information is contradictory, especially in light of what I am now overhearing. I would love to join in and ask them what the truth of the situation is but that would be too cheeky!

If I leave now I will have time to walk back, although it is all uphill, but I enjoy walking and want to take every opportunity to absorb my surroundings. I come to a supermarket. We would call it a mini mart but in Palestine there are no huge superstores, which makes the shopping experience more personal and less stressful. I have a list of items that I would like but would not dream of asking Echlas to buy. She provides the basic food and any 'fancy' European type of food I will buy. I find cheese spread, hummus, jam and yogurt and then put a packet of pitta bread in the basket as I cannot resist its soft, just-baked appearance and aroma, not like the cardboard slabs we get at home. As I queue at the checkout I look round and see a familiar face. It is Jawal from JAI, one of the organisers for the programme. I greet him like a long-lost friend but he looks alarmed, taking a moment to work out who this over-effusive foreigner is but then recognises me. I explain what I am doing in Bethlehem and he invites me to come and visit the programme in February with the information that they will not be staying in the Sahara hotel this time but the Golden Park.

I am disproportionally delighted to have seen Jawal and the phrase 'it's a small world', clichéd as it is, jumps into my mind. Buoyed up by that chance meeting, I climb up the hill with my shopping, refusing all offers from passing taxi drivers who obviously have never experienced the delights of walking uphill while avoiding the many hazards of speeding cars and lack of pavements and cannot understand why foreigners would want to do this.

Arriving hot and a little sweaty back at the camp I find Christina and Layan preparing for the bath/shower. I help to lift Echlas into the manual wheelchair and wheel her to the bathroom where we just manage to position the chair between the toilet and the 'bed'. Layan takes Echlas from the top and Christina the legs, and they lift her onto the bed while I take the chair away and park it outside. We undress her and then Layan takes over. In all my forty-four years of nursing I have never seen anyone bathed so thoroughly. Christina sprays the water on Echlas' body while Layan uses a scrubby and shower gel to scrub every inch of her until I think her skin will peel off. Echlas loves it, giggling when her navel is scoured and chatting away to Layan in Arabic. Christina continually runs the water onto Echlas' body to keep her warm but then the shower peters out so she pours cups of warm water from the full bucket which was prepared for just this situation. Layan sits her up and washes her hair twice with equal vigour, then attacks her back. After the longest bath I have ever known we are finished and rinse the bed of suds, wrap Echlas in several towels and dry her. The bath is ingenious; all the water runs out through a tube onto the floor where it goes into the drain.

We partially dress her on the bed then lift her into the wheelchair and take her back to the bedroom and put the heater on to warm her up while we finish dressing her. Layan gets to work on Echlas' hair which is thick but cut to jaw length, drying and styling it, all the time chatting away in Arabic. It must be family gossip she is catching up on. We tidy up and leave them to chat.

Our task now is to clean since the CL will not be coming for a while and really I am glad to have something to do, not being used to sitting around. We take the carpets up and shake them outside in the garden and vacuum and dust, moving the furniture, which is heavy, to clean underneath and behind. I am not sure that the vacuum is very effective as there is no obvious difference after I have used it on the carpets but at least I feel they are clean having gone through the process.

Last night I had good news when Echlas said I was to move into the garden room, as I call it. I am delighted as it is a much brighter room with an ensuite toilet, sink and shower which does not work but that is a minor inconvenience and does not detract from the advantage of having a more comfortable bed, I hope, and a view of the garden. So I set to and clean my new room, change the sheets and move all my stuff from the volunteers' room, with no regrets whatsoever. Along one side of the room are three cupboards where I find a stack of quilts, sewing items, prayer mats, an iron and some hanging space for my clothes. This was Echlas' mother's room, only slept in by selected people, so I feel privileged. Perhaps it is my age as I am the oldest volunteer Echlas has ever had. Usually they are in their twenties or thirties and a few in their teens.

I had bought some Dettol spray when I was out as the only cleaning material I could find in the house was bleach and decided to tackle the kitchen next. All the cupboards and fittings are pretty old and the sink and the area around it are mouldy and grubby looking. The work surfaces are marble so easy to maintain but the plastic drainer was really dirty. Armed with my rubber gloves and Dettol I set to and make some impression but cannot do a lot with the aged sink. Still, I felt satisfied when I finished. Christina had explained that only two rings of the cooker work and there is no oven or grill so with those restrictions inventiveness is called for. Of course, we also have the microwave with the temperamental door. The washing machine is functional but water is restricted so we put all our washing in a basket together and do a wash when we have a full load. Water is precious. I was always careful at home not to waste water, but here that need is acute when one is reminded daily that water cannot be taken for granted. Every morning, the first one up, usually me, turns on the water tap outside the back door to make sure that water is coming through from the mains. Then I turn on the electric pump, which pumps water up to the tanks on the roof for storage. This is one way that Palestinian houses can be distinguished from Israeli ones: Palestinians' houses always have large black water tanks on their roofs. Israelis have unlimited access to water, taken from aquifers beneath Palestinian land, and enjoy swimming pools and water fountains and irrigation for crops while the Palestinians have their water rationed and in the summer months often have to buy their own water from Israeli companies who fill up their tanks at great expense.

A few facts and figures: an Israeli's per capita domestic water consumption is 350 litres a day while for a Palestinian it is about 60, so 5-6 times more. Water consumption by the 50,000 Israeli settlers in the Jordan valley alone is equal to 75% of the amount consumed by the 2 million Palestinians in the entire West Bank. Water is not scarce. There is more rainfall in Ramallah (619mm) than London (596mm) but the distribution is unequal. The entire water system in Israel and the West Bank has been owned by Mekorot, the Israeli national water company, since 1982, of which the state owns 50%. This company supplies water meters for Southern Water and possibly for other UK water companies which is why I refused to have one of this make installed in my house.

The World Health Organization minimum water in litres per capita per day is 100 and the poverty threshold is 50. Israelis have 300, settlers have 369 and Palestinians 73. The right to water is protected by the International Human Rights Law which "entitles everyone to sufficient, safe, acceptable, physically accessible and affordable water for personal and domestic use". This statement was endorsed by the UN in July 2010. This information was provided by Al Haq 2013.

So we are very conscious of the water we use and do not wash our clothes or ourselves unnecessarily.

Care is also taken to not overload the electricity supply, so if the water pump is on then the washing machine and the water heater cannot be used at the same time. Even using the vacuum cleaner while one of the other three appliances is on can blow the electrics, as I discovered.

The refugees in the three Bethlehem camps have free electricity but for those outside it is very expensive. Echlas told me that when the Pope came – she did not know which one – Dheisheah camp was granted free electricity so the other two camps complained and now they get it free as well. I am not sure how the other camps stand in regard to this.

We make some lunch. Echlas has two boiled eggs chopped with tomatoes and bread and I have pitta with cream cheese and cucumber. The cucumbers here are small, about four inches long, and seem to last longer and taste better than the large ones we get at home. Christina has boiled eggs as well. Eggs are plentiful but very unlikely to be free range. The shells are white and the yolks pale but I cannot think about where they come from. Here you eat what is available without the luxury of choosing free range.

Christina had an interrupted night. Echlas went to sleep at 2am and then was up again at 5am for a bedpan so she goes for a lie down in the volunteers' room while I have my first Arabic lesson. All Echlas' students work from a programme called 'Spoken Arabic for Foreigners' written by a professor of Semitic languages at Bethlehem University which Echlas gets copied at the copy shop (there are no copyright laws here) and I am excited to get mine and get going. I took some Arabic lessons last term at Sussex University in standard classical Arabic but I expect this will be different as it is Palestinian dialect. We begin with greetings – *marhaban* (hello), *marhabten* (reply), *keif halak/halik* (how are you? – male/female) and so on. I know how difficult Arabic is but I love the language for its own sake not because I expect to become fluent in speaking it, and I also love Arabic script – the different shapes of the letters and working out how to write a word from the phonetics, which I usually get wrong. In Brighton I was learning to speak, read and write so I am determined to practise some writing every day so as not to lose what I have already learned.

After an hour, by which time my head is buzzing with unaccustomed concentration, Echlas phones Mohammed to do some shopping for her. He is a ten-year-old boy who lives in the camp with his mother and three sisters. His father is a political prisoner so the family struggle financially but being part of the Al Azza clan, which I am discovering is huge, hence the name of the camp, they receive support from the close-knit community. Echlas helps out as much as she can, as I observe during the course of my stay, in so many ways. Mohammed is a very obliging boy, a result of the respect for their elders ingrained into the culture here, I suspect, and interrupts his game of football or bike ride to come at Echlas' bidding. He does not have a mobile phone so I am always surprised that he is so easily contactable but it must be the fact that everyone knows everyone else so it is just a question of his mother shouting in the street for him and someone will know where he is. This is more or less a nightly occurrence as Echlas invariably wants more cigarettes even if we have been out shopping earlier. Mohammed's English is limited but he is learning it at school and smiles shyly as we exchange greetings in Arabic. He shuffles into Echlas' room in the way that boys do and listens carefully to the list and then repeats it back. Christina gives him a note from Echlas' purse and off he goes, leaving the front door ajar so he can come back in without bothering us. He has known Echlas since he was a baby so is quite used to being in her bedroom and he seems very fond of her. He comes crashing back through the door and deposits two plastic bags on the floor and gives a handful of change to Christina. I am amazed at the amount of plastic bags here. Having come from a country where plastic bags are being phased out it is so environmentally unfriendly and contrary to my habits to see this plethora of bags. Every item you buy you get a bag and when I produce my own bag and refuse a plastic one I do get a strange look. We have a cupboard full of them in the kitchen and use them up to line the small rubbish bins. Echlas gives Mohammed a couple of shekels which he is reluctant to take but Echlas insists he take them to add to his savings. He has been brought up to refuse gifts and money and this is something that has impressed me about the kids in the camp: they never ask for money, even when they carry my shopping.

Now we have some broccoli Christina and I cook the dinner – fried onion and garlic, broccoli and potatoes – all in one big pan. Not quite *MasterChef* but not as bad as it sounds. It is 9pm now, much later than I am used to eating, but meals are very flexible here so I go with the flow.

I manage to go to bed at 11.30pm and sleep well in my large, comfortable bed, despite being pinned down by the heavy weight of assorted blankets and eiderdowns. When I wake in the morning

I open the curtains and the frosted window to look out on the little garden and hear the birdsong. I am no 'twitcher' but even I can hear that the birds are different here from their songs. I wrote the following while looking out of the window one morning:

The View From My Window

This is the view from my window.
Metal bars, twisted like barley sugar, painted green.
A small patch of bare earth, borders for flowers made with breeze blocks.
A sage plant, some pelargoniums, fallen leaves.
A lemon tree, a few lemons out of reach.
A concrete wall, not high, patterns on it made by sunlight through leaves.
Dry tendrils of a vine
Laying over the structure of metal pipes and wires to make a canopy.
A blue plastic sheet fixed over the seating area to provide shade and privacy.
A painted wall, green and blue, a tree, a woman carrying a water jug.
When I look up I see blue sky, passing clouds.
I see other buildings, a satellite dish, rusted metal, water tanks, unfinished houses, washing on the line.
I hear birds singing, a distant hooting of horns, people talking, children playing, hammer on stone, the call of the imam.
Is this all, this view from my window?
Sometimes it has to be enough, to feel the cool air, hear life, observe the resilience of life in the plants,
Consider the past in the relics left in the garden,
Hope for the future in the labour of man to make a better life for his family.

Later on Echlas goes out with a friend and Christina goes to Jerusalem. I go for a walk and come back via Star Street so I feel confident that I know another route to Manger Square. As today is Sunday, the Christian shops are shut but the *souk* is still busy. I feel melancholy today and feel sorry for all these people, shopping for entertainment or just hanging about, but I suppose that is what a lot of people at home enjoy doing. The emphasis is on family so most socialising is done in family homes and celebrations are always taking place for weddings, births, birthdays, prisoners being released from prison, anniversaries of historical events, e.g. the 'Nakba'. Some of these occasions for celebration spill over into the streets and then one can see how the Palestinians love a good party.

Although it appears to me that there is much camaraderie here and people are loyal to each other, Echlas was telling us that there is a degree of suspicion among Palestinians as they are divided politically, e.g. Hamas, Fatah, PFLP, the PA, even in the same family. Very few people can say a good word about the PA but they must not be criticised publicly, e.g. on Facebook, as this carries severe punishment. So the unity I imagined amongst the population is false. There are many spies working for the PA and for Israel so a certain amount of paranoia is inevitable. The family name reveals a lot too, which is why Echlas will always ask this if she meets a stranger. Some families are known as 'bad' but what for she did not elaborate.

A Spanish girl, Amia, comes round to take Echlas out in the evening. She has been here for two years and works for BADIL, a human rights organisation, of which Echlas' brother-in-law is the head, and lives in Aida camp in a flat belonging to Echlas' relatives. While she is waiting for Echlas, Amia tells us something of life in Aida. I remember going there for a cooking evening when a group of us learned to make *mujudera* in the home of Islam and her family. It was one of the highlights of the trip and the food was so delicious but that was my only visit. The camp is much larger than Al Azza and has more facilities but is up against the wall so the Israeli soldiers make frequent incursions into the camp and often use tear gas. This is what Amia told us:

On Tuesday, when I came back from work I could smell it. The soldiers just come and throw tear gas. It gets in everywhere, you have to shut all the windows and put towels under the doors. Two small boys, about six years old threw stones and the soldiers just wanted an excuse to come and provoke the older boys and men in the camp so they threw the gas canisters. There are also frequent night raids. They come in and arrest boys, often children. All the time the people live in fear and anxiety, not knowing what will happen next. Children are frightened to go to bed. Grown men still sleep with their parents. A thirty-year-old man wets the bed, a result of the psychological damage he has received at the hands of the soldiers.

These soldiers are boys. They probably have no idea what they are doing to these people in their day-to-day lives. One day some soldiers came up on the roof of our building and they were there all day on some sort of training exercise but they were polite enough to pee into bottles. They brought food with them and offered apples to the children. They were smiling and friendly but the next minute they could be shooting tear gas or rubber bullets at those children. Bizarre.

They sometimes spray skunk water, the most disgusting, toxic water that ruins clothes, and if it gets on your skin it causes a rash. The smell can take a month to disappear. Last time everyone scrubbed the streets to try and get rid of the smell but still it lingered. It kills vegetation so must be harmful to people. Who knows what the long-term effect of these substances are.

I listen with sadness, anger and frustration. Why should these people, who are only guilty of existing, be punished so unjustly?

CHAPTER TWO

ECHLAS' STORY

Now I have been living with Echlas for a week and she is the reason I am here in Palestine, I must write her story next, or at least as much as she has told me so far.

Her family come from Beit Jibrin, a village near Hebron, destroyed in 1948 by the Israeli forces and the inhabitants forced to flee for their lives. The ruins are still there, the land designated a National Park, but the rightful owners are forbidden to return. This was the Nakba, the catastrophe when 750,000 Palestinians were driven out of their homes and land and 13,000 were killed when Israel declared independence from the British mandate. Echlas' mother fled to Hebron with her family where they rented a flat, and met a man of the Al Azza clan whom she married. Her grandfather became employed by UNRWA in Al Roub camp, near Hebron, a newly set up refugee camp to deal with the vast numbers of homeless Palestinians in that area. Later he was moved to Al Azza camp and appointed administrator of both Aida and Al Azza. Echlas' mother lived in Hebron and gave birth to four children but sadly two died, one of a fever and the other after suffering polio for nine years. Her husband was an active member of the Communist Party and was imprisoned for six years for his politics. Echlas' mother was forced to move out of the flat which she could no longer afford and her father found her a room in Al Azza camp. That room is now the kitchen. The small family lived there, walking approximately a quarter of a mile to the communal toilet and washroom, but being an enterprising and resourceful woman, she picked up materials around the camp and built her own bathroom next to the kitchen. To keep herself and her children she did traditional Palestinian embroidery for the Catholic nuns to sell to visiting pilgrims.

When her husband was released from prison they extended the house further until it was the four-bedroom house, with spacious living area and small garden, in which we are living today. They went on to have another six children. Tragically the youngest died after being detained in the hot sun at a checkpoint for hours. The shock of his death caused Echlas' mother, five months pregnant at the time, to suffer complications with her pregnancy and necessitated a caesarean section to deliver Echlas. She was born with disabilities and was diagnosed as having muscular atrophy.

So Echlas' mother had six children to bring up plus a disabled child who needed twenty-four-hour care. As there were no facilities for disabled children at school, Echlas was educated at home by her loving, close-knit family. Echlas' mother was much respected in the camp, helping out neighbours and providing a sort of 'alternative therapy' clinic where she would dispense advice and traditional treatments for various ailments. Echlas lived in a busy household with all these comings and goings as her mother would not turn anyone away. She has benefited from her mother's legacy of kindness, as her neighbour, and no doubt others if she would let them, will always come and give a hand when required. While I was there one of Ida's children would often knock on the door and be found standing there with a plate of freshly cooked food for us – a great gift to me if it meant I did not need to cook. Ida was also indispensable in changing the gas cylinder for the cooker. When the gas ran out, usually in the middle of cooking, we called Ida, she being the only person trusted to change the gas safely.

Ida would sometimes come in for a chat with Echlas, bringing her grandson Omar with her. Unusually for this culture his mother got divorced and is now living back at home. Ida looks after Omar while her daughter works although she also works as a teacher and looks after her family, so is a busy lady.

It was Echlas' idea to have international volunteers twenty years ago to give her mother some rest and also to provide a different dimension to her life by having interaction with young people from different countries. In return for the work they do in caring for Echlas they live as part of a Palestinian family, learn about the culture and receive free Arabic lessons and board and lodging. Since Echlas' mother died five years ago Echlas has lived independently with volunteers, a precarious existence as visitors to Israel are often denied entry. She advertises through various websites, and then emails and Skypes with the candidate to assess if they will be suitable. They are mostly female, although she does have the occasional male apply. He would not be able to do any personal care so she always has to have at least one, preferably two, female helpers. During my stay two helpers were denied entry through the Allenby Bridge crossing from Jordan, a big blow for all of us.

A lack of volunteers is a big problem for Echlas. She does have a fall back as her sisters in Aida camp and in Hebron always offer to have her but she is reluctant to leave the family home and to give up her particular way of life. She also has a sister in Ramallah who lives with her son and his family and Echlas does go and visit them sometimes but could probably not stay there long term.

As well as having severe birth defects, Echlas was hit by an Israeli settler woman in her car in 1987. As a result of the injuries sustained she spent two years in hospital in Israel, not receiving any visitors for the first six months as her family were refused travel permits. She received no compensation from the woman, the court stating that 'she was disabled anyway'. While in the hospital she was shunned by the Israeli patients when they discovered she was Palestinian. This was not immediately apparent as she does not wear a *hijab* and has short hair.

Apart from the two wheelchairs, a hospital bed and the 'bathbed' Echlas has no other aids. She did receive physio and rehabilitation and used to attend a day centre for disabled people but now prefers to get on and lead her own life and not be defined by her disability. All lifting has to be done manually, a hoist being unsuitable for her body shape. Perhaps if she lived in Europe or the US, aids would be found to help her but then her life would be taken over by various agencies – people checking on her, piles of paperwork to fill in – whereas now she lives her life her way.

When Echlas' mother died the free oil and flour from UNRWA ceased so she receives no benefits and relies on income from the Arabic lessons and the political calendar she makes. She also has some financial support from her brother in America. As well as being something of a linguist, Echlas is an artist and has produced a calendar for a number of years, showing scenes from her life and making political comments, which she sells locally and abroad.

Echlas was brought up to be thrifty. Life must have been hard when she was young and her mother needed to be an efficient housekeeper to provide good meals for her family. There were also the difficult times during the Intifadas when food was scarce and it was a case of making do with what you had. Echlas' mother made all the meals from fresh ingredients, including bread, and Echlas has memorised many traditional Palestinian recipes. She also finds some online and then tells us volunteers what and how to cook a dish. She is vegetarian which makes food cheaper but more of a challenge for us meat eaters. Echlas is at the mercy of the culinary skills of her volunteers but the only food I saw her leave was a savoury dish which included four tablespoons of sugar in the sauce. I had my doubts when making it but trusted Echlas too far on that occasion. It was an unusual taste!

She likes a lot of salt on her food, contrary to all our health warnings, so I was reluctant to give it to her but she won with her argument that she has always taken a lot of salt and remains healthy and is fully aware of the risks, so I had to give in. The worst risk to her health, of course, is the smoking but she will never give that up.

I soon learnt to make just enough food for one day, or we would be eating the leftovers for days until they were finished. Occasionally Christina and I decided that something was past its sell-by date and threw it out. Even though Echlas is frugal she is not mean and we would buy large quantities of fresh fruit and vegetables from the greengrocer around the corner, who pointed out the Palestinian-grown produce like apples, potatoes and tomatoes. We bought kilos at a time and could hardly carry it all home but it all got eaten quite quickly, especially when Echlas took to drinking fresh orange juice. She had been having grapefruit juice from a carton in the morning but then decided that all the sugar it contained was not good for her so she would have fresh juice instead. We squeezed at least one large, sweet, juicy orange for her every morning and sometimes I could not resist having half of one myself. The oranges are wonderful in Palestine. Later she went on to tomato juice of which I made a quantity at a time and kept in the fridge as it took longer to prepare. On one occasion Mohammed came around with a sack of potatoes and then a sack of carrots, enough to keep a family going for a month, but they were cheap and Echlas could not resist a bargain. She shared these with Mohammed's family but even our half was an effort to get through before they started going off.

It was contrary to my practice at home to put vegetable waste in the rubbish bin and I did think about having a compost bin. There was a bin in the garden which I could use but I was reluctant to start putting out food for fear of vermin. Echlas always insisted we keep the screen door into the garden shut to stop 'mouses' getting in so perhaps there was a problem, and with creatures bigger than mice!

The rubbish was collected every night except Thursday and Saturday from outside the front door – brilliant service, better than our councils can manage. However, this only applies to the camps as they are run by the UN.

The volunteers looked after Echlas' purse, giving money to Mohammed for shopping and paying for things when we went out. Although she was not handling the money herself she usually had a rough idea how much she had left in the purse. When we went out for meals we paid for ourselves but it was never expensive and sometimes if I went out to do some household shopping, taking Echlas' purse, I would use my own money. She got wise to this though and did not like me to do it, perhaps a matter of pride, so I had to be very devious after that.

Echlas loves clothes and has two packed wardrobes and a suitcase full. I do not know how she remembers what she has but in the

35

mornings she would choose what she would wear for the day, asking for 'the green top' or 'the blue woolly top' and I would go through the piles until I found the right one. Very few of her clothes are new. There are no charity shops in Bethlehem but even better, there is the 'one-shekel *souk*', a paradise for bargain hunters. Piles of clothes are laid out on trestle tables, and the owner shouts incessantly, "Look, look, only one shekel for this, one shekel for this", holding up some entirely unsuitable garment. After a while one just ignores him and works steadily through the heaps of clothes. The first time Christina and I experienced this we came away with bags full of things and Echlas added to her wardrobe of tops. I could not wait to wash them and try them on and at approximately 20p a piece if they were no good I could take them back or pass them on. They were all good when I did try them and one top that I wore around the house I brought home with me for sentimental reasons. I do not know where they came from as the labels were unfamiliar. Perhaps they had been donated to charity from another country and found their way to the *souk* in Bethlehem. All the rest of the clothes I bought I left behind as did Christina and Hannah so the succeeding volunteers had a selection to choose from. The one-shekel *souk* was also a good source of bedding and Echlas purchased sheets, duvet covers and pillowcases, all in good condition, for a few shekels.

Social media can be a wonderful means of communication and it certainly is for Echlas. Her laptop is her lifeline and she spends hours every day emailing, Facebooking, Skyping, and watching YouTube and Egyptian soaps and films. Through her laptop she keeps in touch with all her hundreds of friends and relatives and is able to continue giving Arabic lessons once her students leave the country. While I was with her she was addicted to an Egyptian soap, a Middle Eastern *EastEnders*. She would watch it for hours on end and on one notable occasion watched seventeen episodes all through the night so that when I woke up in the morning she was still exactly as she was when I drifted off to sleep, sitting up still watching the screen.

The nearest family Echlas has live just over the road in Aida camp, as already mentioned. Every time we visited I met another family member so I have no idea how many actually live there and when family becomes clan. Echla's sister Afaf lives in a flat with her husband and their daughter Layan lives upstairs. Echlas' elderly aunt lives on the ground floor with her daughter and various members of the family live on other floors of the houses that surround the garden and terrace. On the occasions that we sat outside someone would pass by and give effusive greetings and exchange hugs with Echlas so I assumed they were other family members.

LIVING THE LIFE

Echlas has physio every Monday morning, given by a very smart lady with very short hair. We leave them to it after providing the customary pot of coffee, and have some time for ourselves. I decide to make a start on the garden as it has not been touched since the disastrous attempt by CL to clear the leaves. I enjoy being outside and I am a keen gardener at home so this is pure enjoyment for me. I find a few tools in the garden shed, a brick-built store where all sorts of unused things have been stashed. There is not much of interest except the rake and a couple of brooms. I rake all the leaves up, putting them into rubbish bags, wishing I could make leaf mould but I will not be here long enough for that. Then I sweep all the hard surfaces and weed the borders. There is no grass, just earth, and because the lemon tree casts a lot of shade I cannot imagine what can be grown there. A mad idea occurs to me: I could ask Alan Titchmarsh to do a garden makeover. It would make good TV but cannot imagine the BBC taking it on. Too non-PC. I find some parsley growing and some sage which could be useful for cooking. It is still too cold to sow the seeds I brought although I am itching to get on. As preparation I am saving all the plastic cups that Echlas drinks from, as she does not like to reuse them, and making holes in the bottom. The next thing I need to find is compost which could be a challenge as I have not noticed any garden centres locally.

Evidently there is bird flu in Israel; 350 people have it. I hope it does not spread here!

The lemon tree has produced a number of lemons which look ready for picking. Echlas has said she will get Mohammed round after school one day to climb the tree and get them down. I decide to have a go myself, using the rake, and manage to pick seven lemons which I arrange artistically on the garden wall.

The day passes with Arabic lessons for Christina and me, fridge cleaning, clothes washing and cooking. Tonight we make pasta with tomato sauce with courgettes in it – very good.

Some days ago Echlas received a phone call from a man in Hebron asking if she could help at all as he is in desperate need of a volunteer to assist his wife to care for his three daughters with learning disabilities. She explained to him that she is not an agency and advertises for her own carers but if she had any ideas she would call him. This evening about 10pm there is a loud knock at the door; I open it to see two men standing there. I feel slightly intimidated as they are big burly men, one with a black leather jacket on, smoking a cigarette, the other in a policeman's uniform. They are polite and wait while I go to tell Echlas. It seems she is expecting them so I show them into her room and bring another chair. Christina and I leave while they talk for an hour. I take the opportunity to have a shower while Christina watches some awful violent film on the tiny TV in the lounge. When they leave we find out that the man in the police uniform is the man from Hebron and the other is a relative of Echlas' who brought him here. He is so desperate for help with his girls aged thirteen, nine and three but lives in a village outside Hebron so it sounds as if it will not be easy to find a volunteer. Echlas knows of a Danish girl who may be interested so Facebooks her, and Christina and I ponder on why they are all disabled and the burden on their parents and just how awful it must be for them, but how would an international who does not speak Arabic be of any help? I feel like going to lend a hand but of course my place is here with Echlas so that is not possible.

Echlas has an acute abdominal pain and is not feeling well but

Christina says this recurs about every week so we settle her early, hoping that sleep will help.

I am working on my Arabic and try to do an hour in the morning before the others wake up. I am happy in my bedroom and the first thing I do on waking is to open the window to look out and see the sky and feel the air, hear the birds. This morning I am preparing lemon marmalade using the lemons I picked yesterday. I find some empty jars in the kitchen, dozens of huge cooking pots and a piece of worn cotton material in my wardrobe which will do in lieu of muslin. I chop up the lemons and put them to soak in a litre of water. I looked up the recipe online last night but there are no scales so will have to guess the sugar.

Echlas and Christina wake up at midday and Echlas is feeling a bit better, but she will not go out today. She was awake several times in the night so Christina is feeling tired from lack of sleep today.

We see on Facebook that a ten-year-old boy was arrested in Aida camp this morning. Echlas' nephew, Musa, filmed it so we watch the video with disbelief, dismay, sadness, indignation. It is hard to believe that this happened just over the road but it makes it all the more real when it is so close. I think of Mohammed being arrested and I could cry with the injustice of it.

We talk about the cruelty of the IOF soldiers while we are on the topic. One time Echlas was on her own at home; her parents had gone out to visit a neighbour. She was watching TV and the soldiers broke the front door down and went through the house, wrecking it, doing senseless things like mixing the salt and sugar. All she did was turn up the volume on the TV as she could not move and to engage with them might have led to physical violence on her. On another occasion when they broke in, they threw her out of bed onto the stone floor to search in the bed.

She tells us the soldiers will beat this boy as they do all the people they arrest. They usually make the child sign a paper which, written in Hebrew, he will not understand, admitting to a crime he did not commit, i.e. throwing stones, and then they can take him to court. Some of the older boys they will blackmail into being a spy for the IOF.

A bit later on we read that a relative went to get him and he has now been released but what scars this will leave on the boy's mind and what hatred it breeds. I think how this regime is senselessly cruel, apart from all the other crimes against humanity it commits every day, and yet the world governments turn a blind eye. In what other country would this happen without condemnation?

Yom il Arba (I am practising Arabic days of the week)

Marmalade day. I boil up the fruit with the peel to soften it and add the sugar and stir until it reaches setting point. It only makes three jars but it looks good so I am pleased since it was mostly guesswork. There was one hiccough though as lots of tiny black bits appeared as I was stirring so I had to pour it out, strain out the bits and wash the pan thoroughly. I got most of it out. When we came to eat the marmalade it was more like treacle so my guesswork with the sugar was a failure. I wonder if it is still in the fridge?

This evening we are giving a dinner party for the Scottish and Belgian boys who are leaving. As a farewell gift Echlas has prepared certificates for them to say they have successfully completed a course in Arabic. While Echlas is giving a lesson I go to the copy shop where they have printed them out and then call at the garden shop where, to my delight, I am able to buy a few litres of compost. The shopkeeper measures it out from a large bag and puts it in a smaller bag for me to carry. I am thankful I did not have to carry 25 litres home. Recently I discovered a bakers' at the top of the *souk* selling sliced wholemeal bread which Echlas also likes so I buy a loaf and some chocolate to melt and dip strawberries in for dessert.

It is cold and windy but it is good to be out and walking. When I get back Christina and I lift the plastic garden table from the alcove and put it in the middle of the sitting room and lay it with the best plates and glasses. Just as I am getting ready there is a knock at the door and the Hebron family traipse in – five of them plus a toddler. I am alarmed, are they here for dinner and did Echlas forget to tell us? Thankfully they have just dropped in on the way back from visiting another relative in Bethlehem. I find out that Echlas' sister's husband was a nurse and is now a manager in public health. He speaks very good English so we are able to have a conversation. Echlas' sister is a commanding sort of woman, serious and capable, a no-nonsense sort, and she talks loudly with Echlas. There are two young women, one the mother of the toddler, who also speaks fairly good English, and a younger girl who is lively and curious about Christina and I. The fifth person is the nephew who stayed over last week. They all talk at once and there is laughter and noise and a sudden joy in the room but then as suddenly as they arrived, they leave.

As soon as I shut the front door behind them, there is another knock at the door and a lady wearing a *hijab* who I have not seen before comes in to visit Echlas. The boys arrive for their lesson so she cannot stay long and we usher her out, hoping there will be no more unexpected visitors.

It is time for Christina and I to finish the dinner we started preparing earlier. It is our first attempt at making *maqluba*, a very famous Palestinian dish that I had eaten on one of my previous visits, and part of the experience of this dish is the presentation. It is a mix of rice and lentils, spices and vegetables cooked in layers in a large pot and when turned upside down on the serving plate should come out like a cake. This is served with pitta bread, yogurt and salads.

The boys have brought a bottle of red wine with them which we eye with anticipation. This will be the first wine I have had here and in fact I was not expecting to drink alcohol, this being a Moslem home. Echlas is not a strict Moslem so does not cover her head or pray and she enjoys an occasional glass of wine. The fact that she does have alcohol occasionally has to be kept from most of her family as some are very religious. The Hebron crew have just been to Mecca on pilgrimage and the females all wear the *hijab*. I witnessed later that some members of her family do drink on social occasions and indeed a number of Moslem men and maybe women do not practise their faith and have turned away from Islam which I found surprising. As Bethlehem is a Christian community there are what we would call 'off-licences' and they call 'liquor stores' where all kinds of alcohol can be bought.

The wine that we are drinking is 'Cremisan'. This is the local wine made at the Cremisan Monastery in the Cremisan valley 5km from Bethlehem. It was built in 1885 on the ruins of a seventh-century Byzantine monastery and is part of the Salesian Order. As well as the monastery there is a Salesian Sisters Convent and school which has about 400 primary and kindergarten children and a school for children with learning disabilities.

Unfortunately, it lies on the dividing line between the West Bank and Jerusalem and the Israeli authorities want to build the separation wall right through the middle of the area, dividing the monastery, which would be in the Jerusalem side, from the convent school. It would annexe about 75% of the convent's property and enclose it on three sides and would also annexe the farmland of fifty-eight Palestinian families. It is believed that the route chosen for the wall is to enable connection between the Israeli settlements of Har Gilo and Gilo.

In April 2015 the Israeli Supreme Court ruled in favour of the monastery and Palestinian farmers, ending a nine-year legal battle. That will probably not be the end of it though as Israel always gets what it wants. Since writing this the wall has been built through the land despite many protests.

The *maqluba* is ready so now the tricky part: turning the pot over onto a plate in one movement. Two of us grapple with the huge pot and the plate and eventually succeed but it's more of a heap than a cake. I read later that one should oil the sides of the pot first. Anyway, it tastes fine and we all eat and drink but unfortunately Echlas cannot give the certificates as on inspection they are made out in the same name so the boys will come back and collect them at another time.

Our strawberries dipped in chocolate are not a great success. Christina describes them as strawberries with a blob of poo on the end. Cadbury's milk chocolate is evidently not made for melting but we eat them anyway.

The boys are interesting to talk to. The Scottish one is a researcher and has been a 'resident' recording the mapping of the Oslo Accords and the Belgian has a degree in moral sciences and is doing something with architecture.

Yom al kamis

Today we are in a private hospital in Beit Jala waiting with Echlas for a CT (computerised tomography) scan. Some time ago she had an abdominal ultrasound to try and find out the cause of this intermittent pain but nothing showed. The doctor advised that if the pain continued or got worse she should have a CT and because she does get this quite frequently and because it makes her feel so unwell, she phoned up the hospital. Amazingly we are here today. What service! What does worry me is that Echlas has had no prep for the CT. Usually the patient has to drink contrast in a couple of litres of water over several hours but of course Echlas has not done this; it was not mentioned yesterday. After reporting to reception we are sent upstairs where it is confirmed that yes, Echlas is here for a CT and yes, she does need contrast, which means drinking a cup of water every ten minutes for two hours. A blood test is taken first. I get talking to one of the doctors there who, when I tell him I was a nurse in the UK, explains the problems they have with infection in ITU, particularly MRSA. The culture is such that it is impossible to enforce rules about the number of visitors, hand washing, gowning up etc. I can see an opportunity for some health education. Kimberley is with us today. She is a Scottish friend from Edinburgh and lives in Ramallah, working for an NGO. Because Echlas had to go in a taxi to get here she asked Kimberley to come and help as it is quite a performance to get her in and out of a taxi. Two people can do it but I am sure Echlas thinks because I am 'older' I am not strong enough. It is lovely to meet Kimberley and Echlas obviously places a lot of confidence in her.

Kimberley tells us about a friend of hers that she is very worried about as he has been put in a Palestinian prison. His crime was to post a comment on Facebook about the boss of the Palestinian football team who also holds an important position in the PA. Because this man is Hamas they arrested him. Mohammed, the taxi driver, joined in the conversation and confirmed that Palestinians have to be very careful what they say about the PA and get treated as badly by their own police as they do by the IOF, something else I had no inkling of.

We sit and talk and then watch the comings and goings. A lady is crocheting and I have an idea that is something I can do while I am sitting on that hard plastic chair in the evening. Echlas knows where I can buy wool so I must get some. It's a pleasant hospital, not very big and Outpatients has a central atrium with tropical plants and a tortoise. I listen to the Arabic conversations around me and can pick up the odd word, but I like listening to the sound of it. Some of the doctors wear jeans but they all wear white coats so at least you can tell who's who.

At last Echlas goes in to have her CT. We lift her onto the table and after fifteen minutes it is all done and we lift her back into the wheelchair. She is cold and desperately needs a pee but we have to wait for Mohammed to come with the taxi and then have to stop for the certificates at the copy shop. They are not ready so I say I will wait for them and the others can go on home.

Jacob and the Belgian guy come round just after we get Echlas into bed and we have tea and chat for a while. Then Christina leaves to go to Jerusalem and Kimberley leaves for Ramallah so it is just Echlas and I.

I have just put her wheat bags into the microwave when the electricity goes off and we are plunged into darkness. I find my torch and some candles and dot them around. I check the fires and they have gone off so Echlas tells me to knock on Ida's door. She is out but her elder son Mahmood comes across. He is a big serious-looking boy of about fourteen and must be very popular in the camp as we always hear someone calling outside for him: "Mahmood, Mahmood!" He takes a broom from the garden and strides purposefully down the alley but whatever he does with it, it does not work. Ida's husband comes and there is more conversation, then Echlas wants a bedpan. Cigarettes are running low so Echlas calls Mohammed to buy her some and when he comes back she wants him to stay so I try to entertain him by practising my very limited Arabic with him and then showing him pictures on my iPad. Echlas needs another bedpan so Mohammed waits in the sitting room with a candle to keep him company. Another man comes in and talks to Echlas when she is off the bedpan and miraculously the lights come on. What a relief. I had filled some hot water bottles to try and keep Echlas warm as, of course, the heaters were off but now I can heat up the wheat bags and warm up our dinner and we are able to eat at last. Ida comes round while Echlas is Skyping the Danish girl who is supposed to come in two weeks so we sit in the living room and try to converse. Ida teaches Arabic at a middle school as well as looking after her family of five, plus grandchild.

The Danish girl confirms she is coming on 13 February but is slightly apprehensive as she has appeared on YouTube at a BDS demo in Denmark so that news has got Echlas worrying. After a litre of contrast she is using the bedpan frequently. I just hope it does not continue all night.

It is time to reflect on what I am really doing here. I know I am helping one lady who is totally reliant on me but I could be doing that at home. What am I getting out of it? That is easier to elicit: the experience of living in a refugee camp, discovering the Palestinian culture and hearing the stories of other volunteers. Visiting the hospital today was interesting and not so different from ours as one would expect. On one level life seems to be lived normally but the restrictions and dangers of the occupation are always present and can never be forgotten for an instant. Echlas is a good example of the resilience and steadfastness of the Palestinians, although these terms are generally applied to more overt ways of resisting the occupation, but in her own way Echlas is showing she will live her life as fully as possible by making her own decisions and will not be beaten by the Israeli regime. Having internationals to come and care for her in the West Bank is defiance and by inviting them to have this experience she is spreading the truth of the occupation to the world.

She takes a risk by having internationals: firstly, whether or not they will actually be allowed in, then trusting this stranger with her personal needs, her food, home, money. Of course, the volunteer also takes a risk but she can leave, whereas Echlas is dependent on that person. It is a delicate balance between what Echlas needs and expects, and the amount she puts on the carer and what the expectations of the carer are. She is there to work for her board and lodging and Arabic lessons, but more than that she is a companion so has to give emotionally as well. There is also the question of gratitude. If the needs and rewards are balanced then it works well but if one side feels they are not receiving what they expect, then problems could arise. It is a relationship of mutual gratitude, a symbiotic relationship which relies on the goodwill and unselfishness of both parties.

Echlas has had years of experience now and must be a pretty good judge of character. She says she has only had a couple of 'unsatisfactory' volunteers with odd behaviours but the majority she got on with and many still keep in touch. Echlas has to maintain control, after all it is her house. This could be frustrating for her when she cannot move around to see and hear what is going on in the house, but she always seems to know what we are doing even if we are out of sight. I think her hearing is very good.

This is my first night sleeping in Echlas' room but after such a busy and traumatic day she goes to sleep early and sleeps all night. I am kept awake by the lively neighbours for a while and the bed is hard, but at least there are no springs sticking out. I am awakened by the bread man calling out at 7am. Mohammed comes round after school to pick lemons and he climbs up the tree fearlessly, picks the lemons and hands them down to me. We hear shooting. Mohammed makes the action of shooting with a gun and points over the building. Echlas says it is probably tear gas in Aida camp again.

I hear the story of how Echlas came to be in the camp and ask if she has any old photos. She is not sure where they are so I hunt in the likely places like the wardrobe in my room and the cupboard in Echlas' room, but I am unable to find them so we will ask the CL or Echlas' sister.

Mark Thomas, the comic and author of *Extreme Rambling*, is appearing tonight and I am so excited that he is in Bethlehem. I phone up for tickets and enquire about wheelchair access. The guy assures me that Echlas will be able to get in, as although there are a few steps there are always some strong men around to assist. Echlas is hesitant about going and says she will find someone to sit with her while Christina and I go. At the last minute she decides to go so it is a rush to get her ready and then we have to walk for half an hour to get there. It is really cold out. I wear my coat and scarf but Echlas had shunned my suggestion to take a shawl and consequently is not dressed for the weather. None of us are sure where the building is but I see some EAs (Ecumenical Accompaniers) and guess they are going so ask them and they point to a building way up a steep hill. I go ahead to investigate and find a set of about a hundred very steep stone steps. There is no way that Echlas is going to get up these. Dejected I go back and break the bad news but Echlas and Christina have already made a plan to go to a favourite restaurant above the bus station and wait for me there while I see Mark Thomas. After many "Are you sure?"s, I step across the road and up the steps. The place is small and packed with people. I find myself sitting next to one of Echlas' pupils and recognise a couple of others I know. The audience is mainly foreigners with a smattering of Palestinians. Mark Thomas is funny but I am not sure that many of the non-English get many of his very English references. He is passionate about Palestine so it is a mixture of the ridiculous situations that occur because of the occupation and the very desperate circumstances that Palestinians find themselves in. It was certainly worth going to and I am full of it when I meet up with the others. It is just as well Echlas did not go as I think a lot of the jokes would have passed her by.

*

Today we are going on an outing to visit Echlas' sister and her family in their village near Hebron. After the palaver to get Echlas into the taxi we set off south out of Bethlehem and into the countryside. It is lovely to see green and terraced hills and olive trees and crops growing and young boys tending the sheep in the valleys. What is deeply unpleasant is the sight of the ugly settlements scarring the landscape. Mohammed gets a bit lost (no sat nav) but eventually we drive into a wide driveway outside a large white brick house.

Members of the family come out to greet us and we are spared the effort of getting Echlas out of the taxi as one of the nephews just lifts her out and plonks her into the wheelchair in seconds. Sister is here preparing the food, and brother-in-law, also two nieces plus little Esa (Jesus in English) and two nephews.

The view is just wonderful. We can see for miles across to the distant hills and it is so quiet after the camp. I feel there is room to breathe out here and think about those kids playing in the confines of the grey brick alleys and wish they could all come out here. The house is high up and looks down onto a few houses scattered around, some of which belong to brother-in-law's family. The houses have big gardens where vegetables are grown and I learn that sister-in-law grows a lot of produce and is quite a countrywoman.

The house is luxurious compared to the camp and all the furnishings are plush and new looking and we offer to take our shoes off, and are told no, but do anyway. The usual plastic table and chairs are brought out from their storage under the stairs and the women lay the table while we, as guests, sit outside in the sun drinking homemade lemonade which is like nectar. Son-in-law says it is very easy to make and we can use our own lemons.

There is a lot of banter and laughter and Echlas is enjoying the teasing from her nephews. They have a very easy way with her and almost ignore her disabilities and take her needs in their stride. The nephew we had not met looks different from his brother. He is tall and lean whereas the other one is stocky and slightly overweight. His job is training Palestinian soldiers so he must be tough. He is very attentive to Echlas and even feeds her. They are a very warm, loving family, so hospitable and friendly without fussing, and I immediately feel comfortable here. The lunch is wonderful. Sister-in-law is a very good cook. We have chicken and rice with almonds, three different types of salad and a dish made with bread which is mainly for Echlas.

On the way we had stopped to buy *knafa* to take with us so a little later we have that. *Knafa* is a Palestinian speciality and is gorgeous. The best *knafa* is made in Nablus but this one was from the best *knafa* shop in Bethlehem and having no comparison I thought it was heavenly. It is made with a base of *knafa* noodles, baked in butter covered with 'stretchy cheese'. Bakers only use Balcodi cheese, a white cheese sold by Bedouin so probably not available here. This is baked and when ready, a syrup of lemon juice, sugar, flower water, butter and water is poured over. It is made in huge flat pans, and portions roughly cut out to eat in or take away. *Knafa* is made and sold in restaurants selling only sweets and cakes and you can see groups of young men and older men, and families, sitting around a table enjoying the intensely sweet taste of *knafa* and *baklava* and similar. Sometimes it is sold in the street and I was tempted in Hebron but disappointingly it was not up to the standard of Bethlehem or Nablus. I think I am becoming a connoisseur!

Sitting outside in the warm January sun, eating *knafa* and sipping mint tea is heavenly. I have a walk around with the younger daughter who shows me the neighbouring houses of her three uncles and the views from the roof of the house which are even more far-reaching. One of the sons prepares an *aguila*, lighting the charcoal and when it is ready, placing a few pieces in the *aguila,* drawing on the mouthpiece and releasing a delicate aroma of apples. I have seen these all over Palestine – groups of mainly elderly men sitting in a semicircle on their hard upright chairs, wearing *keffiyehs*, puffing on their *aguilas*, watching life go by and exchanging a few words with each other. What must they have seen in their lifetimes I wonder and how do they feel now, still living under occupation? It's a typical scene in any town and village. Sometimes they will be playing backgammon or a card game at the same time. They do not need old people's lunch clubs and suchlike as they are such a close-knit community they probably all grew up together.

It's not just the preserve of old men though as nephew demonstrates. Young people enjoy *aguila* and in most restaurants it is available, where I see women indulging as well. Being an ex-smoker it is too much like smoking for me and makes me cough but I love the smell.

Christina and Esa play football and nephew joins in. The older sister and I are able to converse so I ask her about wearing the *hijab*. Her sister, I think, has only just taken to wearing it as she is always taking it on and off, sometimes enjoying the freedom without it and then trying it again in a different style. Older sister says she likes wearing it as it is part of her religion but no one makes her wear it. She shows me some photos of herself without the *hijab* and with blonde hair at a friend's wedding party where it is permitted to be without *hijab* as they are all women together. She just looked so different but I would not say she was less attractive wearing the scarf. I learn that she is in the last year of her degree and when she graduates will probably be an Arabic teacher. Her husband is a builder and, as he works in Nablus, she only sees him at weekends. Her mother looks after little Esa during the week and they practically live there while the husband is away.

An uncle plus young daughter, a beautiful girl with long wavy light brown hair, drop in at one point, drink coffee, then leave again. Brother-in-law shows me some photos, on his phone, of their pilgrimage two weeks ago to Mecca. It obviously means a lot to him but he is not an overtly strict Moslem from what I can tell. He challenged my preconceptions about Islam, although many have already been dispelled by previous visits and what I have learnt from Echlas. I think it is the exclusivity of Mecca and Medina which make it seem radical and alien, those pictures of men in white robes, thousands around the Kabah, the rituals about which most of us are ignorant. When I lived in Saudi Arabia we were not allowed anywhere near their holy sites and definitely felt alienated and resentful that they are welcome into our churches and holy places and yet we are refused entry to theirs. I resolved to read up more about Islam and try to get to grips with it.

It is comfortable sitting on the squashy sofa, listening to the banter and laughter and even though I cannot understand the words I can sense their family closeness, their easy way of being with each other, and suddenly I envy them and think how wonderful to be part of this large loving family, living in a place where one could almost forget the occupation for a while.

At last we have to go. Brother-in-law puts Echlas in his big four-wheel drive, and we gather up all our possessions and the bags of things that sister has given Echlas: 200 cigarettes, tin foil, 2kg sugar, dried figs and frozen broccoli from the garden, and dates. On the way we stop in a village and they buy a phone, bananas and cooking oil. At one point we slow down and brother-in-law shows us the lights of Gaza, we are that close! He says in the summer assault they saw the shells being dropped and could hear the bombing and felt such horror and despair being so close and unable to do anything to stop it.

Back in the dark camp the huge four-wheel drive, incongruous in the narrow shabby street, stops outside our alley and brother-in-law lifts Echlas out of the car. We go inside and put her to bed while brother-in-law sets up the new phone and sister puts away the shopping.

What a marvellous day we have had and I just admire so much the way they are with Echlas – no fussing, no deferring. She is just one of the family.

We have a couple of quiet days where nothing much is happening and the time is filled with domestic chores and looking after Echlas. She likes to get some sun when it's out so we go down through the *souk* and stop in a Christian centre where there is a garden at the back and they sell drinks. Sitting there in the sun, the noise of the *souk* in the distance, it is like being on holiday. We meander down to Manger Square and sit on the steps of the Peace Centre, eating falafel, and then I see a familiar face. It is Michaela, a member of Brighton PSC who I know, so I introduce her to Christina and Echlas and she comes and joins us. She was in Palestine last year as an EA and is now here for three months doing a research project on emigration amongst Palestinian Christians. Tomorrow she is interviewing the only Palestinian archbishop – he is coming to meet her here from Jerusalem. What a coup! She is living in a flat in Star Street which is fine except it is absolutely freezing so she has to come out to get some warmth. We walk back up Star Street with her and she invites me to go and have dinner with her and Susan this evening but I have to decline as we have to wash Echlas' hair when we get back – a long process.

After seeing Michaela I am envious of her freedom to go and see what she wants to and to be fully involved as an activist, in reporting what she sees and hears. What am I doing? Am I wasting my time? As Michaela said, "You come here planning to write a book and then can hardly string a sentence together." In my case what I can write about seems pretty mundane compared to her 'front line' reporting. In fairness to myself, however, she would probably be unsuited to the role I have and I am not assertive enough to do what she does.

Susan, the other friend I know here who is working as an EA in Jerusalem, is coming to Bethlehem so I manage to arrange some time off to meet her at Casa Nova, a restaurant next to the Church of the Nativity in Manger Square, where we sit in the quiet garden for coffee and stay on for lunch. I find it immensely helpful to talk to her about my experience here and my doubts as to my usefulness, but she answers me that she thinks I have the harder job and I am doing something unusual which will be of interest to people at home, being another aspect of life under occupation.

She tells me she is on a rollercoaster of emotions. It is her first time in Palestine, but she is finding the work very interesting and satisfying. She is living in a house in East Jerusalem with five other internationals and they all get on, taking turns with cooking and housework. They have three bedrooms, so she shares with a Belgian woman, and a lounge, kitchen, bathroom and balcony. When she has time off she receives an allowance which enables her to stay in a hotel in Jerusalem or Bethlehem. She chooses to come to Bethlehem as it is an oasis of calm compared to Jerusalem. It is so pleasant sitting in the sun and as I am in no rush we plan to have a wander about, when I get a call from Christina saying I am urgently needed at the bus station restaurant as she is ill. Saying a hasty goodbye to Susan I jump in a taxi and ask for the bus station. After a few minutes I sense we are going in the wrong direction so repeat that I want the bus station in Bethlehem. I do not know where he was taking me but no wonder he was confused because it turned out that I was about five minutes' walk from the bus station. We get there and it cost me 30IS (Israeli shekels) – about £6!

I find Christina sitting at a table with Echlas, looking pale. She tells me the story of her bad period pain and how she had collapsed in the toilet onto the floor. A waiter had to help her, which must have been so embarrassing, and got her a hot water bottle. She had phoned me from the toilet floor and I feel guilty for taking so long to get here but explain what had happened.

She still feels ill so Echlas phones Mohammed to come and collect her in his taxi and I walk home with Echlas. By the time Christina has a rest and we put Echlas to bed she is feeling just about well enough to go to Jerusalem to see her Jewish friends. Echlas wants to eat the remains of some food her sister had made which is now five days old. Although no meat was involved I am still not keen and say I would prefer a pitta sandwich so she calls Mohammed to come and fetch the rest. I am embarrassed.

Echlas has Skyped an American girl who is coming on 29

March so she will overlap with me and then take over when I leave in April.

Reflection

Being here is teaching me patience and unselfishness. Until yesterday I was thinking about what I wanted to do, where I wanted to go, what time I wanted to go to bed, eat, go out, having lived for eight years as a widow, being able to make these decisions for myself. But now, having been in the house all day with Echlas, on my own, I have had a change of mind. I ponder what it must be like for her all the time, for those people in Gaza who do not even have four walls or enough food and have to live with the boredom of a life severely limited by privations and by a wall stopping them from going outside their small strip of land.

I think of Echlas who is totally dependent on others for her every need, including going outside the four walls of her room, out of her bed. She cannot even see outside as the window looks onto a concrete wall and the other one is too high. All she can experience of outside is the voices she hears through the window, mainly the conversations of the children. Mohammed is her lifeline to outside and she asks him for camp news; being a boy he is not conversant with the gossip, but tells her what he can.

I know she has the phone, the internet and Facebook and has many friends, who visit her here but that is on their terms. She does not have the freedom to go where she likes without a great deal of planning and preparation.

So today I have been more content to just do what Echlas wants and potter about and just be. I just realised that I have not watched TV for two weeks and have not missed it.

Next weekend Christina and I have a few days off while Echlas stays with her niece in Aida camp. She has never stayed with them before and they keep urging her to do so. She is worried about how we will get her up three flights of stairs and so am I, now she has mentioned it, but it all usually works out.

There are two places in Jerusalem I have heard about and really want to stay in: the Austrian Hospice and the Hashima Hotel, both in the Old City, so I book them online for one night each and look forward to the experience of having a proper hot shower.

Christina came back this morning feeling back to her usual self. Echlas needs to buy a present for her niece, to take when she goes to stay, so we go out in the afternoon to a particular shop in the *souk*. Echlas knows exactly what she wants: a traditional wooden box with an embroidered lid, to keep sweets in. While she is choosing I come across some dusty cross-stitch canvases printed with various designs. I choose one of a woman in traditional Palestinian dress and then choose the embroidery silks. The whole lot, with a needle of course, is ridiculously cheap and it will give me something else to do in the evenings. Funny that I am going back to doing cross stitch that I last did many years ago in Saudi to pass the time when we had no work.

Melina comes in for a lesson. She is a very pleasant German girl who works with Crystal for JAI translating farmers' stories into Dutch to be published in a book. She tells us about Zumba classes that Crystal runs and we may go next week as Echlas is keen and it is near enough for us to push her. Uncanny how life here mimics life at home: gardening, buying second-hand clothes, embroidery, Zumba.

I met Roger in the street in Bethlehem earlier. He was the hotel receptionist when I stayed at the Sahara hotel in Beit Sahour for olive picking and planting. I have followed him on Facebook on his travels, but now he is back. He tells me that the Sahara is not so good now and groups do not go there. I am sad as I liked that hotel and felt at home there.

As well as the wooden box Echlas also wants to get a wooden ashtray to give and has seen some in a shop in the road on the other side of the camp. Mohammed comes round and she sends us out with instructions but the shop only has glass or metal. We go to a large souvenir shop where they have a square wooden ashtray but it is in use. Mohammed speaks to the shopkeeper and then we return home to ask Echlas if it is what she wants, but forgot to ask the price. After numerous visits over several days, speaking to different people, I eventually buy the only two wooden ashtrays they manage to procure and, thoroughly fed up with the whole saga, present them to Echlas who thankfully is very pleased with them. I feel I know the guys at the shop pretty well now and have met some of their family. One of them is always asking me to come in for coffee and a chat. He must be so bored, as customers are scarce since the wall was built; tourists rarely venture this far unless they are staying up the road at the Paradise Hotel, so many businesses are struggling. On one of my visits to the shop Echlas also asks me to go to her friend's shop and give him some money. He owns the Bedouin shop and sells the usual souvenirs and some *keffiyehs* and clothes. Echlas has bought things from him and maybe did not have the money at the time or phoned up and ordered something from him, so she owes him some money. She is not sure how much but I give him 100IS; he is not sure either and does not seem bothered one way or the other. I love this casual way they treat money – so trusting. The next time I go to his shop it has been invaded by a group of Africans all in yellow robes who have wrecked it by pulling out all the boxes of sandals and mixing them up and pulling the clothes from the shelves and leaving them on the floor. They leave without a purchase between them. Poor Majde is beside himself trying to match up the shoes, so I set to and fold the clothes and put them back on the shelves. When order is restored we sit down and have coffee while he has a moan about the Africans. That's shopping in Palestine.

CHAPTER THREE

JERUSALEM

The plan was to wake up at 8.30am and be out of the house by 10am but, of course, Echlas had to smoke six cigarettes before she could begin getting up so it is 11am before we get to her niece's home in Aida camp. The stairs up to the flat look impossible and Echlas is very nervous about the whole operation. Musa, her nephew, appears and we discuss how we can do this. Despite protestations from Echlas, Musa starts to pull the chair up backwards while Christina and I push the wheels round towards him to help the momentum. The stairway is very narrow for two of us so it is awkward and Echlas is giving instructions loudly in Arabic to Musa who is trying to calm her. On one of the turns I catch my top on a sharp bit on the banister and tear it so there is some swearing before we can climb up the next staircase. Sweaty and dusty and with a torn top we arrive at the flat. What a relief. I hope going down will be easier. The flat is a big surprise. It is all very modern looking with a beautiful fitted kitchen and when I go to the bathroom I have to take photos as it is amazing – much better than mine at home.

Echlas' niece, Rosha, and her husband have four daughters ranging in age from about eleven to the baby who is a year old. She is very solemn but so cute. Rosha wants us to stay for refreshments but Christina and I really want to go as she has a friend, George, a reporter from Ma'an News and a student of Echlas', waiting for her, and I just want to get going.

We manage to get away at last and George gives me a lift to the checkpoint. This is the first time I have walked through a checkpoint so I am apprehensive and interested in equal measure. I follow some other people up a narrow enclosed passageway, all concrete and wire, and then down the other side into a sort of holding area, again concrete, corrugated metal and wire. It feels prison-like. There is a queue of mostly Palestinians with a few foreigners among them all waiting patiently in line. I think about how they go through this every time they go to Jerusalem, the city that is 7.5km up the road and yet can take hours to get to if you are held up at the checkpoint. Permits to go to Jerusalem are not easy to obtain. Those that work in Jerusalem can get permits but for visitors to the city and age under fifty, they are only given twice a year for holy days to Moslems and three times to Christians. Then a permit may not be given to a whole family, just one, so of course, they do not go. This is a strategy by Israel to keep Palestinians out of Jerusalem, part of the overall plan to have Jerusalem entirely for Jews.

I have no idea what the hold-up is but can only follow the example of my fellow travellers and stand patiently. After a while the queue starts shuffling slowly forward and I can hear the clang of a turnstile. When it is my turn to go through I get my case caught as there is not room for me, my rucksack and case, and the last thing I want is to draw attention to myself, but a kind Palestinian man helps me extricate it and I proceed to the airport-type security where my case and rucksack are X-rayed. Then I walk across an open stretch of ground and into another building. This is passport/permit control and another queue. When the soldiers see my passport I am waved through and I nearly skip off towards the waiting bus. It has taken about forty-five minutes to do the first step of the journey but I expect it to be straightforward from now on. Soon the bus passes through the Jerusalem suburbs and it is strange to see the streets populated by Jews instead of Palestinians. The women are easily identified by their long, drab clothes and their head covering, and many of the men wear black from head to toe including the tall black hats from which their dreadlocks swing. I notice some large detached Arab-style houses among the ugly blocks of flats and think of the Palestinians who have been dispossessed of their beautiful homes and feel resentment towards these people who have taken away the land that does not belong to them.

Jerusalem is noisy and bustling with all sorts of people and I am dazed by all the activity and sights and sounds and smells. I weave my way amongst the crowds on and off the pavement, around street vendors, until I get to Damascus Gate, one of the entrances into the Old City. So far so good, I just have to find the Austrian Hospice in the maze of narrow alleys. I have a fair idea of the location and I have been here before but cannot find it. I walk back and forth, taking directions from three small boys who then demand shekels. At last I come upon it and struggle up the stone steps of the oasis that is the Austrian Hospice. The garden is lush and green and calming and I know it is worth coming here. I check in and then go up to my room which looks out onto the front of the hotel and has a wonderful view over the rooftops of the Old City. The room is white, plain and spacious and has a clean white bathroom with a shower. What bliss. The corridor outside is wide and wood panelled and a window at the end frames a statue of Our Lady. I go downstairs and sit with a coffee in the garden, savouring the peace and planning what to do next. I came here twice with the Olive Tree Campaign but this is the first time I have the freedom to just wander about and discover the city for myself. So I stroll along the cool dark alleys, up and down steps, out into bright sunlight into a square and then back again along another interesting alley full of shops selling spices, all sorts of food, clothes, household goods, leather goods, jewellery, antiques, souvenirs, T-shirts – everything imaginable. I soon learn not to look too interested or I get into a long bargaining ritual with the owner over something I do not want but am just looking at. I mingle with locals and foreigners and hear languages from all over but all the shopkeepers speak English and many speak several other languages as well.

It is mid-afternoon and I am hungry so look for somewhere to eat. I come across an inviting Moorish looking restaurant that is down a few steps. It is like going into a cave hung with colourful Arabic carpets and furnished with traditional Arabic sofas where one can relax with a *shisha*. I have falafel and a lemon and mint drink and feel quite adventurous staying here in the middle of Jerusalem on my own.

My next quest is to find a cashpoint as the hotels want paying in cash, and I think I will not find one here so go out of the Old City through Damascus Gate and up Salah al-Din Street in East Jerusalem where I am sure to find one. On the way I pass the English bookshop, famous among English workers, so stop after I have my cash for tea and a piece of their delicious cake. Books are my addiction so I spend some time perusing the shelves and buy two books. I have to be careful though as any political books I buy will have to be sent back, adding expense, and the books themselves cost more than at home.

Last time I was here I was desperate to buy a political T-shirt, of which there are many in Jerusalem, but did not get the opportunity. One of the most popular has the Google motif and says, 'Israel? Don't you mean Palestine?' Another one says, 'America Don't Worry, Israel is Behind You', and has a picture of a warplane. There are so many to choose from and, as usual, I get talking to the owner Ahmed, who tells me he had been to Manchester and has a friend in London who comes here every month on business. Some of the T-shirt designs were his so I feel I should buy one of those instead of my original choice.

While 'just looking' in the window of a jewellery shop I get enticed inside, given the usual coffee, and before I know it have bought a silver Jerusalem cross, designed with white sapphires and jade. The shop owner tells me he learnt design at university in London, then came back to take over his father's silversmith business as he was getting too old. Not entirely sure I believe him. He asks me about my family, which is customary in Palestine, and unthinking I say I am a widow. He then invites me out for a coffee, which is not customary. Shocked, I make some excuse and leave.

Shopping here is certainly not the tedious experience it is at home. On the Via Dolorosa I pass a small shop selling snacks where a large parrot is attracting much attention from passers-by. He is very old and the owner brings him to work with him every day as he enjoys interacting with people.

I am then invited into a very expensive-looking antique icon shop where the owner does not try to sell me anything but takes me through the shop to show me the 'bedrock' which was part of the original city foundations through a perspex window in the floor.

After a busy and interesting day I am ready to go back to the Austrian Hospice where I sit in the garden again and read and have a drink before having a blissful hot shower. The rest of the evening is spent in bed under my fluffy duvet, reading, sewing and eating chocolate – heaven.

Three years ago before my first visit to the Holy Land, I would never have imagined that I would be in the heart of the Old City in Jerusalem, that name evocative of the Bible, of Christianity itself. The idea was too big to comprehend and yet here I am in this fascinating, troubled city, the focus of the three Abrahamic faiths, that means so much to millions of people. Looking back I do not know why I thought to visit Jerusalem was so improbable; now I know it is the same as visiting any other large city once you have got through security at the airport. After a while anywhere can be normalised, once it becomes familiar. Those are my thoughts anyway when I wake up and look out of the window, down onto the already bustling street below.

At breakfast, after another hot shower, I talk to two ladies, one from Switzerland and one from Vienna, and tell them what I am doing in Bethlehem. They are astonished and very interested to know that that sort of independent volunteering is possible. At 9am I had arranged to meet Susan, my EA friend, in East Jerusalem. We sit and talk in the sunshine, Susan telling me about the horrors of Kalandiya checkpoint where she is on duty two mornings a week. It all sounds very depressing and deeply unsettling and Susan is finding it very hard to cope with. I think if you have not experienced life in Palestine before then it must be extremely challenging.

We walk through the alleys to the Western Wall as I am hoping to get to the Al-Aqsa Mosque but am told curtly by a disinterested soldier that it is closed. We find out it is only open between 8 and 10am so I plan to get up early tomorrow. Susan has to go to work so I continue my exploration of the Old City, less worried about getting lost in the maze of alleys today as I know I will eventually find a familiar landmark from which to get my bearings. Discovering a genuine-looking antique shop full of wonderful furniture, wall hangings, lights, lamps and embroidered dresses, I go in to explore and of course, get into conversation with the owner.

As I am interested in traditional Palestinian embroidery, he shows me different types and explains how one can tell which part of Palestine they come from, depending on the design. Embroidery is a traditional craft practised by village women and is an important symbol of Palestinian culture. It has always been used to decorate the women's dresses and also for cushion covers, purses, bags and in more modern times iPad covers, spectacle cases, wallets. The main patterns are found on the chest, sides, sleeves and lower back hem of the *thaub* which is a long dress with long sleeves. Some older women still wear it but the younger ones tend to have one for special occasions such as weddings. The design and colours have all sorts of meanings and tell all sorts of stories from ancient myths and legends. Some patterns reflect nature and some the supernatural, while others are a commentary on women's life. During the Intifada embroidery was used as a form of resistance when women incorporated forbidden nationalist symbols into their designs.

The shop owner tells me he is a designer so no wonder he displays such a knowledge and love for these embroideries. He shows me two dresses which he keeps in a trunk so as not to let the daylight fade them, which are worth thousands of dollars. I feel honoured that he got them out especially for me to see but he says he saw my bracelet and is pleased to see a Palestinian supporter among all the tourists who visit his shop. Some of them are very rude and abusive and walk into his shop saying he should only sell Israeli goods. It was obvious I was not a customer for any of the expensive items and yet he had given me his time. I buy a small embroidered mat, not because I feel I should, but purely because I like it.

Just around the corner is a tiny shop with old *thaubs* hanging up outside, but inside there are shelves of old dress fronts. I spend a good hour going through the piles, to find the one I like best and that I can afford. The man there puts them out all over the tiny floor space trying to be helpful and brings me the customary coffee which I am fearful of spilling on them but he is not at all pushy and leaves me to it, going across the road to chat with his friends. I finally make my selection and plan to frame it when I get home.

Lunch is falafel and salad in a café near the Austrian Hospice from where I collect my bag to take to the Hashimi Hotel. I had passed it on my wanderings so am able to go straight there and check in. This is a very different hotel from the Austrian Hospice which is in an open square, whereas this is a doorway amongst the shops, the hotel accessed up some steps. My room does not have much of a view but is clean and comfortable with a huge shower space and altogether very satisfactory. I go up to explore the roof for which the Hashimi is well known and am not disappointed. The views are even better than from the Austrian Hospice. I take lots of photos of the Dome of the Rock, glistening gold in the sunshine, and the rooftops of the Old City. It is a pleasant place to sit and have some peace after the stress of shopping so I sit and read, looking up occasionally to re-admire the view. I see a cloud of thick, black smoke on the left, slowly billowing across the horizon and wonder what on earth it can be.

In the early evening I go out through Damascus Gate and across the road to meet Susan in a restaurant past one of the bus stations. She has not been here before but has been told it is good by her colleagues. We go up the stairs and into an area with a bar and a large TV where people are sitting on sofas watching a football match. It all looks very laid back and relaxing but we get as far away as possible from the TV and settle in. I have lamb kebab, trying to get some meat while I can, chips, salad and a glass of wine followed by a delicious chocolate pudding.

A girl on her own, laptop in front of her, smoking *shisha*, comes over to speak to us when we have finished eating. She is Norwegian, called Sterna, and is attracted by Susan's EA jacket and wants to know what she is doing. She is working in Hebron for the women's cooperative there. They sell their embroidery in the *souk* in Hebron as well as online and I see from their website they have recently branched out into weaving so are making carpets now.

Walking back in the dark through the alleys of closed-up shops is in sharp contrast to earlier. Now I meet one or two other people walking but mostly it is quiet, just the clip clop of shoes on stone. Maybe mistakenly I feel no fear or anxiety walking here.

During the night I am awoken suddenly by the sound of gunfire. I can now tell the difference between fireworks and gunshots as the latter have a crack sound which makes me jump. Then all goes quiet again and I drift off to sleep.

The next morning I queue up with a party of Germans to get into the Al-Aqsa compound. The day is bright and sunny but colder than yesterday. Approaching the Dome of the Rock is breath-taking, on a par with the Taj Mahal, in my opinion. The golden dome shining in the sunlight, the intricate patterns of the blue mosaics which are just too beautiful, and the size of it too, I can only appreciate by being this close. The whole compound is vast; there is nothing else like it in Jerusalem. No wonder the Israelis want to get their hands on it. I walk around, feeling the holiness, and taking photos, just blown away by the experience.

Groups of women and men are dotted all around the compound, praying and reading the Koran. As I approach the Al-Aqsa Mosque, a fairly nondescript-looking building compared to the Dome of the Rock, a shabbily dressed man approaches me and asks if he can be my guide. I decline at first, out of habit, but something about him changes my mind and I agree on a short tour as it is so cold. He explains that the Dome of the Rock is for women only to pray, although men are allowed at certain times, and is the site of Mohammed's (PB) ascent to heaven. The Al-Aqsa Mosque is prohibited to women but he told me to look through the window so

I catch a glimpse of the vastness of it before a man inside blocks my view with his hand, obviously not happy for a woman, non-Moslem at that, to peek into this sacred place. My guide rattles through the history which I have not retained and then shows me pictures of his three children, plus his wife, mother and numerous other relatives for whom he has to provide. I have no way of knowing whether he is genuine or whether it is a sob story but I give him 50IS (approximately £10) – a lot for fifteen minutes.

As I walk away from the mosque past the prayer groups, a group of Israelis came in accompanied by a soldier. The women immediately began chanting "Allahu Akbar" very loudly and I wonder why these Jews have to be so provocative and insensitive.

It is time to get the bus back to Bethlehem after picking up my bag from the hotel, to meet up with Christina back at Aida camp and take Echlas home. Travelling back through the Jerusalem suburbs my head is full of thoughts of Jerusalem, about how the Palestinians are gradually being squeezed out by the Israeli authorities, knowing that the aim of Israel is to completely rid the city of all non-Jews and claim it as the capital of Israel. Do they live every day in trepidation? Unless they hide it very well, I feel that they just get on with life day to day, in the belief that one day justice will be done and they will have their rights and property returned. In the meantime they earn what they can for their families and derive strength from each other.

CHAPTER FOUR

HOME AGAIN

I walk back to Aida camp beside the graffitied wall, past Banksy's shop and the house surrounded on three sides by the wall. When I get to Rosha's home, Christina is not there yet but it looks as if we are in no hurry to go anywhere as Rosha is making bread for breakfast. She rolls out two large flat loaves and tops one with *za'atar* and the other with cheese. The left-over pieces of dough she makes into small croissant shapes, filled with Nutella. A niece from Ramallah is staying and she is entertaining the baby and then Rosha's mum drops in and they Skype another family member and all sing 'Happy Birthday' to a one-year-old.

The bread is truly delicious, well worth waiting for. Lucky family. Rosha is an excellent cook and has been away on cookery courses. She has recently set up a business making cakes and the photographs of the ones she has made look spectacular. She made one like a camera for Musa – it is so realistic!

Musa finally arrives and despite Echlas' trepidation, scoops her up out of the chair and carries her downstairs. Much easier than going up.

The smell of stale smoke hits me as we enter the flat, but it now feels like home and I am glad to get back. Rain and possibly snow are forecast so I hope we are not stuck indoors for days.

While I was in Jerusalem, Christina and George had travelled down to the Dead Sea as, being a journalist, George has a car. He came round for dinner on Sunday and showed us the photos he took, on his laptop. It looks stunning, not what I saw of the Dead Sea at all. The area they went to has waterfalls and rock pools, trees and vegetation, and sand where they camped overnight.

As a follow-up to the CT, Echlas has to go to the Holy Family Hospital in Bethlehem one morning to see her doctor and have the result explained. I have seen the report and it shows nothing abnormal except a benign adrenal cyst but Echlas wants to see the doctor anyway. It is a beautiful building with high ceilings, large courtyards with orange and lemon trees and holy statues. It is all very clean and tranquil and on a hot day a welcoming, cool oasis. We sit in the waiting room with a number of mostly young pregnant women with their mothers or husbands and some young children. This is obviously the obstetrics and gynaecology department. The system is mysterious as there is no evidence of patient notes. It seems to be up to the patients to organise themselves and works well until someone turns up and tries to jump the queue. She does not succeed so knocks on the consulting room door where after a short conversation with the doctor she goes off in a huff.

The doctor, a very pleasant man, trained in Scotland, he tells me, explains the CT report to Echlas and suggests she should see an endocrinologist re the adrenal cyst. As she has had no period since November he gives her a blood form to check her hormone levels to ascertain whether she is post-menopausal. The blood test cannot be done at this hospital and Echlas has to find her own endocrinologist. Fortunately, sister Afaf is a nurse so knows the system and will be able to help.

In view of the weather forecast Echlas is stocking up. This morning before the hospital I went with Layan to the greengrocer around the corner and bought so many bags of fruit and veg we struggled to carry them back. Now we have to go to Echlas' favourite grocery shop which is miles away, near the bus station. Two dozen eggs seems excessive to me, but we trudge home with these and bags full of other supplies.

Many days are spent just pottering indoors tidying up, washing, hanging it out, ironing, cooking, reading, sewing, doing Arabic, the day punctuated by the call to prayer which is the only thing that gives it shape. Mealtimes are random; we eat when we are hungry, except for the evening meal. Echlas spends her day on her laptop or her phone giving lessons. We talk, give her a wash, do her hair, make plans and the day passes.

As Christina was out last night at Zumba, I go to AIC tonight to listen to a Palestinian guy from Haifa in Israel so he is what is called a '48er'.

He talks about his book of short stories, all about identity – for Palestinians an important issue. They cannot be called Palestinians in Israel as according to Israel, Palestine does not exist. They are Arabs. However, Palestinians call themselves Palestinians as this is what they are. For those that live in Israel, the issue is even more complex as technically they are Israeli citizens but Israel, since 1948, has made a distinction between citizenship and nationality. The state is defined as belonging to the Jewish nation, so not only to the residents but also those in the diaspora. A group of Jews and Arabs have been fighting in the courts to be recognised as Israelis, a nationality that, according to Israel, does not exist. Although there are more than 130 possible nationalities for Israeli citizens most are defined as either Jews or Arabs. Jewish nationality is used as a way to undermine the status of non-Jews in Israel, especially the 'Arabs', giving special privileges to Jews under thirty different laws, including immigration rights, land, employment and naturalisation.

All citizens of Israel and Palestine have to carry identity cards with them at all times. By glancing at these it is easy to distinguish a Jew from an Arab as the date of birth of a Jew is written according to the Hebrew calendar. Also the Arab ID contains the grandfather's name.

So all non-Jews, i.e. Palestinians, whether Moslem or Christian, are easily identified in order to enforce the state apartheid system, of which I saw many examples. One of the most memorable was in Hebron when I was part of a group. As we approached a road to go down to the infamous Shuhada Street, a soldier stopped us and told us we were not allowed to walk on the tarmacked road; that was only for Jews. Instead we had to pick our way through a rough verge on the other side of a high metal fence. That was a small taste of what it feels like to be a second-class citizen.

After a fascinating talk I meet a couple of people from the Olive Tree Campaign who I know, and have a conversation with a young guy who is researching for his dissertation on how history is taught in Palestinian schools in order to pass on the Palestinian story.

I phone Mohammed to come and pick me up and while I am waiting I talk to an English girl with Bangladeshi origins who is on the planting programme, and she tells me about her five-hour interrogation at the airport. Eventually she gave in and told the truth, that she was there to plant olive trees, and they let her go! She was quite traumatised by the experience but says the planting experience has surpassed her expectations. I remember feeling the same.

When I get home Echlas had her abdominal pain again but does manage to eat some salad and then sleeps early.

Yom al arba

Extract from diary: Got up at 9am, nice and warm in bed, could hear the wind outside but sun shining. Echlas and Christina still asleep and it's 11am. No idea what the plan is for today. Just had tea and toast, put the water pump on, practised some Arabic and writing this.

Quite a boring day. Spent all day indoors as cold and windy out. Popped out briefly to shop and got caught in a hailstorm.

Feel I could have died of boredom! There is a limit to the amount of reading and sewing one can do. Sore throat.

The sore throat seems to be developing into a cold but the next day is bright and sunny so I go out to get some strepsils while Echlas is giving lessons. It is cold but good to be out.

In the evening another Mohammed comes to introduce a new student to Echlas. He is Irish, lives in Sweden and knows a Japanese girl that I met while olive picking. It really is a small world. He is about my age, divorced and staying in the camp guesthouse, the four-storey building at the end of our alley. He has been here eight days and his plan is to give English lessons to older students, being a teacher by profession. Being Irish he talks a lot but I find him very pleasant and think we should befriend him and introduce him to AIC, for instance. His name is Eugene and he gives me his phone number and invites me to go to his place for a cup of tea and a chat.

When he leaves Echlas says I am not to go to his guesthouse, as it would reflect badly on her. It seems ridiculous to me at my age, but camp politics are unfathomable to an outsider so I have to abide by her wishes. She says it is OK to meet outside the camp but not to fraternise inside. I make potato soup for dinner. Should have invited Eugene.

Yom al Jumma

I go to turn the water pump on but only a feeble splutter emerges and it is bath day. I turn the water heater on anyway. There is no way of telling how much water is in the tanks, which is why we have to put the pump on every day. This is another day when I wonder what I am doing here, apart from experiencing the daily hardships and frustrations of living in the camp and learning some Arabic. I write: "Why am I enduring this, will it be of benefit when I go home and what have I learned so far? Water problems, power cuts, medical systems, camp politics, tear gas in Aida, BDS, Arabic. I really need to go out and see and do something."

Looking back now, that is precisely why I came here, to experience life in a camp, and this is the life. A lot of it is routine, boring – exciting things do not happen every day – but even if I think I have learnt nothing on a 'boring' day I am learning to live communally, to adapt, to give, to communicate with all ages, of all different nationalities. I am listening to Arabic a good deal of the time and using my brain to attempt an understanding of it. I am not here primarily for my benefit anyway, but for Echlas, to be her carer, so anything else I should regard as a bonus.

This day promised to be anything but boring with a cooking class and the arrival of Hannah, our next volunteer.

We get Echlas up in the wheelchair and I carry on with the washing as Christina is in a hurry to go out with George.

Hebron sister is late, of course, and arrives like a whirlwind, son and daughter in tow, laden with bags of food. Within minutes she has her apron on and is organising proceedings like the head of military operations. Layan arrives and the three women chop and mix while I try to help but then realise they are more efficient without my foreign ignorance so just watch. Son is sent out for missing ingredients and then leaves and son number two arrives and rather reluctantly takes over the role of shopper. The three students for the cookery class arrive: a Canadian woman employed by UNWRA and her boyfriend, an Italian TV journalist, and Maddie, one of Echlas' students.

I had been to a cooking class in Aida camp on my first olive programme visit. It was organised by a delightful woman, Islam, who with a number of other women in Aida and Al Azza set up a cooking school in order to raise funds for disabled children in the camps to provide them with much-needed equipment. It was held in Islam's house and we had great fun chopping salad ingredients, supervised by Islam's husband who was very particular about the size of the diced cucumbers and tomatoes. He also showed us how to cut a tomato into even-sized cubes using a very sharp knife, without a chopping board. This skill was very impressive but there was the risk of having some blood in the salad so I persisted with the slower but safer method of cutting on a board. Evidently Palestinian men tend to regard themselves as good cooks, not that I ever saw one actually cook a meal; it was always the women in the background who cooked and the men presented the finished dish with great flourishes and fanfares as if it was all their own work. That night we learnt to cook *mujuddara* and a gorgeous pudding made with semolina, eggs, sugar, lemon and coconut. I tried to reproduce it at home but it was nothing like Islam's version. The entertainment was provided by her youngest daughter, a girl of about four, who watched us from the spiral staircase going from the kitchen up to the children's bedroom. Her father had made a swing from an old car seat hanging from the ceiling of the covered way between two buildings, where the shared oven lived. The swing proved a great attraction for all of us while waiting for the food. It was a memorable meal, although very simple, consisting of rice and lentils with spices and topped with caramelised onions accompanied by salads and yogurt followed by the most delicious pudding.

The cooking school is now held in a purpose-made kitchen and, looking on the website, the dishes look a lot more ambitious than the ones we made.

Echlas' cooking class is low key in comparison and different, in that she cannot provide the instruction herself. Her sister is an excellent cook and the participants seem to enjoy joining in. The floor oven comes into use for the chicken, a treat for us non-vegetarians. I am intrigued to see how it works. It is a large round metal dish with a lid and electric elements in the base and lid. The *sumaced* (*sumac* is a spice) chicken is put on another metal plate which fits over the element, the lid is closed and the oven plugged in. Simple. There is no temperature regulation, you just turn off the top or bottom heat by guesswork.

The whole meal takes about three hours to prepare and cook so when it is ready and all laid out on the table we need little encouragement to dive in. Gradually other people start arriving. Rosha and her baby Ru Ru, sister's husband, Amia bringing a cake and another woman who I do not know and Hannah. At first I do not realise she is the new helper, sitting on the sofa looking rather bewildered amongst all these people, but when the penny drops I explain what is going on and reassure her that this is not a 'normal' day.

It is near Valentine's Day, another reason to celebrate, so Rosha is here to talk about how she met her husband. Contrary to popular belief, that all Moslems have arranged marriages, she talks about how they had met and fallen in love. The family approved as he is an Al Azza, so within the clan. Many of the older generation want the young to marry within the clan and if a girl or boy marries someone outside they will not be ostracised but will be met with some suspicion and put under close scrutiny until they are accepted as part of the family.

It is a hectic day with much laughter and chatter and the atmosphere is relaxed and convivial. Christina arrives back from her day out and some people go and then come back, so lots of comings and goings. Meanwhile I do the washing up, tackling the huge pots and the piles of crockery but it is soon done and the kitchen restored to some sort of order. I am beginning to feel quite proprietorial over the kitchen and like things to be in the right place.

Hannah decides to go outside to look around but Echlas is alarmed when she notices she is missing and sends me out to look for her. She has not gone far, just to the end of our alley, and is surrounded by a group of very friendly, chatty small boys but I have to bring her back indoors, under Echlas' wing, much to Hannah's puzzlement. In the midst of all the activity there is a smell of burning and smoke appears to be coming from the settee. Christina has put the heater too close to the soft furnishings and now we are in imminent danger and get ready to evacuate but a cup of water douses the potential fire and the hole is hardly noticeable.

During the evening numbers diminish until it is just the four of us. Hannah has coped remarkably well with her chaotic introduction but does look a bit bemused. Christina is showing her around, explaining the vagaries of the electrics and the cooker, which she is bound to forget by tomorrow with so much to take in. She is very young and has just left school but seems to be self-assured and confident so I am sure she will fit in well.

Since being here in Bethlehem I have not been to Mass. This seems incongruous but up until now I have not had an opportunity and do not feel that I can make an issue of it as my primary purpose is to care for Echlas. Johnny, who I met on the pilgrimage, is picking me up from the Intercontinental Hotel to take me to Mass in Beit Jala, where he lives. He picks me up and takes me to his home, a flurry of activity with members of his family rushing around getting ready. They are all dressed up and made up and I feel a bit dowdy as I am not used to this level of sartorial smartness, living in the camp. Johnny has to go back to work so leaves me with his wife Beryl, who calls me Merrill, two daughters, one husband and two small children. We pile into two cars and take off at speed through the narrow roads down to the church. Beryl finds me a seat near the front, while she goes off to sing in the choir. I have a mass book and hymn book but all in Arabic so follow as best I can. I am amazed at the number of children in the congregation and, halfway through, a nun gathers them up from the pews and brings them to stand either side of the altar: boys on one side, girls on the other. There must be at least fifty children. I count twelve altar servers, all girls, one with blonde hair (the Crusades?). The choir sings very loudly, raucous to my Western ears but very enthusiastic, and there is a great sense of community among the people and real engagement with the Mass. At the end of the service the priest gives out red carnations to everyone for Valentine's Day, to remind everyone that God loves us all. Grabbing a cup of Arabic coffee on the way out, Beryl rushes me into the car and off we go back to Al Azza, not the leisurely after-Mass get together I was imagining. Beryl and her daughter had obviously not been into a camp before and I can sense their horror as we enter the rubbish-strewn, narrow, rough road between the haphazardly constructed buildings. Together they say, "Why you live here?" in shocked voices looking out at the people and houses in disbelief. Matter of factly I reply, "I like living here. It's a good experience."

Johnny is manager of a large souvenir shop near the camp so we often used to pass it and when I saw him outside on a couple of occasions after this he treated me like a saint, saying I was doing such good work and God would reward me. I did not feel I needed any reward as it was not a hardship living with Echlas but it was kind of him to say so.

Echlas is still in bed and has not long woken up when I get in so I help to get her up and washed for our outing to Aida camp. The camp is a maze of streets without names but relying on landmarks it is easy to find one's way around after a while. We go past the large cemetery and the children's playground next to it and the Largee Community Centre and come to the wide road with the gates at the end in the wall where the soldiers come from their military base to terrorise the inhabitants. Turning left we pass an antique shop, a curious place that I would like to explore, but we move on and soon turn left again down a slope into the garden of our destination. This is where Echlas' aunt lives with her daughter, in a ground-floor flat. It is spacious, furnished with large settees and armchairs and a large modern kitchen.

Aunty is a delightful old lady with mild Alzheimer's and diabetes but still insists on several spoons of sugar in her tea. Musa comes and teases her in an affectionate way. I cannot understand what is said but can glean something from the body language and facial expressions and it is funny to watch them. I ask if I can take a photo of her and that provokes further teasing, Musa telling her that she will be on Facebook. Dubiously she lets me photograph her on her own but when Hannah takes one of us together she is much happier. She smiles a lot and seems quite happy but her daughter cannot leave her at all as she has been known to leave the gas on and tries to cook. She loves making coffee or tea for guests as this is her deeply ingrained custom of hospitality and cannot understand when we say we do not want any as we have just had a glass of delicious lemon and mint. In the end she is allowed to make it under discreet supervision and it is left on the table to remind her that we had been offered refreshment.

Christina, Hannah and I go out with Layan for a short tour of the camp, leaving Echlas and aunty to gossip. Layan shows us two of the original dwellings built in 1950 when the UN realised after two years of living in tents that the refugees were not going to be allowed to return to their villages anytime soon. They are breeze-block rooms approximately 12 foot by 12 foot where a whole family lived. Now these form part of a larger house as more rooms have been added by later generations but there is no more room to build out so they have to go up. An unpleasant smell draws me to peer into a dark basement where Layan tells us sheep are kept. They do get out to wander about the streets but there is no grazing around here for them. No animal rights here then but not surprising since there are no human rights. A visit to the Largee Centre, where Musa works, gives us great views from the roof and there is also a polytunnel here where vegetables are grown. The Largee is one of two cultural centres in the camp, where children come and do activities and learn skills like photography, acting, computer skills and *dabka* dancing. She points out the burnt watchtower, set alight by activists, and the hole in the wall they made as a protest. Before the wall was built the camp had views over the countryside and access to green spaces but now the wall forms a solid grey barrier, confining them within the camp. On another wall within the camp, we see portraits of the men from Aida camp who are in prison. Some have been released after twenty years but they are still not really free as they have restrictions placed on them, are watched constantly and are often re-arrested very quickly on trumped-up charges.

Back at aunty's we find Rosha, her mother and Ru Ru there. Rosha's mum does embroidery, the traditional patterns that have been handed down through the generations and are part of the cultural resistance. She has brought some to show us as I had expressed an interest in seeing it. She lays out cushion covers, purses, mobile phone covers, specs cases, bags, all made by her and so beautiful I want to buy them all but I already have a number of items like these that I have bought on previous visits. However, as they are made by a family member I buy some more as these will be even more special to me and good for presents. Meanwhile, Ru Ru is very lively today and is entertaining us all with her antics.

Christina stays behind with Layan to help her with her personal statement for her application to the London School of Economics. It is wet and windy as we walk back and we are glad to get back inside. I put the wheelchair on charge; after we get Echlas into bed we eat the leftovers from yesterday and I am prepared to settle in for the evening but Echlas decides she wants to go out again. So reversing the procedure we have just carried out, off we go out into the rain and wind to the bus station restaurant. As usual it is almost empty and the waiter provides a heater for Echlas, knowing what she needs from her frequent visits here.

Hannah's family is Lutheran and her mother is a priest but Hannah is an atheist and has particularly anti-Catholic views so we have a lively discussion about the differences between Protestantism and Catholicism and the pros and cons of religion in general while drinking red wine and eating chips. The journey home does not seem so bad after the wine, although we get soaked and struggle to get the wheelchair up the wet, slippery slope to the camp.

Yom il tnin

Today we are having a tour of Bethlehem by car, arranged by Echlas with Mohammed as an introduction for Hannah. Christina instructs Hannah how to get Echlas into the car and with a deal of manhandling we manage it between us. Having got Echlas into the seat we put the wheelchair seatbelt around her and the back of the seat to ensure she is firmly secured. Her feet rest on the foam foot pieces from the wheelchair and lastly the seatbelt goes on. Once she is comfortable we can set off. Thankfully it is not raining, the sun is shining and it feels good to be going out into the countryside where the effect of the rain is evident in the greenness of the fields and the many wild flowers blooming. It all feels fresh and new and I feel energised leaving the grey drabness of the camp but I feel for the children who do not have the opportunity to play in green open spaces. Mohammed drives skilfully along the country roads, pointing out places of interest and stopping now and then so we can get out and look at something specific while he and Echlas have a cigarette.

Beit Jala is on a hill and was originally surrounded by orchards and vineyards but these lands were confiscated by Israel to build three settlements, Gilo, Har Hom and Giv'at, as well as two tunnels and two bypass roads exclusively for Israeli use. Only a quarter of Beit Jala municipality is under Palestinian control (Area A), the remaining 75% under full Israeli control. This was news to me as I had assumed that all the main Palestinian towns were Area A as per the Oslo Accords. Over 16,500 people live here, 70% Christian and 30% Moslem. In the Second Intifada Beit Jala suffered shelling from the IOF, causing damage and destruction to churches, mosques, schools and homes, was under frequent curfew and endured food shortages.

Just looking at the town and its people going about their daily business one could not know all this, although the evidence of the settlements is all too plain to see, great fortress-like structures on every hilltop. It makes me angry when I hear and see how the land is being stripped of its natural beauty and its people being deprived of their livelihoods and their freedom by the illegal occupation, acting with impunity.

Beit Sahour is on the other side of Bethlehem, where the Singer Café and the AIC are, and the YMCA from where JAI operates. It has the largest Christian population in the West Bank – 75%. It also has one of the highest numbers of university-educated people in Palestine. What I learnt from JAI is that it is renowned for its innovative resistance actions in the First Intifada. The residents refused to pay their taxes to the occupiers and organised demonstrations using the slogan, 'No taxation without representation. No taxes without a government'. The IOF retaliated by imposing a forty-five-day curfew, arrested hundreds of people and confiscated goods. The film The Wanted 18 *about a herd of cows that had to be hidden from the IOF and was part of the resistance in the Second Intifada, is a story that took place in Beit Sahour and is a wonderful example of the ingenuity of a group of people working together to outwit the occupation.*

 Like Beit Jala it is an attractive town with is renovated, original architecture and a place I feel at home in having stayed here twice. The Shepherds' Fields are just a few steps away from the hotel where we stayed and is reputedly the very place where the angel appeared to tell the shepherds of Jesus' birth. The area is smaller than I expected and has been landscaped so not the rugged hillside one imagines but the caves where the shepherds lived are interesting.

We visit Cremisan Monastery, high up on a hillside in a wooded area, and I just have to get out of the car to take photos of the wild cyclamen flowering there. It is quiet and peaceful, just us here, but unfortunately we cannot see the actual monastery as it would mean leaving Echlas too long in the car. This is where the famous Cremisan wine is made, the only commercial vineyard in Palestine, and while I am here this is the only wine I drink, to support the local economy, and it is very good. Since my visit here the wall has now been built, despite widespread protest, dividing the land from the monastery and spoiling and confiscating yet another piece of land. I am glad I saw it when I did.

During our tour and on previous occasions I had noticed that many of the houses in Beit Jala and Beit Sahour have plaques over their front doors depicting St George and the dragon and was intrigued by the connection, since St George is the Patron Saint of England. One of our guides told us that he lived in the village of Al Khader after leaving his native Lydda. He is venerated for being able to ward off the evil eye and is also the patron saint of farmers, travellers and the mentally ill. Moslems and Christians make a pilgrimage together annually on 5 May to Al Khader Church, built in 1600AD in his memory.

Next we go to Solomon's Pools. A couple of men in uniform, giving the impression of being in charge, are unable to give us any information about this site so we wander around looking in the water and admiring the size of the pools. With a bit of research later I learn that they were built in the first or second centuries BC and are part of an ancient water system to supply Jerusalem. Brooks and rainwater supplied the cisterns and some water was piped to Jerusalem and some to Herodion through aquaducts which remained in use to irrigate crops until the early twentieth century.

Every army which intended to capture Jerusalem first set up camp here, i.e. Crusaders and Saladin's army.

Fortunately we had thought to bring some food with us so we sit here and eat crisps and jam sandwiches and chocolate bars. Not exactly a well-balanced, healthy lunch but that was all we had in the kitchen. On to the mount of Herodion next. This is a man-made hill on which King Herod's impressive palace was built between 24 and 15 BC. It is said to have been his favourite palace and that he is buried here. We drive halfway up the hill and then stop to admire the view but it is so windy the visit is cut short. The site, in Area C, is under Israeli jurisdiction which charges an entrance fee to go any further, so not wishing to contribute in any way to the occupation, we drive back down and see some of the excavated ruins of the lower city.

The last visit of the day is Dheisheh camp, the third refugee camp in Bethlehem. This was somewhere else I had visited previously and walked around its narrow alleys seeing the martyrs' portraits painted on the camp walls and hearing the stories of how they had been killed by the IOF. Invariably they are young men, those identified by the IOF as being the greatest threat.

The camps are always a target for the IOF, suffering frequent curfews, night raids, arrests and tear gassing. From 1987 to 1993, the First Intifada, the Israelis set up a military camp overlooking Dheisheh and installed a six-metre-high barbed wire fence surrounding the camp. Thirteen of the fourteen entrances to the camp were barricaded and the only means to exit and enter was through a heavily guarded turnstile gate. Hundreds were injured and sixteen died and more than 30% of the young people were imprisoned for varying lengths of time. These events become part of the history of the ongoing suffering of the Palestinian people.

After a long but interesting day we settle Echlas into bed straight away. Christina and Hannah go off to Zumba while I cook a vegetable sauce to go with some leftover *maftoul*. This is bulgar and whole wheat flour, made by groups of Palestinian women who hand roll and dry the organic wheat in the hot sun. It is a time-old tradition passed down from mother to daughter and part of the Palestinian culture.

Snow is forecast for the weekend so my plan to go to Nablus may be scuppered.

Yom il talata 17 February

Today I take Hannah down to Manger Square. She is amazed by all the shops and the people and receives a good deal of attention from young men attracted by her blonde hair. Down in the square we eat falafel in pitta bread in the tiny restaurant below street level where they sell the best falafel in town and it is too – fresh and crispy. The man makes them using a special scoop which he fills with falafel mix, levels off with a knife and drops into a huge pan of bubbling oil. In a few minutes he scoops them out to drain and continues like this at lightning speed. Falafel is a traditional Middle Eastern street food made with chick peas and one can buy three falafel for 6IS or a falafel sandwich for 10IS so it is a cheap meal or snack.

Our time is limited so I point out the Church of the Nativity and the Peace Centre before we hurry back up the hill past the tourist shops with their colourful displays of scarves, dresses and *keffiyehs* replying to the cheerful "*Marhaban*"s from the shop owners, some of whom I am on familiar terms with now. When they know you are living here they cease treating you like a tourist and trying to lure you into their shop but they must struggle to survive with so few tourists about.

Echlas is expecting visitors so we buy some cake on our way home and just have time to tidy up before they arrive. Two tall, youngish German men are invited in and offered tea and cake. They come from Ramallah, where they are doing some official-sounding work for the German government on the refugee population and are here to interview Echlas. They ask her about her background and her disability, all the usual questions. Then the conversation becomes more controversial when one implies that the stone-throwing youth are to blame for many of the problems in the West Bank, to which Echlas responds sharply that this is the only way they have of expressing their anger and frustration. A few stones against the might of the armoured trucks and fully protected and armed soldiers is indeed a David and Goliath situation and the continued killings of Palestinians who then become martyrs is a crime that goes unpunished and fuels the tense situation. The Germans look rather uncomfortable at this forthright answer and turn to the three of us to ask what we are doing here and what had made us come to Palestine. We all reply that we are here to support and be in solidarity with the Palestinians by living and working with them, to let them know they are not forgotten by the world even if our governments would like us to. They leave in no doubt as to our convictions that what we are doing is absolutely the right thing in view of the unjust, illegal, immoral occupation of the Israeli regime and that world governments cannot continue to appease Israel.

Now they are gone Echlas vents her feelings about them and how little they understand about the Palestinians. This leads on to a discussion about culture and how it is not possible to begin to understand until you live in the place amongst the people. As an example, Hannah wanted to go out and play football with the small boys in the street but Echlas explained this behaviour would be seen as odd, foreign, as young women do not go out and play in the street. If she did she would be bound to attract unwanted attention from the young men, leading to harassment and lack of respect from the locals. This unusual behaviour would also reflect badly on Echlas and she is very conscious of her standing and reputation in the camp. Already she is seen as 'different' due to her disability and unusual way of living – with internationals. At first Hannah did not understand why she could not do as she liked and could see nothing wrong in it but now she recognises this is a very different culture and we, as foreigners, need to adhere to its customs if we are going to live here.

Christina and I leave Hannah to cook *freekeh* soup while we go to AIC, taking Eugene with us. The taxi driver is friendly – they usually are – and keen to speak English but I practise my limited Arabic on him and manage to have a short conversation along the lines of:

Me: *Marhaba, keif halak* (Hello, how are you?)
Him: *Al humdulila, mabsute, wa inti?* (Good, thank God, and you?)
Me: *Mabsuta, shukran* (Happy, thank you)
Him: *Inti btihki Arabi?* (Do you speak Arabic?)
Me: *Sway* (A little)
Me: *Wen inta sakin?* (Where do you live?)
Him: *Fi Beit Sahour*
Me: *Ana sakne fi Al Azza, ana bastgil ma Christina fi Al Azza wa ihna bnitallam Arabi.* (I live in Al Azza, I work with Christina in Al Azza and we learn Arabic.)

He seems to understand so I feel quite pleased.

The talks never start on time so I have a glass of red wine when we arrive and chat to a few people I know vaguely. The AIC is a very relaxed place and has a seating area, furnished in traditional Arabic style, suiting the old stonework of the building. They sell subversive T-shirts and other printed material. To go to the talk we go outside and down a few steps into another old stone building. The speaker is Jamal, a Palestinian living in England, who I know from olive picking. He is doing a PhD linking occupational therapy (his occupation) to olive farming in occupied Palestine. It sounds obscure but an interesting angle to take and a lot of it made sense at the time but I cannot recall the content of his proposal now.

After a sociable and stimulating evening we are met on our return home by the unpleasant odour of burnt sardines. I bought these to provide us with some protein, being a fish I actually recognised, and told Hannah that I would cook them when we got back. I was right to doubt her culinary skills as the poor sardines are massacred in the frying pan and look like something a cat has thrown up. I berate her for the ruin of half our dinner and just hope the other half is edible. Under Echlas' careful instruction she has managed to cook *freekeh* soup but the fiery hot pepperiness of it I thought too cruel to mention after her catastrophe with the fish, so eat as much as I can bear.

Yom il arba

Echlas is staying in bed today. I wake Hannah at 11am as she could probably sleep all day if left. Christina goes to the *hammam* and Hannah and I wash Echlas' hair in bed. She has a mildly itchy scalp and some dandruff and thinks frequent washing will help. This time we are using Nablus soap, purely olive oil and water, very good for the skin and dirt cheap. Having got her protected with towels and a plastic cape, we rub the soap into her scalp and try to produce a lather to wash her thick, black hair. The procedure is precarious with jugs and a bowl of water balanced on the bed. We manage to soak her T-shirt and a bit of the sheet but dry it with the hair dryer and change the T-shirt. I dry her hair off with a towel and then put it up, damp, in a ponytail. When Layan comes for the bath she spends ages drying and styling her hair but I think that time is as much for the chat as it is for the hairstyle, so today we keep it simple.

The conversation about culture is taken up again by Hannah, who I am realising is a very intelligent girl. She says she is a Marxist and plans to study philosophy at university, a subject she is already conversant with. She is keen to have some serious discussions on politics, philosophy and culture but her other side is quite childlike, acting like an excited puppy, breaking out into mad dancing and singing for no apparent reason. Her bedroom floor is covered in clothes, while the wardrobe is empty, and I only know that because I put some clean clothes back in her room. Perhaps all young girls keep their clothes on the floor? I must remember she is very young and make allowances and try not to act like her mum.

Re the culture conversation, Echlas tells us the story of an English girl who met a Palestinian boy here in the camp and started living with him. She was having Arabic lessons with Echlas which is how she knows her. The couple planned to get married, despite misgivings from both families, but the relationship broke up while the girl was back in England, her visa having run out. The girl wanted to come back to continue her studies at Jerusalem University so asked Echlas if she could stay with her for a couple of weeks until she found somewhere more permanent. Echlas agreed but then was constantly harassed by the former boyfriend and members of his family banging on the door at all hours, until she left.

I think the moral of this story is to respect the culture and if you go against it then it is likely to end in tears. However, there are many more examples of mixed marriages, i.e. Crystal, that work extremely well.

It is pouring with rain and I am still trying to get the washing dry. It is hung on the dryer in the living room with the spare heater underneath and I keep a close eye on it as I do not want to start a fire. The weather forecast, which Echlas takes a strong interest in, is very poor with heavy snow predicted but Christina is determined to go to Jerusalem so that she can get to Petra in Jordan to meet up with some friends there.

I fry fish in egg and flour for dinner. What sort of fish it is I cannot tell but it came frozen so I defrosted it in a large bowl of hot water and it turned out well. We eat it with rocket salad, followed by hot *freekeh* soup, which I decline, for obvious reasons. George stays for supper after his lesson. He admits he is lonely after his best friend left Palestine, and the flat they shared together feels so empty. Hearing Echlas, Christina and George talk about him he sounds like an irreplaceable character. George smokes non-stop except when he is eating but then he has one between courses, and bites his nails too. His job as a journalist must be very stressful being constantly exposed to the extremes of the occupation. I stay up till 1.30am until Echlas is ready to sleep as I am not confident that Hannah is either capable or happy with settling Echlas for the night on her own.

Hannah was up before me! Today it is constant rain. The washing is still drying. My sheets need changing but I dare not do them yet until the weather improves. They have been on the bed for a month but as it is a double bed I have moved them around so not as dirty as it sounds.

Echlas has found Hannah a job to do to keep her occupied. She is taking all the paper cut-out volunteers off the wall with the aim of laminating them. The copy shop is happy to do them and Hannah and I can help arrange the figures on the page for them. Hannah keeps getting side tracked so it is taking ages but I do not offer to help as it is her project.

We have a visitor in the afternoon and it is someone I know so I don't know who is more surprised. It is Deanna (not sure how her name is spelt, but that is how it is pronounced) and I met her on the olive programme when she was working for JAI. As Echlas has company Hannah and I go out to do some shopping but it is horrid out: cold, wet and windy. We buy the essentials: bread, milk, cereals and Echlas' tablets from the chemist. That is another surprise to me: once you have medicines prescribed by a doctor you can take the old packet in and buy another. Even children can do this but they can also buy cigarettes here. Only one of Echlas' tablets is supplied by the UN so I assume they provide only the most basic medicines.

The decision to postpone my visit to Nablus was easy to make in view of the weather and another factor influencing my decision is my slight worry about Hannah's ability to cope on her own: it does not seem fair to leave her so soon. Echlas had given instructions for making broccoli soup so while Ida, our neighbour, is visiting, Hannah and I prepare it. I have grave doubts as to how this soup will turn out as the ingredients include five cups of sugar, so to me it is obvious that it will be sweet. As indeed it is. Sweet broccoli soup. Even Echlas struggles. Then she feels sick and has her abdominal pain again so I give her two paracetamol and when she is feeling better I make her two boiled eggs with toast. There is no toaster or grill, so, ever inventive in Palestine, we use the heater, laying the bread over the elements on the top. Echlas tells us her mother used to cook on it too. I eat an apple and some cheese and Hannah makes a disgusting thing in the frying pan.

During the evening Echlas talks about her experiences in Germany and Sweden. Some years ago – I forget how many – she travelled to Germany and on the advice of a friend there, went on to Sweden where she applied for asylum. While the application was going through, taking five months, Echlas created a problem for the authorities as she had no carer so they were obliged to provide twenty-four-hour care for her. She was refused asylum because the rule is that you have to apply in the first country you arrive in. She returned to Germany but was also refused and by this time she decided she wanted to go home anyway, but generously the German government gave her the electric wheelchair, hospital bed and bath bed and paid for her and a friend to fly back to Palestine. So all the equipment Echlas has is courtesy of Germany. There has been no water today and I should have a shower; it has been three days since the last one but I shall just have to have a wash instead.

Friday

I just know when I wake up by that different light that comes through the curtains that it has snowed in the night. When I open the window and see the garden and the lemon tree covered in snow I feel like the boy in *The Snowman* and just want to put my wellies on and go outside. Acting with restraint and respect to the neighbours, I get dressed first then tentatively step out into this transformed world. It is very slippery so I step gingerly to the end of the alley and take some photos but what I would really like to see is the hills covered in snow. As this is not possible, I carry on taking pictures of boys throwing snowballs, like missiles, from the rooftops down onto unsuspecting pedestrians below. A few people are out, especially the children, enjoying the novelty while it lasts. Inevitably, there is no water again and the electricity is reduced but I decide I really have to take a short shower so brave the icy bathroom and also change my sheets even though there is no possibility of washing them yet. Mohammed comes round, cheeks red and tingling, sensibly wearing plastic bags over his gloves, to do some essential shopping for Echlas, i.e. fags.

I find some beans in the cupboard – no idea what they are but decide to cook them – and make a tomato sauce and have jacket potatoes, cheese and homemade baked beans for dinner. It is a good thing I start early as the beans take ages: one hour boiling, then another half an hour in the pressure cooker. Echlas and Hannah both like it but Echlas is amused as the beans are supposed to be eaten on their own as a snack; in fact it is a street food. They did the job though. Now dinner is over, we arrange ourselves on either side of Echlas' bed and watch *Heart of Jenin*, a true story and very moving, on Echlas' laptop.

Saturday

The phone wakes me out of a deep sleep. It is the guy from the Turkish bath phoning to say they are closed until Monday. I had booked a bath and massage today as I longed to indulge in a hot shower and be in a warm place for a while but that was not going to happen today. Echlas plans to stay in bed again; there is nothing to get up for as she cannot go out in this weather. The snow is mostly gone and it is raining but I go out for a walk as I need some exercise and fresh air. I dress for the cold with a scarf and hat but after a while the sun comes out and it warms up. The remains of the snow lie in dirty heaps by the roadside and waterfalls pour down the streets and steps and off roofs. Walking is more hazardous than usual. As well as taking detours around parked cars into the road I now have to dodge the water cascading down from above. Some shops are closed and it is quieter than usual. We hear on the internet that Jerusalem had come to a standstill due to the storm in the night.

When I get back it is Hannah's turn to go out, down to the Church of the Nativity which she has not seen yet. I remember on the pilgrimage, my very first time in Palestine, how exciting it was to enter the Church of the Nativity and to touch the brass star on the floor marking the place where Jesus was supposedly born, but now, sadly, having visited several times it no longer holds the same sense of awe for me. While tidying up Echlas' room for something to do, I come across a book about a New Zealand nurse who married a Bedouin and lived in Petra. It looks interesting so I will give it a try.

Sunday

Today we have to rev up the energy as it will be a very busy day. First we wash Echlas' hair, then get her into the wheelchair. There is water today, *alhumdulillah*, so I put on a load of washing, hoover and clean the bathroom. Mohammed comes round and together we go to the greengrocer via a short cut, involving passing a ferocious Alsatian dog, but I feel sorry for it as it is tied up, also thankful it is, otherwise I would be going the long way round. We stagger back, past the poor barking dog, loaded down with kilos of oranges, onions, aubergines, potatoes and strawberries.

The weather has warmed up and I am pleased to see that the seedlings that I planted have survived despite being covered in three inches of snow.

Hannah goes into the teaching room at some point in the day and finds the carpet soaking wet and the floor nearest the outside wall under an inch of water. We have to get the carpet out first so roll it up and carry it outside, dripping dirty water as we go, then lay it out over the stone seat to dry out. Then mop the water up. The only sort of mop is one of those long thin ones that you use with a floor cloth, not the best way to mop up a flood. Hannah manages to open the window and I put the big fan on. It seems that the snow and rain have caused water to come up through the floor and wall. Lucky it is the least-used room in the house and it is also the oldest room as it used to be the meeting room for the camp before Echlas' mother came.

After all that drama, I have to get on with cooking as Melena's parents are coming to dinner and I am cooking *mujuddara*. Hannah is sent out to buy wine and returns after an age with the salads still to prepare and I am getting stressed as I know how slow she is. I get the table and chairs out, lay the table and then start making chips, splattering oil everywhere. Melena and her parents arrive and we are still clattering about in the kitchen and I feel like the hired help, waiting on the guests. Melena is one of Echlas' students and is being a great help to her in applying for her visa to Germany and getting letters of invitations from people in Germany, necessary for the visa application. Her father is involved in the Church, in fact I get the impression he is a minister and plans are made for Echlas to give a talk in his church. He speaks very good English and also his wife so the conversation flows, not so the wine. It is Lent and they refuse wine, which I consider over-pious in the circumstances.

The dessert of strawberries and yogurt is appreciated by everyone and is so simple to prepare; then I make tea and coffee and wearily survey the piles of washing up. I wish they would go so that I can make a start. We have enough *mujuddara* left to last the next day and possible the one after so will have a reprieve from cooking, not my favourite occupation.

We hear via Facebook that soldiers are in Aida camp but no one knows why so we go to bed feeling slightly uneasy.

Monday, Yom il tnin

Echlas is expecting the physio to come today so stays in bed but when she is half an hour late it is apparent she is not coming so we all go out to the copy shop to see about laminating the paper cut-outs of the volunteers. Echlas had arranged to meet a man who owns an electric appliance shop to give him the money for an electric heater for Mohammed's mother but she has forgotten to bring the money. I offer to lend her some, but she decides to send Hannah back home to get the money out of her blue bag in the wardrobe. We wait and wait; Echlas smokes several cigarettes and speculates as to the whereabouts of Hannah. She gives the impression of one who can easily get lost but it is a straight road back to the camp so even for Hannah getting lost would be difficult. After half an hour she appears minus bag. She could not find it, so I lend her the money after all and Echlas calls the man to come and meet us. It all seems rather clandestine. While we are waiting for him we go to the nearby stationery shop for Echlas to buy a children's Arabic storybook for Melena's birthday – genius idea. The shop is a treasure trove for someone like me, who cannot resist a new item of stationery. I am overwhelmed by the selection of notebooks and pens and although I have plenty I buy another pen as a spare. The man appears, Echlas hands over the money and we continue with our shopping. It is so warm I have to remove my jacket and cardigan – so different from the last few days.

We arrive home starving and like a miracle, there is a knock on the door and Ida's son is standing there bearing a plate of steaming chickpea *mujuddara*, just what we need. It is no warmer indoors despite the rise in temperature outside so we put Echlas to bed as she is cold. Rain is forecast for tonight so we lug the carpet in and arrange it on three chairs in the lesson room to continue drying. I do some ironing in an attempt to finish drying some of the clothes but at least we have been able to put it out on the line today. We see on Facebook what the soldiers did last night when they entered Aida camp. One hundred soldiers came to arrest one man who was not there so instead they harassed his family, shot seven people with live ammo as they were angry and hit a pregnant woman who had to go to hospital. They broke down doors to get into homes and shot people who had come outside to see what was going on. Musa was filming the events and had his camera smashed. He filmed two boys continuing to play their computer games in the internet café, since they could not go outside to go home, oblivious to the soldiers filing past behind them.

Today there is worse news. A nineteen-year-old boy in Dheisheh camp was shot dead last night by the IOF. As in Aida the night before, soldiers raided the camp at 5am, supposedly to arrest someone, and using silent bullets killed this boy for no reason. We all feel stunned and horrified and I am suddenly plunged into the reality of why I am here. This is not the death of 'another Arab' in the Middle East, which would not even get reported in our Western media, but a young man who I may have passed in Bethlehem, someone's son, brother, friend, murdered by invading trigger happy soldiers who kill with reckless impunity, knowing they will not be held to account for killing an Arab. We wonder what the repercussions of this will be.

Layan comes round and cuts up some broad beans for a dish I am making tomorrow. I have never seen the whole pod used before and am keen to try this dish as it seems a brilliant way to avoid wasting so much of this vegetable. Hannah goes out early today to Banksy's shop and the wall before I go to the Turkish bath. Echlas warns me to be careful on the way back as I may run into a demo at the wall, after the boy's funeral, and she asks Hannah to shut all the doors and windows in case of tear gas.

At the grand age of sixty-five this would be my first visit to a Turkish bath. I have been to spas and had massages but this promised to be more than that. There are some very old *hammam* in Palestine in the old cities of Nablus and Ramallah and no doubt elsewhere but this one in Bethlehem is modern, on the second floor of a tall building just down the hill from the camp. I have borrowed a swimsuit from Echlas, never imagining I would have need of one here. It is adequate but not flattering, not an issue as there is only one other woman there when I arrive, wearing her swimsuit pulled down to her waist. I am instructed to start with a shower, absolute bliss, and could stay here all day, feeling the stream of hot water pouring over me, and I keep returning to the shower in between the sauna, steam room and jacuzzi. That is so hot it is like being boiled alive so I can tolerate it for only a few minutes and the cold plunge pool I avoid completely. I am sure it is good for one but having been cold for so long I am not going to make myself deliberately so. Having been through the preliminaries, I then lie on a large, round, marble table in the middle of a large, glass doored room. The table is heated so I can relax and enjoy the sensation of being warm, but after a while I begin to wonder what is happening, my limit for lying on a table being reached. Fortunately, my masseuse appears and begins throwing bowls of warm water over me, followed by a brisk rub all over with what feels like sandpaper, until I am sure she has removed several layers of skin. It is painful while she is doing it but the pain is relieved when she throws more water over me. Next comes a soapy rub, more water and now the massage. As she is attacking my spine, I have concerns that I may not be able to get off the table but endure it for half an hour and to my relief find I still have use of my legs. It certainly has been a great experience and would have been even better if my Arabic had been adequate to request a little less vigour on the spine. I have another shower and a hair wash and feel so clean and relaxed but also invigorated. Amazing what water does to one's wellbeing. The walk home uphill takes some of the edge off the feel-good factor and I can see no signs of a demo or tear gas thankfully, but I cannot stop thinking of that poor boy and his family.

If a neighbour gives you food then it is bad manners to return the plate empty so Echlas suggests I make Baba Ganoush and give a plateful to Ida. It is quite quick and easy to make, and involves aubergines, cooked and whizzed up in the mixer with olive oil, tahini and lemon juice. Debt paid, I then proceed to fry the broad beans briefly to stop them going black as instructed by Echlas.

Hannah and I go to AIC together in the evening as George is here for a lesson and will stay until we get back. The talk is by a guy from BADIL about the privatisation of security in Israel. What I learned from the talk is that Israel outsources security thus avoiding prosecutions for violations of human rights, since all responsibility is the company's.

One of the main companies used is Blackwater, an American one, not surprisingly. This is an international phenomenon, where conflicts involve contractors who benefit from war having a vested interest in it. Israel is sixth in the world as arms exporters and are leaders in 'homeland security'. The industry creates jobs and millions in revenue. All Israeli products are 'battle tested' and the evidence of their effectiveness is there for all to see, in the devastation and the 2,700 dead in Gaza in the summer of 2014. Israel also trains police around the world and many retired Israeli military start their own training companies. In some of the settlements private contractors are doing the jobs of the police, i.e. in Silwan and where this is the case, it is private employees who take the rap for any deaths, not the company or the Israeli government. Most of the employees are poor people, i.e. Druze, Ethiopians, Russians who have no redress.

Regarding the checkpoints, in 2006 they were privatised and are now controlled by two companies. Israel, in an attempt to legitimise the checkpoints, is using the term 'civilisation' not 'privatisation' and saying to the world that the IOF no longer controls the checkpoints, but what they fail to reveal is that most companies employ ex-soldiers. It is trying to pretend that Palestinians are well treated at the checkpoints, meanwhile planning to transfer power to the border control agency and make the wall a permanent border.

George had been to Gaza today for Ma'an News to report on the number and type of supply trucks entering the strip. He was only allowed to enter the border area but no further and was under constant surveillance by Israeli guards. For the Israelis this was a PR exercise to show that they are being generous in allowing all these supplies in to counteract the accusations that they are systematically starving the Gazans to death. George had filmed the convoy of trucks rumbling across the border and although it looked a lot to us George said the number is far less than ten years ago and now more supplies are needed to rebuild the destroyed homes and infrastructure and to feed the increasing population.

Today is bright and sunny and we have water so I am able to do some washing and hang it out in the garden. It is also housework day. Hannah and I carry the still damp carpet outside again and put a different one down on the lesson room floor. Later, Echlas has a lesson so Hannah and I go out for a walk to Aida camp and for the first time I see the Banksy of the girl searching the soldier. It is protected from the road by a perspex screen so I had never noticed it before. Last time we came to the Largee Centre my camera ran out of battery so I am keen to go up on the roof again and take some pictures. It is a lovely warm evening, with the sun just going down and the views from up here, although not stunning, being of buildings and the wall, are liberating after the claustrophobia of the streets below. Two large polytunnels on the roof are used for growing vegetables, an initiative I am pleased to see.

On the way back we stop at our friendly greengrocer where the owner always tries to engage us in Arabic conversation and corrects us when we are wrong, which is most of the time. Fortunately, something makes me buy some more broad beans. The gas has run out and Ida, the only one who can change the cylinder, is out, so dinner will be late. At 6.30pm another student turns up and I have the feeling that Echlas had forgotten she was coming. She is a friend of Deanna's and such a pretty girl with coffee-coloured skin and a mass of black curly hair which she has artfully wrapped a scarf around. I detect an English accent but there is no time to talk to her. Very generously she has brought some shortbread for us, which I immediately rescue from Hannah's hands before she eats it all.

Ida appears at 8.30pm to change the gas, so we can eat at last. The beans that Layan had prepared yesterday had mostly gone black so it was serendipitous that I bought more and they take minutes to prepare. I really like this dish, made with onions, cumin, stock, rice, beans, water and *laban*. It is creamy and tasty and we eat it with salad. *Laban* is made from sheep's milk and is sold in cartons like yogurt in the shops. Unlike cow's milk yogurt it does not curdle when cooked. In the market I had seen piles of round white balls for sale and wondered what they were until Echlas explained they are made by Bedouins from sheep's milk and left to dry in the sun until hard. They keep for ages and to reconstitute you cut off the amount you need and, using your fingers and some water, rub the hard yogurt against the sides of a special bowl which has a rough surface, until it becomes a milky liquid. I suppose without the bowl it could be made with a grater or possibly a food processor.

Echlas then asks me to make hummus with the chickpeas we had bought and cook some other beans and then wash up. Hannah's contribution was the salad, so not feeling hard done by at all, I feel justified in going to bed at 11.30pm, leaving Hannah to settle Echlas.

Yom il kamsa

Loud banging on the front door wakes me up at 9am. Startled, I open the door to find Rosha's mum there with some money that I had paid for Layan on my debit card for her application to the LSE.

Another warm, sunny day and a bright blue sky entices us out early to go and pay the telephone bill. It seems that monetary transactions are mostly carried out in person, so when we get to the office, in the bus station building we take a numbered ticket and sit down to wait with about twenty other people to be called. It is a bright, modern space and not a hardship to sit and observe the other customers. They are mostly men, although there are a few women in *hijabs*. A few impatient men try to chat up the security guard to get them through quicker but I can see he is a jobsworth by his neatly creased trousers, peaked cap and air of importance. Most of us wait patiently and at least we have seats. After about half an hour Echlas gets served, pays her bill and now we are free to go up to Manger Square to sit and eat falafel in the sun, feeling hot for the first time this year. Bethlehem is still quiet but the good weather has brought a few tourists out and I feel glad for the restaurant and shop owners.

Echlas is planning a trip to Ramallah to see her sister and to go to the Turkish bath there when Christina gets back so Hannah and I need to find something suitable to wear. It is unlikely that we will find a swimsuit at this time of year so we will have to improvise. I find a stretchy, all-in-one body which does up under the crotch and Hannah finds a pair of cover-up pants which she can wear with a bra. These are so cheap in the *souk*, so even if I never wear it again it has not cost the earth. Next stop is the copy shop where we assist a very pleasant woman, Maryam, to arrange the volunteer figures on the laminating paper and she puts them through the machine. They come out very well and take no time at all so that is a job well done.

During Amia's lesson later on in the evening, Echlas' Hebron nephew and younger niece arrive unexpectedly. We have no idea why they are here but gather it is something to do with milk. Another knock on the door reveals Mohammed and his sisters carrying a bag and a box which nephew and niece take away. Very mysterious. Echlas explains later that Mohammed's mother gets UN powdered milk and Echlas' sister buys it from her to use in bread so that Mohammed's mum can use the money to buy other necessities. I like the way that the better off help the needy, not by giving them money, which would be offensive, but in ingenious ways like this.

I start cutting out the laminated helpers for something to do after dinner. Hannah is going out to a birthday party tonight so I will be sleeping with Echlas, which necessitates a change of bedsheets as I am still fussy about sleeping in someone else's bedding. Echlas is not feeling too well before she sleeps. She thinks it is the falafel that upsets her system and vows not to eat them again.

Friday

What a terrible night. Echlas had complained of feeling very cold inside and could not get warm, despite the two heaters, two wheat bags, a hot water bottle and lots of blankets. She kept dozing off and did not want to eat anything. At 10.30pm she wanted to sleep, very early for her, so I settled her on her side and I went to bed myself. At 2.45am she woke me to move her shoulder and when I touched her I discovered she was soaking wet, her T-shirt, undersheet, topsheet, blankets and her whole body drenched in sweat, as if someone had poured a bucket of water over her. In forty-odd years of nursing I had never seen anyone sweat like that. I removed the blankets and put them on chairs in the living room to dry and found a couple of clean ones on a wardrobe. I removed Echlas' T-shirt and dried her off with a towel, then changed the sheets and drawer sheet, drying Echlas as I moved her from side to side. She kept insisting it was too much work for me but I could not leave her like that and said I would give her a good wash in the morning, not wanting to cause her more disturbance at this time in the morning. Settled and dry she went off to sleep but I only dozed, hearing the call to prayer at 5am and the bread man shouting his way around the camp.

This morning I give Echlas a good wash in bed after her breakfast and thankfully she is feeling better today. A call from Layan to collect some food from Aida means a trip out for me while Ida's son comes to sit with Echlas. It feels really hot outside. Friday is the day when the army are most likely to provoke trouble in the camp so I am not surprised to see some police and Palestinian army hanging around at the entrance to Aida.

I find a group of female members of the Al Azza family sitting outside in the garden having coffee, while Ru Ru toddles about, falls over and generally entertains herself. Having established what I am there for with our limited communication, Rosha calls up to the window for Layan. She comes down with a bag and a covered plate and thanking her and saying *"Marsallama"* to all, I plod back in the unaccustomed heat. The food turns out to be *taboun* and cauliflower fritters made by Echlas' sister so that saves me cooking tonight.

While Echlas is designing a mug online for Musa's birthday, I have a doze, being so tired from my disturbed night. Hannah arrives back at 5pm having enjoyed the party but did not find it brilliant.

Today she has been to Bil'in for a tenth anniversary demonstration there and had been tear gassed, but luckily missed the worst of it.

Bil'in is a village about five miles west of Ramallah and weekly protests are held there against the building of the 'security' wall which separates the village from 60% of its land. Since 2005 the case has been taken up by an Israeli human rights lawyer to represent the village in the High Court of Justice. Palestinians cannot make their own petitions to this court or appear at it so are obliged to hire Israeli lawyers to fight on their behalf. In 2007 the court ruled in favour of Bil'in and the government was ordered to change the route of the wall. Four years later the IOF began dismantling a section of the barrier to reroute it. To complicate matters an illegal settlement had begun construction before the court announced its decision in order to claim ownership of land belonging to Bil'in. The court decided that the settlement could stay but that 160,000IS must be paid by the state, settlers and construction companies. The court stipulated that further expansion of the settlement would not be carried out but this has been ignored. The people of Bil'in, along with many international activists and left wing organisations, i.e. International Solidarity Movement, Anarchists against the Wall, Gush Shalom, protest weekly and march from the village to the wall with the aim of halting construction and dismantling some of the wall. In 2005 undercover Israeli soldiers admitted throwing stones at other Israeli soldiers in order to put the blame on Palestinians and justify crackdowns on peaceful protests. The protests have become symbolic of the continued Palestinian resistance and over the years many incidents on both sides have drawn media attention and participation by high profile internationals.

The film 5 Broken Cameras *was made by Emad Burnat, about the continued struggle of the villagers of Bil'in and is now a famous film. The maker's brother, Iyad, has written a book about the non-violent resistance of Bil'in and I met him on several occasions. On the first he talked to our group and showed us the so-called 'rubber bullets' used indiscriminately by the IOF against protestors. We were all appalled to see that they are steel covered with a thin layer of rubber and not as harmless as they sound, and they can kill. We went to the wall where the protests are held and I noticed many spent tear gas containers just lying on the ground amongst the bright red anemones. The death of twenty-nine-year-old Bassem Abu-Rahman in 2009, due to being struck in the chest by a tear gas canister is depicted in the film and his memorial lies on the road to the wall. The case his family brought against the IOF is ongoing despite three separate videos of the protest showing that his death was in no way justified. The last time I went to Bil'in in February 2016, I was appalled at the sight of two settlements, one on either side of the village, and an Israeli-only highway, where only two years before there had been open countryside. Iyad said they had sprung up in a year. It was devastating to see how quickly these massive settlements could be thrown up, destroying the land that belongs to the Palestinians. How they live with seeing this every day is unimaginable.*

Hannah had been talking about going to volunteer with the ISM (International Solidarity Movement) and despite all of us trying to persuade her that she would be putting herself in danger she seemed undeterred. However, after Bil'in she has stopped talking about the ISM and admitted later that having had a taste of the frontline activism she had changed her mind.

CHAPTER FIVE

TRAVELLING

Our big trip is coming up, a chance to do a bit of travelling and see another part of the West Bank. I have been Googling Jenin to find out where the Cinema Guesthouse is as it seems like a good place to stay. After reading Susan Abulhawa's book *Mornings in Jenin* I have a rather romanticised view of the place but I am prepared to be disappointed as the reality is rarely comparable. We are all travelling to Ramallah with Echlas to stay for one night with her sister's family then the three of us will go to Nablus for one night. Layan has given us a contact there in the refugee camp. After that Hannah and I will travel on separately and Christina will go back to Ramallah and travel home with Echlas. That is the plan but as I am quickly learning, plans do change.

Christina returned from Jordan safely, having had no trouble at the Allenby Bridge crossing, in fact she was given another three-month visa, when she is only planning to stay for a further two weeks. Because of the bad weather she had stayed in Jerusalem with her friends until the transport was operating again, travelled to Jordan to see her other friends there but decided against going on to Petra as they had insufficient time to do it justice. As compensation, I pass on the book that I have just read, about the woman living in Petra – absolutely fascinating but sad at the end when her husband dies.

Hannah continues sleeping with Echlas and Christina sleeps in the volunteers' room until we leave in a couple of days.

Mohammed drives us to Ramallah along the Jerusalem bypass road, the only road Palestinians can take to reach the north of the West Bank, as they are not allowed to enter Jerusalem without a permit. We sing raucously along to 'C'est La Vie' by Khalid on the radio feeling like rowdy teenagers off on a school trip and talk about the obsession we in the West have with everyday showers, all agreeing it is not necessary and is probably bad for the skin. Are we trying to convince ourselves? Part of the single lane road winds down a steep hill, drivers overtaking creeping lorries on hairpin bends, making the journey nerve wracking, but I put my complete trust in Palestinian drivers; they are so skilful. In the rain the road can be treacherous and in the snow impassable but this is a vital road for trade. The journey, if it was straightforward, would take about half an hour but now takes at least an hour due to the inevitable traffic jam around Qalandia checkpoint, notorious in the West Bank. Our first stop is the *hammam* and we arrive slightly late but time is not a major concern here, so after we extricate Echlas from the taxi and wheel her down the slope to the entrance we then have to lift her out again and onto a bench while Christina negotiates the wheelchair up a step and around a corner. Now we lift Echlas back into the wheelchair and take note of the surroundings. This *hammam* is old and traditional, quite different from the one in Bethlehem. It feels cramped but has plenty of atmosphere with its mixture of stained glass, rich red, green and gold furnishings and dark stained wood.

We undress quickly before taking Echlas' clothes off to reveal her swimsuit and wheel her to the steam room. The woman in charge obviously knows Echlas by her effusive greetings and all the staff are very accommodating of the wheelchair and treat Echlas like a long-lost friend. We take turns going into the sauna and shower so that one of us is always with Echlas. Feeling and probably looking like a boiled lobster I wheel her into the *hammam* proper. This is quite different from the one in Bethlehem. In the centre is a circular heated marble table again, upon which young beautiful women are draped, and then in alcoves around the sides are more slabs for lying on. In the four corners of the room are anterooms with stone sinks where you can wash yourself off. The lighting is subdued and relaxing and with the warmth and the gentle sound of water it would be easy to drift off. No time for that though as Echlas is to have her massage here on one of the side slabs, so being very careful not to slip on the wet floor, the three of us manoeuvre her out of the chair and onto the slab, making sure she cannot slide off. There is a fair amount of suppressed giggling amongst us but the beautiful women ignore us and lie serenely like mermaids on their rock.

The masseuse comes along and scrubs Echlas' limbs and body while we pour warm water over her, then, as in Bethlehem, she is soaped and rinsed and a gentle massage follows. Trying to preserve Echlas' modesty we strip off her bathing suit, dry and partially dress her and lift her back into the wheelchair. Christina is called next for her bath, then Hannah and lastly me. I am prepared this time for the sandpaper scrub and it is just as painful but in a masochistic way enjoyable this time. It is followed by the soothing soapy wash and the bowls of warm water. I feel so sparkling clean and I can see this could become an addiction. Echlas is sitting in the relaxing area waiting for us and we spend time sitting with her before our massages. Christina and I are having full body massages and we are lying next to each other in a quiet, darkened room on comfortable benches while we are pummelled, slapped, stroked into a feeling of complete submission. My body has been taken over by someone else and I exist just in my mind for that short time. No wonder it is so relaxing.

I have a last shower to rinse off the massage oil, get dressed and sit with Echlas waiting for the others. The whole process has taken about two hours and is remarkably cheap for such a wonderful experience – about £20 each. Mohammed is waiting for us when I take the bags up to the car and I see that the road is empty and lined with policemen and the streets deserted. Apparently, Mahmoud Abbas, the President, is driving through and this is security. We miss seeing him as he passes while we are inside paying but it's no great loss according to Echlas who, like most Palestinians, has no time for the PA.

Now we are on our way to the family's house, a nondescript block of flats in a side road facing the wall. Various members of the family greet us and a jovial-looking man appears and lifts Echlas out of the wheelchair and carries her up the stairs as if she is a small child. It is a relief to us all that we did not have to pull/push the wheelchair up two flights of stairs. The flat is enormous; just as well as ten people live here. We are introduced to Echlas' sister who speaks no English and looks old but is the same age as me. She is obese and has very painful knees, probably arthritis, causing her to hobble about as she prepares the meal. The man who carried Echlas is her nephew, married to a pleasant, young-looking woman, the mother of one daughter and six sons. The youngest is about two and a delightful little boy.

We are invited to sit in one of the two spacious and sumptuously furnished sitting rooms in comfortable armchairs and I could easily doze after the relaxing *hammam* but try to be sociable by attempting to converse with the children. Most of them have smartphones and are taking a great deal of interest in their screens while taking surreptitious peeks at us from time to time. The meal is served in the dining area between the two sitting rooms and I am glad to see chicken plus the usual rice and salads and pitta and olives. We are all so hungry and hope we do not look like ravenous animals as we dive into the food. At least we do it justice.

Three of the boys have given up their room for us and we are very appreciative. The three beds stand in a line like those of the Three Bears and the blankets actually have pictures of bears on them. Next to their room they have their own 'den' with a TV, an excellent arrangement. Echlas is sleeping with the daughter in her double bed. Her room is very girly and frilly and she also has a friend staying, presumably to help with Echlas. After the gorgeous meal Echlas is ready to retire, so we settle her into the big bed, arranging plenty of pillows around her. I feel doubtful about how she will manage in this soft, bouncy bed, sleeping with someone else but ever adaptable, she takes it in her stride and they both sleep well, the friend sleeping on a mattress on the floor.

In the morning we plan to be off as early as is polite but in the end we have to wait forty-five minutes for Echlas' nephew to come back from wherever he has gone, to give us a lift to where we can get a taxi to Nablus. Depending on where you are departing from and going to you may be able to take a bus, such as the one from Bethlehem to Jerusalem with a set fare of 4½IS or a 'service', a minibus where the cost of the trip is divided between the passengers, or a private taxi where the price is negotiable beforehand.

The journey is only half an hour; I always forget how small this country is and expect journey times to be longer. The taxi drops us in the centre of Nablus but when Christina calls our contact he is waiting for us at the refugee camp so we have to get another taxi to take us back to Jacob's Well. I have been to Balata camp before on a very short tour so I know where it is. Our contact introduces us to our guide for the day, a very good-looking, smartly dressed young man but first we go to the camp centre and meet the director. He will tell us about the camp and says we are welcome to stay in the guesthouse if we have nothing booked. Delighted, we accept immediately.

Fortified with Arabic coffee and crammed into his small office we listen with interest to Mahmoud Subuh, an eloquent, passionate, charismatic man of about sixty as he tells us about Balata refugee camp. It is the largest refugee camp in terms of population, in the smallest space. Maybe five or six generations live in one house and live so close to each other and to their neighbours that inevitably tensions arise, erupting into rows quite often.

The First Intifada started here and many people were killed and in the Second Intifada the camp bred suicide bombers, young men with no prospects for a better life and with nothing to lose. Consequently, the camp was punished by surrounding it with security fences and by severely restricting movement. It was like a huge prison and tensions led to fighting and clashes with the IOF. Two hundred and forty-six people were killed inside the camp and hundreds injured, many disabled for life. Ninety-five per cent of the inhabitants at this time worked outside the camp but because of the blockade they were unable to travel so massive unemployment added to the problems. When the

Second Intifada ended the rest of the West Bank began to change and settle down but in Balata the collective punishment continues to this day with frequent night raids and arrests. Only 5% are given permits to work in Israel and there is great resentment towards the PA for their perceived lack of leadership.

Guns and drugs are freely available in the camp and this is a growing problem. The levels of poverty are higher than in Gaza – 49%, with 63% unemployment and three quarters of the population are under thirty. They feel there is no improvement politically and that no one cares about them, least of all the PA. Consequently, there is a general feeling of frustration and marginalisation in the camp. Hundreds of teenagers were arrested in the Second Intifada, 500 of whom were released from prison last year, 290 from Balata. They are grown up now but still young and nothing has changed regarding the conditions in the camp. They feel their time in prison has been for nothing and they deserve some recognition from the PA for the price they have paid by resisting the occupation. However, Israel will not allow the PA to hire anyone who has a prison record. These young men, resentful and bitter, form gangs, become outlaws and make Balata a centre of serious crime.

The Yaffa Centre, so called as many of the refugees here came from Yaffa, is a cultural centre providing psychological support for the few who can be helped. They also have a literacy programme as 50% of the ninth grade are illiterate despite being in school. The UN school in Balata used to have the reputation for being the best school in Palestine; now it is the worst, accommodating over 2,000 children, 50–60 in each class. No one can control the children. There is constant fighting, the outcome of all the history of the camp and the overcrowding of today. The children display aggression, violence, depression, hate and bitterness and with only two trained counsellors for 1,000 children the problem is overwhelming. Volunteers from Norway used to come to help with the children and some benefit was seen but since Gaza they have stopped coming. Whether this is because Israel denies entry to Norwegians since they officially recognised the state of Palestine, or for another reason we could not ascertain.

The centre is run by a non-profit organisation. Everything is free to *participants but to obtain funding is ever more challenging. Most funding comes from NGOs. The PA provides nothing and the UN has cut down its support. The centre was founded in 1996 with the aim of providing and increasing awareness and education of the Palestinian culture and the history and political rights of the people. Through programmes and activities led by skilled counsellors, the younger generation are guided to believe in the concepts of justice, freedom, democracy and human rights. They also learn about the refugee situation and the milestones in their history, in particular the 194 UN Resolution which upholds the right of return and compensation for the loss of their land. The centre also works to enhance the status of women and their role in the community by changing perceptions towards them and encouraging their participation in progressive change and development of the community.*

The various activities that take place at the centre aim to cater for all ages and include media training, the A'andoon band for folk art and drama, the mental health programme, computer lab, community unit, children's library and the guesthouse, but the enterprise struggles for funding to keep all these vital amenities going.

It was such a depressing picture and Mahmoud spoke with such compassion for the children and young men, it was very moving. Christina asks him if he felt like giving up sometimes and he openly admits that he has felt like putting a gun to his head when it all seems so hopeless and he wonders if he is wasting his life here. On the other hand, he is compelled to keep going no matter the cost to him and his health as these young people need someone to show them that life is worth living and it can get better. When and how he does not know himself but he has to believe it to keep hope alive.

In response, Hannah speaks with such anger and passion for the situation that he has just described that he laughs and says it is good to see such feelings in a young person but wisely advises her that expressing her anger injudiciously would not be helpful to her or those she seeks to support.

I am full of admiration for this lovely man, denying himself a comfortable life in order to work unstintingly for a pittance and giving everything to the children of Balata. I think we all feel frustrated at our inability to do anything to make things any better but Mahmoud says the main thing we can do is to tell people in our own countries about Palestine and how it is suffering. Hannah asks about volunteering at the centre but Mahmoud says at the moment it is too dangerous in the camp for volunteers. We will, however, be safe staying in the guesthouse tonight.

Mahmoud had spent more than an hour talking with us, something we had not expected at all, and I feel very grateful to have been given so much of his time. This is how the Palestinians are though. No one is too important or unimportant to spend time with and share information with. He hands us over to our guide, another Mohammed, and I can sense straight away that he and Hannah are going to get on very well. He leads us upstairs to the guesthouse, explaining the keys to get in the building and then to unlock this door. What a pleasant surprise when he opens the door into the lounge area, complete with a flat screen TV and a well-equipped kitchen. We explore the rest of the floor and find there are four dormitories of four beds each and two bathrooms and we are the only ones staying so can have a room each but instead choose the cosiest room to share, a decision Christina was going to regret.

The best surprise is the heating/air conditioning. To actually have heat is indeed an unexpected luxury. Mohammed is waiting for us so we cannot linger as he wants to show us the camp and Nablus and we need to eat. Although this is my second visit I see and hear different things this time that would not have been possible in a large group. Mohammed lives in the camp so is at ease and knows most of the people. I am not sure I would feel quite so relaxed had we been on our own. Having him as our guide legitimises our presence here. We walk along the wide main street similar to Aida camp but then turn down a narrow passageway, just wide enough for one medium-size person. The buildings are so close together, no wonder there is no privacy. You cannot get away from your

Echlas and Christina in Al Azza.

Dismantling the Christmas tree in Manger Square.

Our first dinner party. Maqluba!

Aunty and me.

Snow in Bethlehem.

The wall at Aida refugee camp.

View from Hashimi Hotel roof.

Children in Jenin refugee camp.

Someone suggested a photo competition

The guardian of the church and my Moslem guide discuss St John's gospel.

The Easter party, painting eggs.

Preparing for Echlas' birthday party with avocado face masks.

Echlas on her birthday.

Settlement construction at Bil'in.

The sea, the sea! My first sight of the sea in over two months, at Yaffa.

neighbours here; not only would each hear the others' conversations but you would smell their food and be disturbed by their noise. The children here frequently suffer from vitamin D deficiency caused by lack of sunlight and it is easy to see why. Looking up, a sliver of sky is visible between the roofs of the buildings and at ground level it is dark. There is nowhere for the kids to play, except in their school playground or in the narrow alleys where there is no space to kick a football or ride a bicycle.

Leaving the confinement of the camp, Mohammed stops a taxi for us and we speed off down the wide main road towards the centre of Nablus. The first time I visited here, with the pilgrimage, our guide was very nervous of taking a group of foreigners through the *souk* and indeed, seemed on edge all the time we were here. He told us that few tourists came to Nablus and although it may not be on the pilgrim routes I had seen plenty of foreigners on subsequent visits. It may also be the fact that for the first time we heard a priest speak with vehemence about the situation of Palestinian Christians under occupation and some in our party were shocked to hear a priest talk politics. They gradually realised that politics cannot be avoided in this land as life is politics and you are reminded of this every day.

I like Nablus. The atmosphere feels hospitable and harmonious.

The town has a reputation for being a centre of resistance, having a history from the early nineteenth century of leading the movement against colonisation and occupation and earning it the name of 'The Mountain of Fire' (Jabal en Nar). In 1963 the liberation movements of Palestine declared the 'Republic of Palestine' in Nablus, resulting in tighter control by the occupation forces of Jordan. Under Israeli occupation the people of Nablus suffered even more repressive measures, i.e. assassinations. The town is now surrounded by Jewish settlements, paralysing the economy of the city as many small manufacturers are restricted in exporting their goods.

During the Second Intifada the city was repeatedly bombarded by Israel, putting it under siege and subject to a more or less continuous curfew for four months. During that time only seventy-nine hours of movement were allowed. Israel considered Nablus 'the centre of terrorism', hence the brutal treatment of the people.

Now all seems peaceful as citizens go about their business, filling the streets with noise and bustle. Our first stop is for food and as Mohammed is not sure where to take us I suggest the place I went to on my last visit, just across the road. It is a very basic eating place and Mohammed looks surprised at my choice. Maybe he thinks we should be going somewhere more Westernised but I assure him this is fine and the food is good. One of the waiters recognises me and I am amazed that he remembers me after all this time but maybe it is my hair that makes me stand out. We go up the narrow stairs and sit at one of the four oil-cloth-covered tables in a room with no windows. I order falafel sandwich and chips and the others have *koubah* and salad and a kebab and drinks. This is fast food Arabic style so within no time the food is in front of us. I am so hungry, having had only an apple for breakfast, and that was hours ago. The food is pronounced very good, the bill ridiculously small and we leave with promises to return, well satisfied with our fast, cheap, filling lunch.

Mohammed takes us through the *souk* where the photo opportunities are such that my memory card fills up and I have to insert a new one while walking and marvelling at the sights. By now Hannah and Mohammed are deep in conversation and Christina and I follow on behind, pausing now and then to look at something particularly intriguing, strange, wonderful, quaint, incredible, beautiful... Seeing chickens in cages is not pleasant but I have to take a photo of a large cockerel, pecking about freely in the cracks between the paving slabs, the only free-range chicken in Palestine. Nablus reputedly has the best *knafa*, so even though it is not long since lunch we have to stop at the best *knafa* shop in town and sample some. Men are serving it from huge round metal platters onto paper plates at the open window of the small crammed café where mostly men sit, enjoying this traditional very sweet sweet. The servers cut very rough portions, passing them into outstretched hands like a conveyor belt. Mohammed takes one and we all dive in with our plastic spoons and wow, it is delicious! It has just the right balance between sweet and salt, a smooth creamy consistency and a crisp sugary top. I could have eaten a whole portion really. Mohammed asks if we can see it being made so we all squash into the kitchen on the other side of the alley, keeping out of the way of the cooks. One deftly covers the base of the flat round pan with vermicelli dough, tops it with soft sheep's cheese, puts another layer of dough and when cooked a lemon sugar syrup is poured over the top. This is possible to make at home but according to the recipe looks a long and complicated process, even if you can source the ingredients, so the best option is to eat it ready made by the experts.

Thanking them very much we head off again, taking a turn off the main street, and find ourselves in another world. This is a secret that only locals would know about. We are standing in a ruin: parts of walls and arches, stone steps and ledges, all overgrown with weeds and wild flowers, sprouting up from the stone floors and in between the brickwork. Luckily Mohammed knows his way around here and leads us up through piles of rubble, up precarious stone steps, under low arches until we reach the remains of a two-storey house. Here we stand and admire the view of Nablus. He and Hannah and Christina climb even further until they are on the roof of the house, but I know my limitations and have no desire to ruin the day by falling and breaking something. I was right not to go any further as they all have difficulty getting down again and it looks very hazardous with a long drop on one side. We marvel at this hidden oasis in the heart of Nablus and I assume it was caused by a bombardment but Mohammed tells us it was an earthquake and there have not been the finances to restore it. To my mind it is better like this: an adventure playground, a secret hideaway to fire the imagination, unrestrained by health and safety or the occupation.

Negotiating the fallen bricks, the broken stone steps and crawling under the arch again, we come out into the *souk* once more and Mohammed leads us to a very old, traditional tea/coffee house. This is somewhere we would never have dared entered on our own as it is full of elderly men, playing cards or backgammon at small tables, puffing on their *shishas*. My impression is of dustcovered windows, pale green faded woodwork, bentwood chairs, authenticity and antiquity – a haven for men to meet their friends, relax and gossip away from their female-dominated homes. The café has a large garden, shaded by citrus trees with a dried-up fountain in the middle, weeds growing between the paving slabs, a general air of dilapidation and neglect and with a sense of timelessness. It is a treasure in the heart of the *souk*. Mohammed orders four mint teas, brought out to us with some ceremony by the owner who sets them down on a very small green metal table, which I covet for my garden. Relaxing in the shady, quiet garden, sipping our tea, someone suggests a photo competition to take the best photo of the glasses of tea before we drink it all. I am the only one with a 'proper' camera – the others use their phones – but it is the 'eye' of the photographer, not the equipment that counts so I have heard, and Christina wins by general consensus for her cleverly angled picture, taking in the café behind the glasses of tea. Mohammed is good company and I can see why Hannah is attracted to him. He is twenty years old but very mature as Palestinians seem to be, due to their upbringing and unusual living conditions.

Reluctantly we leave the café and meander down through the furniture and carpet *souk* to the square and mosque. Brightly coloured bunting festoons the buildings giving a festive air. Mohammed leads us up the steps to the mosque to look inside. Without him this would not have been possible but no one takes any notice of us so I am able to take a photo of the interior. Further on we peek inside a *hammam* and see beautiful Palestinians lounging on couches, smoking *shishas*, their long black hair uncovered, wearing bikinis in the all-female environment, like something out of *The Arabian Nights*. This *hammam* is very old and looks very glamorous and exotic to me.

The sun is going down and there is a chill in the air, reminding us that the day is nearly over. Mohammed has to leave us but promises to see us in the morning before we set off. Thanking him profusely for such a wonderful day, we wave down a taxi and drive back to the camp. Having eaten a fairly substantial lunch and *knafa*, none of us are hungry so Hannah and Christina go out again to get some snacks to see us through the evening. I enjoy a hot shower and luxuriate in the heated sitting room, feeling thankful to all the kind people we have met today for showing us such generous hospitality.

After a warm and comfortable night, for me anyway (Christina had to go and sleep in another room as she was disturbed by my snoring), a knock on the door reveals a man carrying a large cardboard tray with our breakfast on it. It is enough to feed ten let alone three dainty eaters. There is pitta bread, hummus, falafel, olives, *foul*, tomatoes, cucumber, *za'tar*, pickles, cheese spread and oil – more than enough to set us up for the day.

Today I am going north, to Jenin, Christina and Hannah are going back to Ramallah and then Hannah will go on to Jericho or maybe back to Nablus? We tease her about Mohammed and she admits she is attracted to him and they have arranged to keep in touch.

With *Mornings in Jenin* in my mind my expectations of Jenin are high and I cannot believe I am actually going there. I travel in a 'service' through green countryside, passing through the occasional ramshackle village but with no settlements to spoil the landscape. Alighting at the bus station I find my way fairly easily to the Cinema Jenin guesthouse, a place that appeals to my sense of romance. It is an old home, about a hundred years old and is in the middle of Jenin. As well as being a guesthouse it is a cultural NGO established in 1958. In 2010 the cinema was renovated and reopened with funding from Germany and now shows films and runs courses for Palestinians in the creative arts, focusing on Palestinian culture. I am not disappointed with the guesthouse and Ayman, the owner and actor, is friendly and welcoming. He takes me upstairs to the communal dining/sitting room running the length of the building with a balcony at each end. The bright, airy and spacious dorm rooms open off this main room. I seem to be the only occupant though Ayman tells me that four German girls are expected later but now I have the pick of the beds. I choose one by an open window and unpack a few things from my rucksack, while admiring the beautiful old tiled floor, the high ceilings and the design of the windows and doors. Ayman told me to help myself to tea or coffee so I make a black tea, adding some mint leaves from a plant on the balcony. The front balcony has a view of the road below and the hills in the distance so I sit here for a while, enjoying the sun.

My first quest is to find the Freedom Theatre in the refugee camp. According to the map Ayman has given me it is very straightforward and I find the road easily and walk along its dusty way until I reach the beginning of the camp, where the road peters out into more of a track. A little further on and I see the theatre on my right set back from the road. There are people outside, smoking and talking, and I approach nervously not knowing if I can just walk in and what I will say if approached. No one stops me so I carry on into the dim coolness of the building. It is smaller than I expect and as I am looking around, a smiling young man comes up to me and asks if I want some help. Thankful that someone has spoken to me, I explain that I have come to have a look at the famous Freedom Theatre and hope that is OK. He is so welcoming and takes me into a dining room, introduces me to several people there, some Palestinian but other nationalities as well, including the director who comes from London. He explains that they are rehearsing *The Siege*, a play about the siege of the Church of the Nativity in the Second Intifada and it would be touring in England from May. What exciting news as I will be back home in time to see it. They are eating lunch and ask me to join them but having only just recovered from another large breakfast and also feeling it would be something of an imposition to eat their food when I have just stepped in from the street, I decline but someone makes me a cup of tea and I sit and listen to their conversation. An English guy, Andy, has just arrived that day to do the lighting and to teach some apprentices, so he is as lost as me and we chat a bit about what I am doing here. He tries to get me into the rehearsal but comes back saying it is all rather tense in the theatre and he does not know what the protocol is for visitors. I thank him for his efforts and with an invitation to return the next day I walk back to the guesthouse as the children are coming out of school, wandering along with arms around their friends or sucking lollies, kicking up the dust, all in their school uniforms. No yummy mummies in their four-wheel drives doing the school run; here they walk.

I decide to have a look around the old market but after a while, jaded with *souks*, I find somewhere to eat, feeling conspicuous in my foreignness as I seem to be the only Westerner in the town. I have the usual falafel and salad and mint tea. At one point, I think I am lost in the maze of streets but Jenin is a small place so I find my way back eventually to the guesthouse. Ayman advises me it is too late to go now to the village of Burkin and see the church so I plan to do that tomorrow morning. I go out again and buy some strawberries and chocolate and a DVD, *The Heart of Jenin*, a very moving true story about a father who donates his dead son's heart to an Israeli child.

Later on, in the evening after a rest on my bed, I feel hungry so have to go out to find somewhere to eat. When I had arrived this morning, I had gone into a pleasant coffee shop called Delicate, five minutes away from the guesthouse, so make for there. I walk past, looking in the window to assess how busy it is, and someone sitting inside waves to me. It is one of the actors from the theatre who I met this morning so I go in and happily accept his invitation to sit with him and his friends. The guy who waved to me is Ali, a very jolly, funny guy, but he has to leave soon to go back to the theatre, leaving me with Mumtaz and a German girl, who amazingly knows Echlas. It seems like the world knows Echlas! Mumtaz is a young man of twenty and an actor and talks eloquently and at length about why he acts. He explains it is not because he enjoys it and it is a nice thing to do but because it is his way of resisting the occupation and his way of expressing '*sumad*' (steadfastness), by taking the message out to people through another medium. He goes on to talk Palestinian politics and about Islam and the IS plot. He is clearly a very intelligent young man but he is full of anger against the Israelis and says he could never be friends with an Israeli as, all being conscripted to do National Service, one day they could be friends and the next day he could be shot by him. He admits he sometimes feels doubtful for the future but knows he has to maintain hope in order to survive. In answer to my question about his religion he says in his eyes religion does not define a person and there is no difference between a Christian and a Moslem. This same opinion was to be stated by many people I met but it was a while before I could stop myself from asking the rather pointless question. Over time I found out that many young men have turned away from Islam and Christianity but culturally are still classed as either Moslem or Christian.

He tells me that his friend was shot dead by the IOF and he has seen things in his young life that no one should have to see. He had been very angry and sad at the murder of the founder of the Freedom Theatre, Juliano Mar Kamis, in 2011. No one was charged with his murder but Mumtaz is convinced it was an Israeli trained marksman since he was shot with his two-year-old son sitting on his knee and the nanny at his side. Although he is only twenty years old, Mumtaz seems much older in some ways but with the passions and emotions of a young man. He is particularly angry that so many people are unaware of the situation of the Palestinians and finds it hard to comprehend that they are still living under this brutal occupation and the world does nothing. I can empathise completely with his anger and frustration and feel the same about the indifference of people at home. I so admire people like Mumtaz and the guy in Balata who are not afraid to be open and express their hopes and despairs so honestly.

As I leave the restaurant, having eaten a burger to assuage my hunger, despite being so enthralled by Mumtaz that I forgot to eat for a while, I walk across the dark square to the guesthouse. The four German girls have arrived and settled in, their large rucksacks and cases spread about and their chatter and laughter filling the dorm.

They are very pleasant and I sit and talk with them for a while at the long table in the dining room. We are joined by a Turkish guy who I had met earlier and is some sort of freelance writer. The Germans are here for a month, teaching a course on media in the cinema to Palestinian students.

The next morning, I apologise to my roommates for my snoring but they are very polite and say it did not bother them. I take a shower, passing through the dining room to get to the bathroom but luckily no one is about to see me dishevelled in my pyjamas. Ayman brings me a huge breakfast of hummus, pitta, salad and falafel, enough for dinner as well so I put the remains in the communal fridge for later.

THE FREEDOM THEATRE

The founder of the theatre, Juliano Mar Kamis, had a Jewish mother, Arna, a communist, and a Palestinian intellectual, communist father. Arna was an activist and among her many activities, opened an alternative education system for Palestinian children to better equip them to cope with life under occupation. She realised that art and theatre offered a powerful tool for young Palestinians to express themselves. In 1989 she and Juliano, an aspiring actor, opened the Stone Theatre during the second year of the First Intifada. It closed in 1996 after Arna's death from cancer. Juliano made a film called 'Arna's Children, a tragedy about the consequences of the Jenin siege on the children who had such hope and promise for a brighter future, but who succumbed to the desperation, nihilism and violence that occupation produces.

After his mother's death, Juliano teamed up with one of his former students, Zakaria Zubeid, and Jonathan Stanczak, a Swedish nurse, to re-establish the theatre in 2006, to be a major cultural resistance, using not guns, but words. Palestinians, internationals and even Israeli artists come together for a common purpose but there is opposition to it from both the Israelis, who see it as a threat, and the conservative Palestinians, who see it as corrupting Islamic morals. The theatre has been physically attacked by the IOF on many occasions and numerous actors and other associated with it have been arrested and badly treated. A group of ultra-conservative Palestinians who oppose any international participation in the resistance last summer distributed flyers warning all foreigners to leave Jenin and threatening to destroy the town's cinema.

Many young Palestinians who had given up on their future had their lives transformed by drama therapy, enabling them to release their inner fears and anger, and went on to become professional actors through the three-year theatre school course. Young men who had previously been denounced as terrorists were now finding another, non-violent way of resistance through art.

Due to the controversy that the theatre provoked through its outspokenness against both the IOF and the PA, the history of the theatre has been turbulent. When it restarted in 2006, the Second Intifada was ongoing, and fighting between the IOF and the resistance fighters in the camp took place daily. Despite the difficulties and dangers of getting in or out of Jenin, volunteers and guests still kept coming. Bullets were received in envelopes at the door, verbal threats made, but still the theatre thrived.

This year the theatre plans to bring its latest production, The Siege to Britain but the artistic director has been refused entry into the country. Undeterred, Ahmed Tobasi, a former acting student at the theatre, now with a Norwegian passport, will fly out to replace him and the tour will take place.

BURKIN

Finding the bus to Burkin in the bus station I climb aboard amongst the country folk, already returning home after bringing their produce to sell in the market. The countryside is fresh and green and exhilarating after the dusty town. Arriving all too soon in the quaint old village of Burkin, perched on a hill, I get off with everyone else and then wonder where to go as there are no signs pointing to a church. A young girl in a *hijab* asks me where I want to go, as I must look lost, standing in the village square, deserted now the bus has driven off. I tell her I want to visit the church so she very kindly offers to show me the way. As we walk along the narrow, neat and tidy old streets, she practises her very good English, asking me what I am doing here. She says it is unknown for a foreigner to come here on their own as they always come with a group so I feel like a pioneer, venturing into this very traditional, isolated village but which feels completely benign if this girl is representative of the people here. I would never have found the church on my own as we had walked some fifteen minutes up and down and around before reaching it. No one is around but the door is open so we enter the cool, dim interior and I am immediately awed by the obvious antiquity of this beautiful, small and unusual church. According to both Moslem and Christian tradition this is the site where Jesus cured the lepers. A man I met yesterday in the *souk* told me that Burkin church is very important to both religions as Moslems believe in Jesus the prophet and in his miracles. I expect the girl to leave me now but she shows me round, pointing out things of interest, like the ancient chair carved out of stone with heads of lions on the arm rests. I learn that it is the fifth oldest Christian holy place and the third oldest church in the world – 1,800 years old.

Just as we are about to leave, the custodian of the church appears and is very keen to show us around again. I feel obliged to hear what he has to say as he is obviously very proud of 'his' church and probably does not get many visitors. He leads us outside to a part we had overlooked, to a room where groups can sit and have coffee and talk and another small room which has its own altar. He invites me to climb down the vertical metal ladder into the well where Christians hid from Romans and more recently in April 2002 members of the congregation hid during the Battle of Jenin but there was no possibility of me going down into that dark, dank hole, so I decline. He tells me that some pilgrims do actually venture down. Despite my reluctance to spend more time in the church I have to admit that under his expert guidance I am being made aware of features previously missed like the hole in the roof, through which the lepers would receive their food, being completely isolated from the community. The young custodian and the girl, Christian and Moslem, are discussing something in Arabic, then he reaches for a New Testament on the shelf behind him and I gather he is instructing her in some part of the gospels, which she appears to be familiar with. I have to take a photo of this touching scene, in the church, an example of what Mumtaz had said last night: that there is no difference between a Moslem and a Christian. Outside, the neat garden is very well tended and the views to Jenin show me that it is much too far to walk – my original intention.

Saying goodbye to this gentle, kind man, I feel immensely touched by the generosity of Palestinians. It would be interesting to walk around this attractive village but when we reach the square, now busy with locals, I feel the eyes of the villagers upon me and decide it is perhaps not such a good idea to be walking around here on my own. I thank my friend over and over for her time and kindness and she goes off smiling, no doubt pleased to have a story to tell about the strange Englishwoman with white hair, travelling about on her own. The bus arrives and takes me back to Jenin. In the now familiar Delicate restaurant I have coffee and a pastry, passing time as it is too early to go back to the Freedom Theatre. I do not want to gate-crash their lunch again. Jenin is a small town and not a popular tourist spot so further options for sightseeing are limited to another tour of the *souk*, not appealing just now.

Judging the time right to go back, I walk slowly along the road, passing children going home from school but few saying, "Hello, how are you? What is your name?", as I have become used to. Ahmed who had invited me to come back, is not here so I ask another man if anyone is available for a tour of the camp, which is advertised on the wall. He assures me I will be fine to wander about on my own so off I go up the climbing streets, deeper into the camp. It is all very pleasant, the streets more airy, due to the height and views across the town and soon I am joined by the inevitable entourage of curious children, asking, "Where are you from? What is your name?" Seeing my camera, some of them ask me to take their photos and they pose, smiling for the camera. By now I have a group of six boys aged from approximately nine to fourteen; the girls have got left behind. One boy seems to dislike me taking photos and keeps leaping in front of the others, trying to spoil the shot. I think he is having fun and play along but then the atmosphere changes. I cannot understand what they are saying but one boy now keeps pushing my shoulder bag, then another kicks a football at me. Saying "*la, la*" (no, no) sternly at them, I turn to retreat down the hill but one boy starts shouting and the bag pusher gets more aggressive. My Arabic being very limited, I turn to them and say "*Haram*" very loudly, meaning 'not allowed' but this seems to inflame the situation and they pick up bits of rubbish and throw it at me and then stones, not hitting me, just intimidating and threatening. Walking fast downhill I soon lose them but feel shocked and disappointed that I should be subject to such aggression. This is the first time that I have felt any animosity in Palestine but I have sensed that Jenin is not as friendly or tolerant as other places I have visited. I am puzzled too and annoyed that I could not understand them. What had happened to change the friendly atmosphere?

To console myself and get over the traumatic experience, I visit a café I have read about and have a piece of chocolate cake and tea and feel restored again. My knee has been troubling me on and off and is quite painful so I go back to the guesthouse for a rest. On the way in I meet the manager who tells me he lived in Manchester for five years and loved the curries there so now his wife makes them for him. He is a very charming man and says he is glad I made the effort to come here as Jenin gets overlooked being the northernmost town in the West Bank.

The evening passes quickly. The German girls and the Turkish guy have been joined by an Australian girl, travelling on her own and planning to go to Nazareth the next day. This means going into Israel and through the checkpoint which closes at midday, so she has to leave early in the morning. She is concerned about her visa, a small slip of paper inserted into one's passport on entry, and in her case, removed by a soldier at another checkpoint who told her it did not matter. I feel sure it does matter and hope she makes it through the checkpoint without difficulty. Ayman joins us for a while and another guy from the cinema who I get talking to and mention my experience in the camp today. Inexplicably I feel hesitant to talk about it; perhaps I feel it is my fault in some way or do not want to admit that Palestinians can behave like this but I want a Palestinian to explain it to me if he can. This man, Ahmed, lives in the camp so would have insight into their way of thinking, I reason. He is surprised when I tell him what happened and says he has not heard of this sort of behaviour towards a foreigner before. He thinks it could have been because I was on my own, a single, fair-haired woman, unusual in the camp, so they may have thought I was Jewish or a spy as I was taking photos. It still does not explain why they were friendly to start with and then changed but it seems I will never really know. I will just have to accept that I cannot expect rational behaviour from children who have suffered under occupation and who live constantly under threat from their occupiers.

For dinner, I finish my 'all-day breakfast' and eat some dates the German girls are sharing before going to my bunk. Eighteen Italians are arriving tonight so I am expecting a lot of noise and not much sleep.

The next morning there is no sign of any new occupants in our dorm so they must all be men. As quietly as possible I slip across to the bathroom to have a shower before it gets really busy. Returning through the dining room I am alarmed to see two men with long hair, one with a beard, sitting at the table focused on a laptop. They must be two of the Italians, I surmise, but fortunately, so engrossed are they my towelled presence is ignored. One Arabic breakfast yesterday was enough so having packed and now ready to go I say goodbye to my roommates and to Ayman and pay my last visit to Delicate for coffee and a pastry.

The 'service' to Ramallah is efficient and speeds through the scenic countryside. It seems less crowded here in the north with barely a settlement to be seen, lots of agriculture and market gardens and stalls at the side of the road selling vegetables. As we near Ramallah it starts raining. It seems every time I go to Ramallah it rains; everywhere else may be dry but Ramallah has a high rainfall being higher up. I have seen the roads running with torrents of water during a sudden downpour but this looks like a light shower. Echlas' birthday is imminent so I hope I may find something here for her. The bus station is in the centre of the city, so making a mental note of its whereabouts I search the busy streets looking for a shop selling a traditionally embroidered top, something Echlas has expressed a wish for. Long dresses are difficult for her to get in and out of so a top would be ideal but despite finding several likely shops, none stock what I am looking for. Tired of the busy streets I go back to the bus station and return to Bethlehem, an hour's journey.

As I am in no particular rush to get back and feel hungry, I go to Casa Nova in Manger Square and have something to eat before wandering up through the *souk*. A place I have passed many times but never stopped to explore catches my eye – The Bethlehem Museum and Women's Cooperative – so I go in. I am most interested in the embroidery adorning the walls and tables in all sorts of patterns and colours in placemats, bags, purses, clothes, pencil cases – all sorts but no tops.

CHAPTER SIX

CELEBRATIONS AND GOODBYES

The usual smell of cigarette smoke greets me when I get home. The rack of clothes drying, washing up in the sink, yesterday's dinner on the cooker – home, sweet, home.

We chat for a bit and wonder where Hannah is. No one has heard from her and her phone does not work so we cannot phone her, but surely she will turn up sometime today. I stay at home in case she comes back while Echlas and Christina go to Aida to give Musa his birthday present. Still no sign of Hannah when we go to bed. Where can she be?

It is an early morning start today as Echlas and Christina are going to Aida for Christina to say goodbye to the family there. She is going off with George today until Saturday and then leaves for Jerusalem on Sunday. I stay at home again, enjoying the small patch of sun in the garden. My seedlings that I saved are doing well and the blossom is out on the peach tree, so spring is definitely here. Hannah arrives back at 11am. She has been to a party (Israeli) in the hostel in Jerusalem and looks as if she has not slept, so she is relieved that it is only me at home, so she can have a nap.

This afternoon includes another trip to the hospital in Bethlehem to get Echlas' blood results. We go for 2pm as Echlas understands the clinic starts at 2.30pm but the receptionist tells us it is 3.30pm. Deciding to wait rather than go home and then come out again means I have to go back and wait at home to tell a student his lesson at 4pm is cancelled and can he come back at 6pm, as he has no phone. I am eager to go, it being an ideal opportunity to visit the shop near the wall where Echlas has seen embroidered tunics. I rush up there but find they cost 500IS – far too expensive – but I must get something and time is running out so I decide on an embroidered black T-shirt top, hoping it will fit and it only costs 100IS. As I am paying my phone rings and it is Hannah summoning me back to the hospital as the student has phoned and the lesson time changed and Echlas needs me. I set off at a fast pace and arrive red faced and sweaty only to find the doctor has not arrived yet but we decide to wait having waited so long already. Eventually we go into his consulting room and he explains the blood results show Echlas is going through the menopause. She is young for that but apart from amenorrhoea she is not suffering any symptoms at present.

To reward ourselves for such a tedious afternoon we go to the *knafa* shop and indulge in a piece of heavenly sweetness, sitting outside in the sun with the parked cars, as there is no wheelchair access.

The new student who comes at 6pm is Austrian, a tall young man, a bit shy, but interested in all of us and Echlas. He is a volunteer at the Natural History Museum, working on a research project there. I heard about this newly set-up branch of Bethlehem University last time I was here and it sounded very exciting so I am keen to go and see it. It is close by, so next time we go out for a walk we will go and visit. I cook vegetable patties for dinner – very messy to make and I manage to fill the house with frying fumes. Ida calls with, coincidentally, spinach patties, so we have a good dinner.

Excitement is building for Echlas' birthday. After weeks of deliberation she has made a final guest list, including Kimberley coming from Ramallah, but Eugene still has a question mark over his name. We have whispered conversations about our plans for the celebration: the presents, cards, cake. Birthdays here are great occasions with celebrations often extending into days in order to include all the family so we are expecting Echlas' family to fly in at some point and just hope we will get some notice of their ETA. I am making a card using her paper and crayons and also designing my own wrapping paper, crafts I have not done for years but I really enjoy being creative.

On Friday Echlas arranged to meet a German friend of hers, Anna, who had been her first helper, many years ago. We meet Anna and her boyfriend in Manger Square and, as usual, go to the Peace Centre restaurant. The boyfriend is fairly uncommunicative and when asked, in an attempt to draw him into the conversation, if he likes the country, he replies he enjoyed Tel Aviv. There is almost a sharp intake of breath and a moment of uncomfortable silence, quickly covered by Anna who, realising this is not the thing to say to a Palestinian refugee, sitting in Manger Square in the occupied West Bank, tries to justify his statement by explaining he liked the shops there. Unfortunately, it goes further downhill when his reply to enquiring how he felt on seeing the wall for the first time, is a short "nothing" accompanied by a shrug of the shoulders.

Suddenly and providentially, as it breaks the hostile atmosphere at our table, a large group of young men armed with wooden sticks come running across the square and begin to smash the windows of the souvenir shop and restaurant opposite. I stand up to see what is happening and to take some photos but Anna is nervous and keeps telling me to sit down. More and more men run into the square, closely followed by the riot police wearing helmets and shields. The waiters from our restaurant are outside watching and say it is a personal dispute but Echlas says it is a Christian/Moslem fight. I really hope that is not the case as I still believe, from my own evidence, that there is no religious animosity. There is rivalry between the residents of Beit Jala and Beit Sahour, both Christian, but I fail to see any deep religious divide. Later on, we find out that the marauding crowd, Moslems, had gathered in support of a family with a personal grievance against the shop owner who happens to be a Christian, over some perceived injustice towards his employees. I think it was more a personality feud than a religious one and unfortunately anger turned to violence. After all this excitement, Anna and boyfriend have to leave to go back to Jerusalem, thankfully, so we say goodbye and go to the bus station to meet Kimberley and tell her about our eventful afternoon.

I cook *maqluba*, Hannah makes the salad when we get home

and when Christina arrives back there is quite a party of us and we have a lively evening.

Tonight is the eve of Echlas' birthday and we are having a party for her and to say goodbye to Christina. Echlas made her decision re Eugene and asks me to invite him. I think it is short notice but fortunately he is free and not offended that he is invited at the last minute, and is delighted to come. What else would he be doing anyway?

As there are four of us in the house, I go out to get some shopping and for some air. Later Christina and I go to the photo shop with my camera to get some photos printed for the collage she is making for Echlas. It takes ages to download the particular pictures Christina wants as we have to go through each one on my camera and by now there are several hundred but eventually she chooses twenty that she wants and the shopkeeper is very patient and obliging and prints them all out. She also buys a frame from him. We find a shop that sells birthday balloons and also buy three DVDs that we think Echlas will like: *Bridget Jones's Diary*, *Jenin Jenin* and *The Imitation Game* for 5IS each – all copies, of course.

Layan is there when we return and everyone has a green face due to the avocado face mask Kimberley has made, so we join in and take some photos. It turns out to be a real girly sort of day with Layan doing hair, nail painting, make-up by Kimberley and just lounging about and chatting. Getting Echlas into her traditional Palestinian dress is challenging and causes much hysterical laughter but finally she is ready and jokingly we call her 'the Bride' and Christina, wearing Echlas' other dress is 'the Groom'. Eugene calls around, looking the same as always, but I hope he has put a clean shirt on for the occasion.

Our merry group sets off down the road to our usual restaurant above the bus station where we know they can cope with our festivities, but had pre-warned them of our arrival and need for a table to accommodate us all. Deanna is already there and George and Musa join us a bit later. The food is really good. I have lamb kebab, taking the opportunity to indulge my carnivore appetite, and sample some of the various salads and dips we choose for our starter. The wine flows and Eugene, much to everyone's surprise and delight, plays Deanna's guitar wonderfully well, singing Irish folk songs and encouraging us to join in with the singing or just clapping along. The waiter produces an *oudh*, a traditional Palestinian instrument, and a tabla and Musa plays an Arabic song then beats out a rhythm on the tabla, with he and Echlas, Layan and Deanna singing Palestinian songs and the rest of us clapping along. Eugene, sitting next to me, talks about his involvement in another community centre in Aida camp and is keen to introduce me to the people there when I have some time off to go. His lessons in Al Azza have been problematic in that his pupils often fail to appear or arrive late and the younger ones mess with his things in the flat, so he is thinking of stopping them and doing something else – teaching but in a different location.

At the end of a wonderful evening we all leave together except Eugene who is still finishing his wine. I notice that he has drunk a pint of beer and a bottle of wine but does not appear at all affected by it. I know he does drink regularly so must be used to it. The beer, a local one, 'Taybeh', is brewed in the Christian village of that name, here in the West Bank. In the New Testament it is called Ephrain, where Jesus spent the night before his Passion. The Taybeh Beer Brewing Company was founded in 1995 by a returning immigrant, Nadin Khoury, and is the only brewery in the Middle East. The beer is such a high quality, up to the standard of any German beer, and in fact there are Taybeh breweries in Germany and the UK. There are five varieties of the beer including a non-alcoholic one for the Moslem community.

George comes back to the house with us, bringing a bottle of wine, then Eugene arrives, none the worse for his mix of beer and wine, hoping to carry on the party. Echlas is already in her bed with Kimberley and Hannah keeping her company so we four sit in the lounge looking at George's photos on his iPad of the places he has been in his car out in the country. The scenery is amazing, from stark desert places to meadows of yellow flowers but only accessible by independent means. At least there are places left that the Israelis have not yet destroyed but it is only a matter of time unless they can be stopped before it is too late to save this beautiful country.

I am concerned that Eugene is going to make a night of it but he takes his leave when George and Christina say they have to work on the collage for tomorrow. George is sleeping in the lesson room but goodness knows when they will get some sleep with Echlas' present to make.

*

Today is Echlas' birthday and I am the last one up, much to my shame. I blame it on the wine. There are six of us to sing 'Happy Birthday', crowding into her room with the balloon and presents. I think she is pleased with her top and the DVDs, and Christina and George made a lovely job of the framed collage, a record of the people and times during Christina's stay. George has to go to work, Kimberley is going to Ramallah with Musa and Christina is leaving, so Hannah and I prepare Echlas for the relatives and the second part of her birthday celebrations. They arrive like a hurricane as usual: Hebron sister, two daughters, one son and Esa. Then Layan arrives to help and the kitchen is a flurry of activity (oh dear, they are messing up my kitchen again) as food is produced from bags to prepare and cook. A huge fish is cleaned and put in the floor oven and a quantity of smaller fish are coated in something for frying later. A cacophony of chopping produces potato chips and a variety of salads. The table is laden with fish and chips, Palestinian style, and is absolutely delicious, devoured in a loud, hectic free-for-all by ten hungry people with much laughter and joy. My job is the washing up and I am glad to do something and, feeling the kitchen is my domain, am keen to get it back to some sort of order. As suddenly as the family arrive, they leave. A phone call from brother-in-law to say he is locked out sends them hurrying home, leaving us becalmed. Christina has to go so we say an emotional goodbye, she and Echlas crying on each other's shoulders and promising to Skype very soon.

When we have almost given up hope of any more family coming and Echlas is thinking of going to bed, they arrive bringing two elaborate cakes and we sing 'Happy Birthday' again. Rosha made both cakes, one covered in chocolate and decorated with chocolate dipped strawberries and the other a sponge covered with strawberries and jelly. The five women who arrive are Rosha and baby, Layan and her mother, Echlas' niece and Amia. As is customary I cut off chunks of cake to give to Ida's family and Mohammed later and we tuck into the rest. Once they leave we put a very tired Echlas into bed and spend a quiet evening until another visitor arrives. It is Musa on his way back from the court in Ramallah. He brings a present and also one from Kimberley as she had forgotten to buy anything. Musa is tired and fed up after a disappointing and frustrating day.

Two years ago, he was shot in the face by the IOF in Aida camp, the bullet just missing his eye, but had to spend some time in hospital and the scar is still apparent. At the time, he was doing his job of photographing the incursion by the IOF when this happened. He prosecuted the soldier who shot him but after two years of going to court to pursue his case, he is now the one being prosecuted, although he is the victim. Today his lawyer was not present (an Israeli lawyer, as Palestinians are not allowed to work in the military courts) but the judge told him he could pay a large sum of money and that would be the end of it. Musa refused and so it goes on. The injustice is unbelievable and so provocative. My ire is roused again on his behalf, so what he must feel I cannot begin to imagine. I begin to understand what suicide bombers must feel: utter frustration against the might of the Israeli regime. What have they got to lose? A life they feel is not worth living in this repressive and cruel occupation.

*

Today is very quiet and Echlas stays in bed, changing her mind about going to visit the Natural History Museum. I go out on my own for a short while for a walk, enjoying the warmth, even in the shade. It really feels like summer. Hannah and I talk about simple pleasures, one of mine being hanging out the washing. We usually have a few tussles over who will hang it out and bring it in again – ridiculous. But it seems we both take pleasure in hanging out the wet washing on the line and the drying rack, knowing that in a few hours it will be dry and ready to sort and fold and put away. Perhaps this is a reflection of the reduced level of pleasure to be found in a refugee camp. I note in my diary that we have a strange dinner: smashed avocadoes with lemon juice (left over from the face masks) on toast followed by fish with carrot salad for Echlas and Hannah and stuffed courgette with pitta for me, followed by chocolate cake. Our menu is varied at least and often surprising.

A loud banging on the front door wakes me at 9am the next morning but as I am still in bed and not fit to receive visitors I ignore it. Apparently it was Eugene, as he comes around again at 10am to say he cannot come for his lesson as he has a meeting about a volunteer post. I would ask him in but feel like a character in a Jane Austen novel, convention dictating the impropriety of a gentleman caller to an all-female household, so early in the morning. He is talking about having a party for St Patrick's Day but I am not getting involved in the planning of it as he keeps changing his mind about where to have it.

Hannah's black jeans have split in an awkward place and are no longer fit for purpose so our mission today is to find her a pair for under 50IS. We battle the *souk*, Echlas valiantly manoeuvring through the people and the traffic until we come to an old-fashioned-looking shop, where Echlas knows the owner and asks her to show Hannah some cheap black jeans. While she is trying them on Echlas chooses a knitted woollen dress for her niece's birthday present. Hannah finds a suitable pair of jeans for only 50IS so is pleased with her purchase, which no doubt will last her another few years. She has little money to spend, being a student, and I think her Marxist principles define her attitude to money and possessions. I wish I could be more like her instead of a compulsive spender.

We buy a large quantity of broad beans, peas, a green leafy vegetable, along with two dozen eggs, garlic and lemons. I make the broad bean dish again for dinner and let Hannah go to AIC in the evening. My right knee has been giving me trouble and tonight it is more painful so I would rather rest it than go out again. My visa runs out on 20 April but I have booked my flight two weeks earlier. Now I am not sure why I did that. Did I think I would find ten weeks enough or was I concerned about my garden and allotment needing attention now that spring is here? That seems unimportant now and the decision to stay on or go as planned is weighing on my mind. The two extra weeks would be travelling time but the places I really want to go to, the Negev and the Golan Heights, are probably inaccessible without a car. I could go to Haifa or volunteer somewhere else for a couple of weeks or visit another NGO like Women in Black. The choices are bewildering.

Yom Il Arba

How can I sleep so long? Today I wake at 10am. Perhaps it is because I have nothing much to worry about and no compulsion to be up and doing 'things'. I just follow Echlas' plans for the day. This life must be relaxing if I can sleep so soundly and so long. Happily I put on another load of washing, clear up the kitchen from last night and then sit in the garden trying to get to grips with declining the word '*sahib*'. When it gets to 11.30am I wake Echlas and Hannah; just as well I left them to sleep as Echlas did not sleep until 2.30am.

Echlas wants the peas and beans frozen so I shell a kilo of peas and cut and blanch the beans. This takes a good while. Veronica comes at 2pm for her lesson, reporting it is really hot outside. We have no idea how warm it is, as indoors it is always cool or even cold. Layan comes to bath Echlas and the shower actually works.

After our dinner of peas and carrots in a tomato and garlic

sauce with rice Hannah decides it is 'Party Night' so Echlas finds some loud rock music on her laptop and we prance around for a bit like 'Men Behaving Badly' but without the beer until we are out of breath, then calm it down with a game of I Spy and twenty questions while eating strawberries. Hannah washes up while I have a shower, appreciating the comfortable temperature in the bathroom now the weather is warming up. The outside temperature was 26 degrees today but the forecast is for rain and a drop in the temperature with the possibility of snow!

The forecast was right. It feels cold getting up this morning and it has rained a lot in the night. Echlas decides to stay in bed so I do some ironing and pass the day reading, practising Arabic and listening to music until six when the Austrian guy comes for his lesson. We have another strange dinner tonight: chips, rice and leafy green veg like spinach cooked with onion to which I add some toasted almond flakes. It sounds like a bizarre concoction but actually tasted OK.

The next day starts early as one of the Al Azza clan is coming to install two new water tanks on the roof, making four altogether, in an attempt to increase the water pressure for the shower. I am no plumber and do not fully understand the water system, but cannot see the science behind this. Anyway it will be a diversion to see how they get the tanks onto the roof just by manpower alone. Echlas is up in her wheelchair by 10.30am and shortly afterwards a knock on the door announces the arrival of the tanks. They are huge but, being made of plastic, not too heavy to manage. The two men manhandle the first tank down the alley, tie a rope around it and with one of them on the roof, haul it up into position. The operation is repeated with the second and in no time and with no fuss it is done. I wonder how much weight the roof will take and hope this has been considered.

Echlas has a visitor so Hannah and I take the opportunity to visit the Bible College library, just over the road. I have passed it so many times but did not realise it is open to the public and has mainly English language books. They are not all theological either we discover, although the majority are and a wonderful resource for students as so many areas are covered. It costs 70IS to join but as I am only here for another three and a half weeks I wonder if it is worth it. Hannah goes home letting me go to Bethlehem University to look at their library but unfortunately for me it is in the process of being refurbished so is closed except to students. Back I go to the Bible College, bibliophilic tendencies getting the better of me, join up and take out five books, one on Islamic philosophy, two on the Koran and two Palestinian autobiographies.

Happy with my armful of books I return home eager to make a start on reading but first have to cook the dinner – rice and vegetable stew – and watch *Bridget Jones's Diary* with Hannah and Echlas. I have seen it at least three times but still find it funny and the others both enjoyed it despite its very English sense of humour. Hannah thought it sexist and offensive to women's rights, which if you take it seriously it is but I can only see it as a harmless, feel-good movie.

On Saturday Hannah is meeting up with Mohammed from Nablus and going hiking near Jericho with a group so I will be on my own with Echlas on Saturday night but if she can get a sitter I would like to go to AIC.

We get up reasonably early and are out before lunch. The day is warm and sunny but the *souk* is too crowded, so having got a third of the way, Echlas decides to turn around and go home and start again by a different route. We have a bit of lunch and go out again, this time along Star Street – much easier to negotiate. Echlas likes to get some sun so we sit for a while in Manger Square and people watch, trying to guess the nationalities of the groups of tourists who are coming out with the sun. Hannah leaves us at 4pm to go to the bus station to get the 'service' to Ramallah, and Echlas and I go to the restaurant for a lemon and mint drink but as soon as the sun dips behind the buildings it gets cold. Stopping at Echlas' favourite shop on the way home just to get some cigarettes we hurry the rest of the way back to the warmth of the house and put the heaters on. Feeling in need of protein I buy a tin of tuna and make salad nicoise but Echlas cannot eat tuna so I make her a separate salad. Mohammed's mum and sisters come to visit while I go out to AIC for which I am very grateful.

The talk is by an elderly Israeli who is one of a group forming a 'secular' political party with Palestinians. He speaks in Hebrew with an interpreter so I think something is lost in translation as a lot of it passes me by so is rather disappointing. I do have my usual glass of wine though.

Echlas sleeps at 12.30am, reasonably early for her and only wakes twice in the night, sleeping through till 10.30am. The gardener and his young son come to prune the lemon and peach trees and the other unknown shrub. It is too late for the lemon but he tidies up the vine and it looks more under control now. A delightful French nun called Sister Lucille calls in the afternoon. She is from the Sisters of the Sacred Heart of Jesus and met Echlas when she was having rehabilitation after her 'accident'. She speaks English fairly well with a delightful French accent and also speaks Arabic fluently as she has been here for a long time. She is probably in her sixties but still working hard. She tells me about the work the Order does, i.e. running the orphanage here in Bethlehem. I am surprised to learn that unmarried mothers are not uncommon in Palestine but that keeping their babies means social isolation and disapproval, not surprisingly, so babies are left at the orphanage. Sometimes the girl is engaged and becomes pregnant before marriage, the boy leaves her, so she is forced by her family and culture to give the baby away. Adoption is thankfully more common now so some of the children are lucky enough to grow up with parents. The others go to the SOS children's village when they are old enough, to be brought up in care. In Palestine it is very important to know who your parents are, as I have learned from Echlas, especially when getting married, so a child brought up in care has to live with the social stigma of not having a family name.

The Sisters also work with the elderly in East Jerusalem. Many are, unusually, on their own, their families having moved out due to lack of space and the almost intolerable situation of settlers moving in to drive out the remaining Palestinians. The older members of the family sometimes refuse to leave so need care. To make an income some of the sisters make icons and religious pottery figures.

The discussion moves on to death and funerals and I ask why women do not go to funerals. It seems to be a combination of women not being able to control their emotions and men not being able to handle the crying and wailing and fainting of the women. Funerals, traditionally, happen very quickly after death, even the same day sometimes, so grief is very new and raw and emotions uncontrolled. This is the case for both Moslem and Christian. The whole family unites for three days, the women meeting in the house of the deceased and the men gathering in a community hall or the house of close relatives. In the case of martyrs (*shuhada*), i.e. people who have died for the cause, their bodies are not washed or clothes changed and the whole community of men and women accompany the body to the graveyard.

After this morbid but interesting discussion, Sister Lucille has to go but I hope we will see her again. Hannah returns in the evening having had a wonderful day walking through Wadi Qelt, near Jericho with a group of Palestinian women in their long coats and ballerina-style shoes, plus three men and Charlotte, a German student of Echlas' who Hannah persuaded to join her. Admirably the Palestinian women managed the walk in their flimsy shoes but refrained from joining in the water fight with the boys which Hannah described to us. Hannah said she felt sorry for them that they did not have the freedom to enjoy the fun, but since everyone involved appeared to have got drenched, I was inclined to agree with the Palestinians.

Monday 17 March

While I am out buying chillies for tonight's curry, I drop into Wi'am on the Hebron road, just up from the Aida camp entrance. I had passed it many times but it always looked closed, however, today the gate is open so I want to see what they do here. Wi'am in Arabic means 'cordial relationships' and in English the NGO is known as the Conflict Resolution Centre. It started in March 1995 with the aim of helping to resolve disputes within the Palestinian community by implementing the traditional Arabic form of mediation, known as *sulha*, as well as Western models of conflict resolution. This is achieved by empowering women and providing facilities for youth to meet. They also have an international link and the very hospitable man there tells me that the director is doing a tour of England and may need venues so I give him my email and Facebook name.

On the way through the camp I meet Nicole, another student of Echlas', outside the centre where she volunteers. Lots of boys are playing about there and I can see by the various colours streaking their hands and faces that they have been painting the wall of the centre, renewing the faded mural. The facilitator of this project is a priest cum painter who is repainting the less than perfect efforts of the boys. Nicole says it has been mayhem, with forty boys all trying to get hold of the brushes and paints at once. They so lack out-of-school facilities that anything different draws many more young people than can be accommodated. In the circumstances, it is a pretty good job and at least it is bright and better than grey concrete.

This evening I am still mulling over whether to stay or go and considering the pros and cons and what I will do if I stay. Nicole gave me an idea today which is quite bizarre but not impossible. She is looking into going to Italy by freight ship from Israel to Germany. It takes about three weeks by sea. If I did the same I could drop in on my friend Barbara in Sienna and fly home from Pisa. What an adventure but probably quite costly.

Tuesday 18 March, St Patrick's Day

Eugene finally came up with a plan for this evening. We are meeting in our usual restaurant above the bus station as he likes the friendliness and flexibility of the staff and has asked them to provide some Irish music and he will bring his guitar.

He comes for a lesson this morning but does not stay, saying his brain is not fully engaged with Arabic as he has already drunk two beers. I am not sure I want to go to this party but in support of Eugene I make the effort. Eugene and two of his English students are already there and then four Swedish girls arrive, people Eugene met at Wi'am. Mohsin, who owns one of the camp shops, comes later and is great entertainment. Eugene has told me about him, how he buys all his food from his shop and has long talks with him when the shop is quiet and what an entrepreneur he is but frustrated doing what he does. He would like to go abroad and study but it is so difficult to get a visa. The other two Palestinians, Ahmed and Munjad speak excellent English too and tell me they are at university and although aware of their limited prospects of employment once qualified, they consider it is important to get a degree. Munjad started his degree in law but found it too rigid so changed to social sciences. Mohsin and Ahmed sing some Arabic songs (why is it that all Palestinians can sing and are not afraid to do so in public?), and Eugene plays the guitar and sings while we all clap along and I sing the bits I know. The wine and beer flow freely and I can see Munjad and Mohsin getting more inebriated. Despite the amount they have drunk they proceed to have a discussion verging on argument in fluent, fast English about their lives as Palestinians and reveal to me how young men really feel about the occupation, the IOF, the neglect and indifference of the world's governments, their lack of freedom and religion. Although they both say all this in a humorous way and I can see Munjad uses his humour to cope, there is a deep seriousness and maturity about them. As Mohsin says, they learn responsibility very early in life and are exposed to the harsh conditions in the camp from childhood which makes them tough in order to survive. I can empathise with them and feel so keenly their frustration and sadness that they cannot live the lives of free men.

Munjad said, "I only have one life. How do I really live when I have no freedom?" He also reveals that he is not religious but believes in human beings and in one God who preaches the same message of love in all religions and in nature. What profound thoughts for such a young man. Although he cannot live in freedom at least he thinks and uses his mind to try to find answers to his life, so in some way is freer than his materialistic contemporaries in the West who accept the status quo and never question the way they live. The evening has not been quite the St Patrick's celebration I anticipated full of singing and laughter, although we did have some of that, but I am so glad I came and have had the conversations and got to know these young men. We say goodbye to the Swedish girls and walk up through the dark, shuttered *souk*, so quiet and peaceful, a very different place at night.

*

Today Echlas has a new pupil, Robert, an elderly American who describes himself as 'an international, married to a Moroccan lady'. As Echlas' house is not so easy to find I go to meet him at the Paradise Hotel and bring him into the camp and happen to meet Eugene. As they are both retired teachers, I introduce them, thinking they might get on and Eugene tells us about an event at Wi'am that Robert may be interested in. I am interested too, so when Veronica comes for her lesson at 2pm, I am able to go to the talk. We sit outside under a canopy for shade, and refreshments of tea and cakes are offered. There is a good mix of nationalities: four Swedish (the girls from last night), two American, two Polish, one English, one Irish and five Palestinians. One of the Swedish girls has prepared a short talk on ISIS and the director, Mr Zoughbe Zoughbe, who seems very knowledgeable, carries on the discussion about what it is, theories of how it came into being, why it is so successful and possible solutions. In his opinion, from what he has researched, ISIS is so successful partly due to its clever use of social media, a means for recruiting so many disaffected young Moslems from around the world. Bombing and other forms of violence will not stop them; we have to be more clever than that. He also addressed the reason why ISIS has such a following, i.e. treatment of Moslems in Western countries and their reasons for feeling alienated from society. Theories that Israel and the US are behind ISIS abound and no doubt there is some truth in that as the US is usually involved somewhere in conflicts.

19 March

My birthday. How amazing to spend it in the birthplace of Christ. It cannot get better than that. I am awoken by a strange noise outside my room. At first I cannot tell if it is coming from the garden or the lounge but as I surface from sleep, I am suddenly alarmed into wide-awakeness by the realisation that someone is trying to get into my room. I lie, frozen, heart thumping, imagination running wild but not reaching any rational explanation, until I force myself to get out of bed and open the door very slowly to find, not a burglar or monster outside but Echlas and Hannah. They have been trying to open the door but it is very tricky from the outside and they were just wondering what to do when I open it. What a relief! The shock of seeing the two of them up and dressed before me sends me scuttling back into bed. Is this a dream or a nightmare? No, it is my birthday surprise. They come in bearing flowers, cards, orange juice, chopped banana, apple, ginger and chocolate in little bowls, no doubt Hannah's idea. I express my astonishment, read the cards made especially for me and drink some orange juice, thanking them for such a wonderful surprise. There is more. Leading me into the sitting room, there on the table, Hannah has prepared breakfast of cereal and tea which we eat with the chopped-up bits, although it is too early in the day for me to eat chocolate or ginger, but the thought is so sweet and imaginative. Today I am having a day off, leaving Echlas with Hannah, so after breakfast, I set off for the bus station to get a 'service' to Jericho, the oldest continually inhabited city in the world and the home of the sycamore tree into which Zacheus climbed in order to see Jesus, and the Mount of Temptation.

I am the only person waiting to go to Jericho and the driver keeps hassling me to pay 250IS to go on my own, there and back, including taking me around when we get there. It is far too expensive and I keep explaining that I want to go on my own, which is a concept that Palestinians seem to find hard to understand. Fortunately, another lady appears, so now he tries to get both of us to go for 75IS each, which I would agree to as time is passing, but she wants to wait for more people, making it cheaper. We start talking and I learn that she is a German Moslem and is here visiting the SOS children's village. She sponsors a child in Gaza and is aiming to try and visit him. I tell her about George and his experience but she says she will try anyway. I often wonder if she ever got there. Another ten minutes passes, during which time the driver of our bus has gathered some of the other drivers around him and I get the feeling that we are providing them with some entertainment but then another two people arrive with big boxes of cakes. Finally we leave at 12.45pm, two and a half hours after I arrived at the bus station and we pay 50IS each.

The German lady and I talk more in the bus and I learn she is called Fatima, is a Moslem convert and lives in Spain. She converted from Catholicism, but she was not practising, and Islam just spoke to her and she knew it was the right path for her. When we get to Jericho, passing through the flat fertile agricultural lands of the Jordan Valley, the driver takes me onto the cable car for another 30IS, so an expensive journey. The cable car is outside of the town so I would never have found it on my own. It is quiet and I am the only passenger in my car. As I climb higher, the views are amazing over the flat landscape to the Golan Heights, hazy in the sunshine. It is definitely hotter here, being so much lower than the rest of the West Bank, and the profusion of date palms emphasises that change in climate. My destination is the Mount of Temptation, where Jesus was reputedly tempted by the devil. It is easy to see why this place would have been chosen as the views from the top stretch away far and wide.

Alighting from the car, I realise why it was so quiet on the ground. Everyone is up here. Crowds of schoolgirls swarm over the tourist destination, in the shops and cafés, up the steps to the monastery and fill the silence with their excited chatter. They are well behaved and polite, just noisy. My first stop is the restaurant as it is hours since I had that surprise breakfast, and I find a table outside so that I can look out at the view. I order what I imagine is a light meal of a few *koubah*, salad and chips but when it comes my table is full of food that I will never be able to eat. The waiter has brought me the main course rather than the starter but being English and not liking to complain, I set to and eat as much as is sensible in view of the long climb ahead of me.

A group of headscarved girls ask to take my picture on their phones. Usually it is the other way around but having obliged them, I feel it is only polite to take theirs in return. Climbing slowly and steadily up the winding stone steps I am stopped by another group of girls, keen to engage me in conversation and take my photo. I am beginning to feel like a celebrity. They tell me they are on a school trip from Tulkerum, a town in the North West, so quite a journey for them. They are having a grand day out and meeting me is a bonus as being English they think I must know One Direction, a boy band they are all mad about. I have to disappoint them but we exchange photo shots anyway. I continue uphill, smiling to myself, thinking what a surreal moment: here I am on the Mount of Temptation having a conversation with teenage Moslem girls about One Direction.

There are few opportunities or places to go for days out but Jericho seems to be a popular destination as the cable car is such a novelty for the children. The twelfth-century monastery is still occupied by monks and I walk past their individual cells, built into the side of the rock, to stand in the very spot where Jesus is supposed to have stood and surveyed the land that the devil offered Him. I cannot help but ponder where God is in all this mess that is the Holy Land and is Jesus weeping still? Having exhausted all the attractions of the Mount I wait with a throng of chattering girls for the cable car and get in a carriage with a teacher and three girls. One of them is terrified and is crying and the others are trying to console her but not until we reach the ground does she calm down.

I hail a passing taxi, thanking providence as I had no idea how I was going to get back but was just trusting to luck. It takes me back to the town square where I see the 'service' is already waiting. I debate whether to get on this one or stay longer and hope there will be another. It is hot and I am tired from the unaccustomed exercise so rest for a while on a bench in the small public garden, enjoying the sight of elderly men relaxing there, smoking, talking with their friends, and on the other side, a group of middle-aged housewives, with huge bags of shopping, sitting having a gossip. It is now 3.30pm so I decide to return and meet Fatima again. She has been to the mosque and wandered about in the town and like me is feeling the heat. She talks about Islam some more, about how her family had misgivings at first but now accept her faith, how it has enhanced her life and made her a more thoughtful person. The journey back is slow, the road crowded with transport bringing men home from work, presumably from Israel. Reaching Bethlehem, I notice the change in temperature and feel really cold on my walk back to the camp. Passing a fancy cake shop I buy a selection to take home.

Hannah has cooked *foul* and chips with salad but I am still full from the enormous lunch so eat a little since Hannah had gone to the trouble. Then another surprise: presents! Echlas gives me a lovely warm gold and black shawl – she always chooses good presents – and Hannah gives me an Arabic diary and tiny address book, all totally unexpected. We finish the day with the cakes and I can honestly say it was the most wonderful and memorable birthday.

It is bath day for Echlas and we are expecting Layan at 12 noon then at 2p.m. When Layan knocks on the door Hannah moves so fast to open it, I am immediately suspicious and even more so when Layan goes straight to the kitchen while Echlas engages me with choosing her clothes for the day. It feels to me like a carefully orchestrated plot. Layan and Hannah bath Echlas and I am sent out to do some shopping, even more suspicious. I play along, acting the innocent and avoiding the kitchen. Perhaps Layan is cooking something?

When I return with the shopping, Hannah takes it from me thus preventing me from going into the kitchen and Echlas calls me into her room on some erroneous excuse about her phone that she wants help with. It is so obvious that she is keeping me in her room but I continue to play the game and suddenly, Layan and Hannah appear at the door carrying the most beautiful cake I have ever been given. It is covered in white icing with an olive tree piped in brown with green leaves and says 'HAPPY BIRTHDAY' in Arabic. I am overwhelmed and totally surprised. Rosha has made the cake, of course, but did not know who it was for, otherwise she would have refused payment for it. I take lots of photos of the cake with Hannah, Echlas and Layan and then Echlas says I should put it in the fridge.

We are expecting Kimberley but her phone is switched off and Ramallah sister who was going to visit has to stay as someone has died, so it is just the three of us but personally I am pleased not to have visitors. We eat some cake – gorgeous, moist, rich, chocolate cake – and watch a film called *The Salt of the Sea*. It is about a Palestinian/American woman who returns to Palestine to claim her grandfather's money that he had deposited in a bank but had to leave it at the Nakba. Because the bank will not give it to her she resorts to stealing it with the help of two young men she meets. They all pretend to be Israelis and go off to Yaffa. One of them has not seen the sea for seventeen years. Inevitably they get arrested in the end. She is deported and presumably the guy she is in love with goes to prison, so not a happy ending but a good film.

Saturday 21 March, Mother's Day

The weather is cold and windy but Echlas wants to go out so we walk to Beit Jala and see a bit of the town but are unable to get up to the centre of the old part as the road is too steep for Echlas' wheelchair. A lot of rich Christians live here and looking at the large houses and well-kept gardens, I can believe it. We stop at a 'supermarket' to buy some chocolate and the owner gives us each a carnation for Mother's Day, a thoughtful gesture; I cannot see Tesco or Sainsbury's doing that.

The pizza place is on our way back and as Hannah has not been there Echlas suggests stopping since we are all hungry. I remember the last time I was here and everything was still so bewildering to me but this time I feel so at home. The lady serving us is the mother of the owner and amazingly she recognises me from my one visit to the church so we are immediate friends. The pizza is as delicious as I remembered. A strange man who is noticeably mentally unstable is being a nuisance to this lady and keeps pestering her for something, coming in and going out and back in again. The woman tells us he comes every day and they feed him as he has no family to take care of him but it is difficult to get rid of him and he proves disruptive to the paying customers. She is very patient with him even when he becomes threatening and I am thinking we will have to go to her aid but finally he leaves.

Braving the cold again we hasten back home to the electric fires. Poor Echlas is frozen and it takes several wheat bags to thaw out her immobile legs. Hannah has taken up meditating five times a day when she hears the call to prayer, although I think it is only four as she has not managed the 5am one yet. While she is having a lesson the *muezzin* calls out his '*Allahu Akbar*' over the loudspeaker and taking up her challenge I set myself to meditate but instead find myself thinking that hearing *Salah* gives me a sense of belonging, of being part of a community that is hearing the same thing at the same time and it has a unifying effect, whether you are Moslem or not. Whether you are alone at home, out in the street, at school, at work, *Salah* unites everyone for a short time to turn their minds to God. This is contrary to how I reacted to *Salah* in Saudi Arabia, where it felt alien and divisive and threatening even, because to be non-Moslem there sets you apart as an infidel but here in Palestine I experience a more benign Islam, an inclusive, embracing faith.

Hannah and I are discussing whether to go on the political tour of Bethlehem tomorrow or go to Hebron. I am more inclined to the political tour as I have been to Hebron before but because she has not been there she is favouring Hebron. I leave it up to her and she decides at the eleventh hour to go on the tour as she prefers to go on her own to Hebron in the hope that she may meet a young Palestinian with whom she can discuss politics. Echlas has arranged for the cleaning lady to come and spend the day with her as she has now recovered from her fractured wrist, so it means an early start and sensibly an early night for Echlas – 11.30pm. I go to bed and ponder two pressing questions: should I stay for another two weeks and what leaving present can I get for Echlas?

CHAPTER SEVEN

POLITICAL TOUR

Sunday

We are up and out early and meet at the Singer Café for the tour. Not realising we were supposed to book we just turn up but fortunately there are spare seats on the minibus. Ba'ha leads the tour, a guy who wears a Rastafarian hat, who I have seen around on previous visits. The group trickles in gradually while Ba'ha explains to us early birds what the tour is about and gives a general introduction. It was Deanna who recommended this as she found it extremely informative, despite already knowing a fair amount about Bethlehem and the surrounding area, so I have high expectations. The other members of our group are from Italy, Belgium and two from Poland but the common language is English, always good for us Brits.

The tour starts in Beit Sahour, where we are. There are seven clans here so all other family names mean they are refugees. Now I understand the importance that Echlas places on family names. Thirty-five per cent of Beit Sahour is in Area A (under Palestinian control) so 65% is in Area C (under Israeli control). Fourteen thousand people live in Area A, but far more live in Area C. In 2004, when the wall was built here, existing Palestinian property overlooked the wall and was consequently demolished despite the residents producing their licences to show they were the legal owners. The Israeli authorities insisted on permits which the Palestinians had never had so twenty-seven properties were demolished. At present there is a demolition order on the Greek Orthodox Church property, some low-cost housing for young people. No consultation takes place with the PA over demolitions. This is all new to me; I assumed that Bethlehem, being a major town, was all Area A and am shocked to find that most of it is Area C. In order to justify its land-grab strategies, Israel uses old Jordanian, British and Ottoman land laws from which it takes a pick-and-choose approach to confiscate land according to what suits the situation.

The 730km-long apartheid wall was ruled illegal in 2004 by the International Court of Justice and its demolition ordered but Israel ignores this and carries on building. We stand on a hill and look down at an example, Ba'ha pointing out the land on the other side of the wall, owned by Beit Sahour farmers but denied access since 2005. Here the Israelis are using the Ottoman Law of 1538 which states that land not cultivated for three years becomes state property. By denying access they can virtually take whatever they want. Ba'ha points out a large building below us, built on land belonging to four Beit Sahour families. One family took the authorities to court, appointing an Israeli lawyer as they themselves are not permitted to attend court. The decision? The land was abandoned because the families wanted to abandon it. It does not make sense to us but this is precisely the sort of nonsense that is used as judgement. In this particular case, Jordanian law was applied, i.e. the land was confiscated for public service; the building is a grey water refinery system servicing the nearby settlement, not the people whose land it is built on. If none of these laws fit the situation then one or more of the 1,600 military laws, which make up the Israeli judicial system, are applied. The Palestinians receive no compensation for their land. They may be offered the value of the land pre-1967 but Palestinians will not accept money for land theft.

B'tselem, the Israeli Information Centre for Human Rights in the Occupied Territories, to give it its full name, is a reliable source of information. It found that 60% of land built on by Israel belongs to Palestinian families. Only 14% actually sold their land.

Moving on in the bus to another vantage point, we get out and focus on the settlement, gleaming white and fortress-like on the opposite hill. We learn that there are twenty settlements in the Bethlehem district. Har Homa, a large and strategic one, was built on land, a forest of 70,000 trees, belonging to Beit Sahour villagers. On the day in 1999 when Israeli Prime Minister Ehud Barak met Yasser Arafat after signing the Oslo Accords, an agreement promising peace, the Israeli authorities burnt down this forest to make way for settlement construction. This was one of the last remaining forests in the area and its proposed destruction had met with years of campaigning by locals and internationals to stop it. Har Homa was the final link in the chain of settlements which separates Bethlehem from Jerusalem and its expansion continues, the aim being for it to accommodate 30,000 settlers. The proliferation and concentration of settlements around Bethlehem is solely to prevent any continuity between the West Bank and East Jerusalem, as openly declared by Binyamin Netanyahu in an election speech in 2015.

Ba'ha tells us a story about the field we see below. During Jesus' time, He walked in these hills and met a farmer sowing chickpeas. Jesus asked him what he was sowing and the farmer sarcastically replied, "stones". Jesus' reply was "May you reap what you sow" so ever since the field has been full of stones, perhaps a warning against sarcasm?

The building of settlements in occupied territories is illegal under the Geneva Convention Article 49. It prohibits the forcible transfer or deportation of the population, ignored by Israel, and states that if evacuation takes place then the people should be transferred back to their homes as soon as it is safe to do so.

The number of Jewish immigrants continues to increase, encouraged by the state, using enticements of cheap housing and subsidies. Some of these incomers are not even Jewish but the authorities are not too fussy, their aim being to increase the Israeli population by any means to populate the settlements in Area C.

Ba'ha points out a gate in the fence and explains it is there for the farmers to access their land on the other side, a promise that was never kept since the gate has not once been opened. The climate here is perfect for olive trees. They are central to the culture, planted for future generations, and many are thousands of years old. They need minimal care but are generous in their production of olives, providing oil, soap, fruit, fuel, and wood for carving. An olive tree survives and endures, much like the Palestinians themselves, and it is sacred to all religions. The hills have been terraced over hundreds of years to provide

149

an irrigation system for the trees as even these hardy trees need some water.

All the aquifers in the West Bank are controlled by Israelis who take 85% of the water for the settlements and West Jerusalem. Palestinians are not allowed to irrigate their land by pipes so all water used on the land has to be brought in tanks by truck. Recently in August 2015, the Israeli water company Mekorot, which incidentally supplies Southern Water with water meters, lowered the water quota for several villages, because of increased consumption by the settlers, leaving some villages without any water at all. Neighbouring villages brought in tanks of water to help out but as the Mayor said, "Why do the Jewish settlers get a quota of 300 litres per person and we only get 70 litres per person?"

Leaving Beit Sahour, the bus takes us up the hill to Bethlehem while Ba'ha gives us some background information on Bethlehem. King David was reputedly born here and was the first stone thrower (laughter). The name comes from 'Beit' meaning house and 'lehem' which has several meanings: war, bread and, in Arabic, meat. We get out of the bus opposite the wall on the Jerusalem–Hebron road, the oldest road in the area. Ba'ha points out the large gates in the wall, opened once a year on 24 December to allow the Roman Catholic Patriarch to proceed to Manger Square from Jerusalem to say Midnight Mass.

On a different note Ba'ha indicates a remote-control skunk water gun on top of the wall, used to spray a vile, toxic substance onto Palestinians. Put bluntly, the wall is a crime against humanity, preventing inhabitants living normally and destroying the commercial life of Bethlehem. It is a man-made disaster which Palestinians have to live with. I can think of some other descriptions, e.g. a prison wall, a restriction on movement and dignity, a total violation of human rights, a provocation to violence.

Rachel's Tomb is the place where Rachel is supposed to have died in childbirth en route to Hebron. Until 1977 the shrine, venerated by all three faiths, was Islamic property and accessible to all. In the Byzantine period there was a mausoleum here but the present-day building was built by the Ottomans. In 1841, in order to mollify the

Moslems who frequently had their ceremonies disturbed by crowds of Jewish pilgrims, an Anglo-Jewish philanthropist, Sir Moses Montefiore, financed the building of a dome and vestibule. The site, comprising a mosque and burial ground, was of major importance to Moslem worshippers. In 1995 the wall and watchtowers that we are looking at, were built and an Israeli military camp set up on the other side of the road. The Israelis destroyed the dome and vestibule in 1998 and prohibited Palestinians from entering the site. Since 2006 the whole area has been enclosed by the separation wall and the neighbourhood completely devastated to accommodate the expanding military base and a car park for visitors. According to Ba'ha not many Israelis know who Rachel was so an information centre has been built. There are plans for similar annexations of the mosque in Hebron and in Jerusalem but the Israelis act slowly, by stealth, to avoid international condemnation and isolation. Already, Hebron settlers have access to two thirds of the mosque since a settler massacred Moslems at prayer, leaving twenty-nine dead and 125 wounded, causing protests and riots throughout the West Bank. This happened in 1994 and although generally condemned at the time, the murderer is now lauded as a hero and martyr by right-wing Jewish settlers and it seems they have been rewarded for his act of terrorism.

The aim of Israel is to make Jerusalem the capital of Israel but to do this they must drive out the Moslems and Christians remaining there and curtail visitors from the West Bank. Consequently, permits are restricted and it is known that only 1.5% of Palestinians pass through the checkpoint to go to Jerusalem.

Something I had noticed but not questioned before are the large concrete bricks on the side of the road. Ba'ha explains that they denote the boundaries between different areas, i.e. from A to B or C. Standing by the wall we are in Area C (Israeli controlled) but now near Aida camp we are in Area A. Very confusing. At the entrance to the camp, rather incongruously, I have always thought, stands the magnificent Jacir Palace Hotel, now owned by the Intercontinental chain. I am interested to learn its history. One of the richest Christian families in Bethlehem built it as a private residence in 1910 and lived there until

151

*1931 when they lost their money and abandoned the house. It served
as HQ for British soldiers, was a hospital; and under the Jordanians it
became a school before being taken over by the hotel chain. In the large
reception area there are some wonderful murals representing sixty-two
families in refugee camps, here and in Lebanon and Syria. So not so
incongruous after all. Ba'ha tells us that Islamic radicalisation does not
exist here due to the Christian influence.*

*At the Nakba in 1948, when whole communities fled from the
massacring Israelis, Bethlehem had to absorb three times its population.
Due to the hospitality of the residing Christians, the Moslem refugees
found refuge here and the older generation remain thankful to their
Christian hosts. So the locals are the Christians, hence their ownership
of the large houses and much of the property.*

The bus miraculously appears at the moment Ba'ha finishes talking
and we jump on for the short drive into Aida camp where Musa
takes over. He tells the group a bit about himself: that his family
came from Beit Jibrin, that he works for Largee and is also a
photojournalist. He points out the huge key that stands on top
of the archway above us, signifying the thousands of keys that
Palestinians took with them when they were driven out of their
homes, believing that they would soon return.

*The key is the symbol of the 'right of return', which under the Geneva
Convention Article 49 they are entitled to do, and they will never give
up this right. Many of the walls are covered in artwork (I hesitate to
call it graffiti as it is not illegal) depicting various aspects of Palestinian
life and history. One shows a UNWRA identity card, issued to all
Palestinian refugees, stating among other information the village where
the person originally came from, of great significance to refugees. Now,
Musa tells us, that piece of information is not on new ID cards, another
small but insidious attempt to disassociate Palestinians from their past.
We walk on, noting a water tank full of holes, a result of IOF bullets
in the Second Intifada when even their water supplies were targeted.
Many of the walls are painted and Musa explains that the residents*

only paint on their own walls but will not beautify 'the wall' so all the work done on that is by internationals, usually messages of support for the cause. We pass the school with some windows blocked out. The school was attacked in 2002 so now the windows are covered for safety and the soldiers still, on occasions, shoot at the school. Behind this part of the wall is open land where the children used to play but now there is no access to any countryside.

We notice the cameras on top of the wall and Musa explains they are positioned every 300 yards so the people are always watched and they also endure frequent incursions by soldiers into the camp. He stops by a burnt-out watchtower and says this one is now out of action after youth in the camp set fire to it and also succeeded in making a hole in the wall, which was immediately blocked up. Musa stops and talks to us about the refugee issue, the most significant problem in the 'peace process', now dead, but any solution, be it one or two states, must include giving Palestinians the right to return. UNWRA, the UN organisation, was set up in 1955 and deals solely with the worldwide Palestinian refugees. Seven out of ten Palestinians are refugees. Israel has attacked every refugee camp in Lebanon, Syria and Jordan, the most infamous being the Sabra and Shatila massacre in 1982 when between 762 and 3,500 civilians were killed by the Phalangists acting under orders from the IOF and caused the resignation of the then Defence Minister Ariel Sharon but who later became Prime Minister.

After this quick but informative tour of Aida camp we say goodbye to Musa and drive up to Beit Jala. This is the highest point in Bethlehem and produces the most expensive, so I assume the best, olive oil. It is also the source of very good stone for construction and is known as 'The Green Carpet' or 'The Pile of Stone'. The majority of the town's original inhabitants do not live here now, having fled from Ottoman persecution and many live in South America.

After 1967 and the Six-Day War, when Israel redrew the borders and claimed more Palestinian land, Beit Jala lost access to a third of its land as Israel decided it was in part of Jerusalem and confiscated it to build the large settlement of Gilo separating Bethlehem from Jerusalem and has thus changed history. The two cities are 7km apart and have always been closely linked but now Israel is expanding Gilo in order to join it to Har Homa and create a barrier around Bethlehem. Ba'ha points out a bypass road, for settlers only, to enable them to reach Jerusalem in ten minutes, built on Beit Jala land but prohibited to Palestinians. Many of Beit Jala's olive groves are in the path of the proposed settlement expansion even though 34% of this land is in Area A. We see a small brick building in the distance which Ba'ha tells us is about 150 years old and was used by farmers when they were harvesting their crops. Now they are camping out in them again even though there are no facilities, in an attempt to protect their land. Having lost many of their fruit orchards to Israeli land grab it now looks as though they will also lose their olives.

Postscript, August 2015. Bulldozers move in to the area, uprooting olive trees hundreds of years old to make way for the wall. A Roman Catholic priest says Mass amidst the destruction of life. Anger, fear, distress is tangible.

Five families living in a valley are now declared illegally living in Jerusalem as they have never been issued with Jerusalem IDs having lived for generations in what was Beit Jala. Daily life is intolerable for these families being trapped between the wall and Jerusalem. Every day they must pass through a checkpoint in order to access basic facilities, i.e. water, education, food. No one is allowed to visit them so they are virtually isolated.

Ba'ha then goes on to talk about identity. Israel knows the identity and whereabouts of every resident over sixteen. Every Palestinian has to carry his ID at all times and there are different coloured cards depending on where they live. Green IDs are issued to West Bank residents and blue for permanent residents of East Jerusalem. These can easily be revoked by Israel if the person lives outside Jerusalem for any length of time and cannot prove that Jerusalem is the 'centre of his life'. Palestinian citizens of Israel, 1.3 million, are barred from living in 68% of all towns in Israel and carry a darker blue ID. By managing the population Israel aims to divide it and so exert absolute authority – divide and rule. Even the cars' number plates can be identified at a glance: yellow for Israelis, green for Palestinians.

As we pass Al Khadar Gate Ba'ha tell us about the town of Al Khadar and its connection to St George, depicted with the dragon in stone on top of the archway. The church of St George is in Al Khadar, cared for by the only Christian living there, a Greek priest. He is looked after by his Moslem neighbours as is the church building. Both Christians and Moslems pray there. Al Khadar has the largest farming community in the area but the proposed wall will cut off 90% of their land, depriving the majority of residents of their livelihood. Those living in the seam zone, the area between the wall and the green line (the 1967 boundary), will be completely cut off from their families and will have no facilities.

Al Khadar is surrounded by encroaching settlements, reaching to within a kilometre of Palestinian homes in some places. These settlements start out as outposts, a caravan or mobile home parked on a hilltop, gradually becoming permanent structures. The Israeli government has to provide the infrastructure to enable the settlers to stay there and they become established towns on Palestinian land. Illegal in international law they are also illegal under Israeli law but this is conveniently ignored. After 2003 outposts increased when the then PM Ariel Sharon told Israelis to "grab a hilltop", giving the people carte blanche to steal whatever they could. Only settlers are allowed to build. Palestinians are not allowed to construct even an animal shelter on their legally owned land without an impossible-to-obtain permit. They are also forbidden to have piped water anywhere except in their houses. People who rely on wells for water frequently have these blown up or contaminated by settlers, knowing that their victims will be forbidden to construct a new one.

Nearing the end of the tour we stop at a vantage point while Ba'ha talks about Teqoa, a small town of 23,000 built on a Bedouin legacy. This is sheep country; a few shepherds remain here. The prophet Amos was born here and in 1978 a settlement was built to 'revive' the life of Amos. None of the settlers are shepherds and have no interest in Amos but the settlement is built over the richest aquifer and now pumps water to Jerusalem and the settlements. The biblical history of this area has been destroyed and Palestinian grazing land stolen. Avigdor Lieberman, a notorious Russian immigrant, leader of a far-right party and a *prominent figure in the Knesset, lives in this settlement of Nokdim. He has been accused of corruption and racism towards Palestinians and intolerance towards religious Jews. He maintains that Israel is his homeland despite having no religious beliefs.*

The mount of Herodian is a landmark for miles around, a man-made mound, unique in its time. It was built between 24 and 15 BC and is said to have been Herod's favourite palace and where he is supposed to be buried. According to the great Roman historian Flavius Josephus, his funeral procession brought his body from Jericho to here and Israeli archaeologists claim to have found his tomb in 2007. Despite being a good builder he was a mass murderer, ordering the slaughter of the innocents after hosting the Three Wise Men here. He killed two of his sons and his wife. At the base of the mound there is evidence of Roman ruins, the lower city fed by pipes from Solomon's Pools. Herodian is 16km from the State of Israel but Israel declared it a National Park and now administers it, charging an entry fee for the palace.

On the way back to Beit Sahoor, Ba'ha draws our attention to the large red sign on the side of the road, declaring we are now entering Zone A and Israelis are forbidden to enter as it is dangerous to do so. This is to prevent Israeli citizens from mixing with Palestinians and perhaps developing an understanding of each other, something the authorities want to prevent at all costs, as peace is not part of their plan in seizing the whole of the West Bank. They can be fined a large amount if caught, however, the IOF and settlers are exempt.

Returning to Singer, I am so glad I made some notes, however scruffy, as Ba'ha gave us so much information I will never remember a quarter of it. Our heads buzzing, we sit in the café and eat a sandwich and chat to a lovely Spanish girl doing an internship at the Spanish Consulate in Jerusalem. By now it is 5.30pm and I am feeling anxious to get back for the cleaning lady but by the time we get back she has already gone and Mohammed is with Echlas counting his money to see if he has enough to give his mum to get the internet reconnected. Echlas gives him the balance and he runs off happy to know he will soon be back on his computer.

CHAPTER EIGHT

SETBACKS AND SOLUTIONS

The house looks strange. It takes me a few minutes to work out what is different. CL has had a blitz. All the furniture covers have been removed and washed, all the carpets have been taken up and the kitchen rearranged. This is the 'summer look' and it makes the room look much bigger and brighter but the fridge is in the wrong place and I keep going to its old position. She has even prepared some vegetables for me to cook. Echlas has been up all day so our first job is to get her into bed and make her comfortable before any cooking starts. We leave her reading her emails when suddenly there is a shout and we run into her room to see her looking shocked and upset, staring at her laptop screen. The new volunteer has been denied entry at the Allenby Bridge crossing. She was interrogated for seven hours by border control and then sent back to Jordan. She is American with no Arab connections, apart from one visit here five years ago. Echlas is very distressed and we are stunned but busy thinking what, individually, we will do now. This bombshell has made my decision easier as now there is no possibility of me going until contingency plans can be made for Echlas. Hannah is supposed to be going on Sunday after the marathon but offers to stay on. Echlas declines her offer, admitting to me privately that she cannot cope with Hannah's exuberance for much longer. I would like her to stay as she is fun but it is not up to me, despite my best efforts to change Echlas' mind. To complicate matters there is an exciting political camp, organised through JAI, next week that I have signed up to, for four days, thinking the new volunteer would be here to cover. Hannah and I work out between us that we could do two days each of the camp if she stays but as that was not going to happen, I selfishly worry that I will not be able to go at all.

We spend the evening worried and despondent but need to do something positive to offset this state of mind. Echlas has been Facebooking all her friends, informing them of her position and asking if they know anyone who can come and be her companion for a few weeks at least. I email Lauren and Susan in Jerusalem asking for their help and design a flyer to get printed off in the copy shop to distribute in Bethlehem and Jerusalem. By the end of the evening Echlas has come up with her own plan to enable me to go to Jerusalem on Palm Sunday and to the political camp, although I have not said a word about either since the 'bombshell'. Despite her own bigger problems, she was thinking of me, typical of her, and I feel guilty worrying about myself. On Palm Sunday, she will find someone to stay with her and on Tuesday she will go to Aida camp and stay in her room there until Sunday afternoon allowing me to go to the camp and to church on Easter Sunday. As Hannah has been left out of these plans I worry that she will have to find somewhere else to stay, but as I know well, plans change.

When I see Eugene I tell him about our predicament and he says he will ask at Largee Centre and Al Rowwad and Wi'am and anywhere else he can think of. I sit in the garden while he has his lesson and it feels really hot. Echlas' sister and Rosha and some other members of the family are going on Haj to Mecca later today so Echlas and I go over to Aida to say *bon voyage*, or the equivalent in Arabic. We sit in the shade of the olive trees and drink coffee for a couple of hours and it is very pleasant even if I do not understand the conversation, but we have to go back into the heat again and to Magde's shop to buy a Handela T-shirt for Hannah's leaving present.

I make jacket potatoes, cheese and salad for dinner and George comes to be with Echlas while Hannah and I go to AIC. The talk is entitled 'What now?' as the Israeli elections have just taken place and Netanyahu has got in again. I thought that would be a negative result as far as the Palestinians are concerned but most people think the alternative would be even worse so it is a case of 'better the devil you know'. The talk was given by a man with a heavy Italian accent and as I have not made any comment in my diary I assume that I did not understand most of it. We meet Munjad and Ahmed again so talk with them and Hannah gets talking to a Swedish couple, deciding to walk back with them. I am not entirely happy with this from the point of view that Hannah takes it for granted that I take responsibility for getting back to relieve George without any discussion. Anyway I get in a taxi with a guy who I do not know and go home.

Echlas is not pleased that Hannah is not with me and I explain she wanted to walk home with some new people she has met. She demands to know who they are and when I say Munjad and his friend she becomes really angry. I try to call Eugene to get Munjad's number but there is no reply, so Echlas calls the other Mohammed, the older one who is also friends with Munjad. He comes around and has to listen to Echlas' wrath, in Arabic, and then goes off to find Munjad's number from his mother. He comes back after a short while, Echlas still seething, to say his phone is switched off. By now it is 11pm and even I am a little concerned as Hannah has had ample time to get back. Echlas is imagining kidnap, rape, arrest, and generally working herself up into a frenzy of anger. I try to diffuse the situation by saying that in Denmark she would be used to being out at midnight and she is with other people, not on her own and is used to looking after herself. None of my reasoning helps at all and Echlas says she is not allowed in if she comes back now, as punishment for her irresponsibility and thoughtlessness. I think this is harsh and worse for all parties concerned since Hannah has nowhere else to go and no phone, and a volunteer of Echlas' roaming the camp at night would reflect even more badly on Echlas so I decide I will let her in no matter what Echlas says. Whatever happens now it looks as if I will be sleeping with Echlas so I set to changing the bedsheets when there is a knock on the door and before Echlas can say anything I rush to answer it.

There is Hannah, bright and cheerful, oblivious to the upset she has caused until I whisper, "You're in trouble", and her expression changes to one of alarm. The barrage of accusations, swearing and anger that meets her is like an attack of poison darts but although some may penetrate Hannah's cheerful façade, many fail to make their mark. Unfazed, Hannah replies reasonably, saying she does not understand what all the fuss is about. Nor did I fully, but there are still many layers of Palestinian culture that we could never fully comprehend. As the argument calms down but shows no sign of ending soon, I retreat to bed, leaving Hannah to her clean sheets.

The next day the atmosphere is subdued after last night but no one mentions it again. I go out for lunch with Susan, our last meeting before she leaves Jerusalem. She relays her experience at a threatened home demolition, a very fraught situation, and I am momentarily envious of her involvement in such frontline incidents. The downside to being an Ecumenical Accompanier is the number of reports she has to write using proscribed language so as not to appear partisan and the strict timetable she has to follow. My experience is very different from hers but equally valid in terms of solidarity with Palestinians.

On the way back I buy some large bars of chocolate and two pairs of shoelaces for Hannah. Every time we go out she is stopping to tie her laces, so perhaps a new pair may help, unless it is, of course, her technique, in which case little can be done. I also pop into the Peace Centre in Manger Square where registration for the marathon is taking place, to see if I can buy a race T-shirt but am told not until after the race. I reason that if I cannot run it, I could console myself with a T-shirt. The 10k may have been possible if I took plenty of painkillers for my knee but it is too late now. When I get back Hannah is helping Mohammed with his English homework and all is calm.

Thursday

While Hannah helps Layan bath Echlas ready for the big day tomorrow, I go over to the library to change my books, glad that

I joined now that my stay is extended. I plant the sweet peas and marigolds in the garden, the weather being so warm, and give them plenty of water.

I also wash my cashmere jumper that I have been wearing on and off for the whole of my stay, depending on the temperature, in what I take to be delicate fabric liquid. It does not produce many bubbles but I finish and hang it out to dry and then check with Echlas that it is indeed for wool. I had not noticed that the bottle has Hebrew writing and Echlas does not read Hebrew so when Layan comes she deduces that it is fabric conditioner. Oh well, the jumper has not come to any harm and I can wash it properly when I get home.

Later Echlas and I go down to Manger Square to meet up with Hannah who had gone earlier to see her Danish friends here for the run. Two Spanish friends of Echlas' meet us in the restaurant where we have a good view of all the preparations for tomorrow. There is a festive air as groups of runners go into the Peace Centre to register and linger in the square enjoying the atmosphere and the sun. Hannah recognises many Danish but I do not see any English runners at all. It is very amusing to watch the locals' interest in the portaloos dumped in front of the Peace Centre. I really hope they are not going to stay there. Men are approaching them as if they are the Tardis, gingerly opening the door and having a good look inside. I notice that no women do this and also observe that there are three male and one female – definitely not right. The loos are an endless source of amusement and we sit here for a good two hours enjoying the entertainment.

On our way home, having said goodbye to the two delightful Spanish ladies, we stop at a pizza restaurant that we have not been to before, it being Hannah's last night with us. The front entrance is at street level but the back looks out over the lights of Bethlehem, twinkling in the darkness. The pizza is excellent and Echlas and I have wine, a fitting end to a good day.

When we get home, Echlas gives Hannah her leaving present, the Handela T-shirt that I bought from Majde. She is delighted with it and says she will wear it tomorrow for the run. Echlas also gives me a present, much to my surprise: a watch with Arabic numerals. I also am delighted as I have been looking for one and Echlas obviously took note and found one for me. I always wear it now.

At 11.30pm Hannah is Skyping a friend on my iPad, having not packed a single thing, but I go off to bed as we have an early start in the morning.

Friday 27 March

We all get up at 6.30am, put Echlas in the wheelchair then Hannah leaves to get down to the square in time and I do the rest of Echlas' washing and dressing etc. At 8.30am, the earliest I have been out while here, we are walking down the hill towards the Hebron road and it is a joy to be able to walk in the middle of the empty road and not be harassed by traffic. Echlas loves the freedom and cannot get over the absence of cars. We have the whole of one side of the road to travel on and are able to be alongside the runners. Hannah had decided to wear the Handela T-shirt and kindly gave me her race one so I am wearing it today. Thinking we are in the race, one runner shouts out "Well done" as he runs past causing us great amusement. We manage to see Hannah waving her Palestinian flag and I take photos as we go. Quite by chance we meet one of the Spanish ladies, a free lance photographer, and she comes with us down through the *souk* – empty today and mostly traffic free. We encounter one snarl-up where a rogue van has stopped for a delivery and we cannot get past but after a lot of shouting and theatrical gestures he moves and we make it to the square. The pumping music hits us as we mingle with the crowds. It is a big party, locals and internationals all enjoying the occasion together. I catch a glimpse of Mohsin at the finish and see Hannah, squeezing through the crowd to get to her to give her a drink and make sure she is OK. She looks a bit dazed but after some water and a banana I leave her to look for her friends.

Annoyingly my camera battery decides to give up so I am unable to take any more pictures. We stay for a bit, enjoying the fun, but our usual restaurant is full so we leave the noise and the crowds, go along Star Street and down the road leading to Beit Sahour. It is eerily quiet except for a few runners; the hardy ones who are doing the whole marathon. A group of people sitting outside a café are cheering them on and it seems quite lively so we go in and have a snack and a drink. Incredibly, Hannah appears, on her way back home, so she stops and eats with us as she is clearly in need of energy and a rest. Despite no training she had managed to run/jog the whole 10k and feels pleased that she has taken part, running alongside Moslem women wearing *hijabs*, leggings and T-shirts, an unknown freedom for them to run in the street. We cheer on the few runners still passing the café, urging them on to the finish. I feel their pain, having run a few marathons myself and have great admiration for their perseverance as this is a hilly course and by now it is hot. Reluctantly, we slowly walk home, savouring the luxury of walking in the empty road, clapping and cheering those runners we meet on the way.

Johnny, my friend from Beit Jala, is standing outside the large souvenir shop, Nissan Bros, where he is a manager, so I introduce him to Echlas and Hannah. He invites me to his home again and I say I will try but now it will be even more difficult with Hannah gone.

Sadly, for me anyway, we say goodbye to Hannah. She does her packing when we get back, leaving a quantity of clothes behind as they will not fit in her rucksack. She is going to Jerusalem and then wherever fate takes her, so I wish her all the very best in her travels and promise to keep in touch.

After all the excitement of the morning and the loss of Hannah the house has a melancholy gloom, or perhaps that is just how we feel, so we need to go out somewhere. Echlas comes up with the plan of visiting aunty, cousin and Layan in Aida. Relatives are always a good fallback when one is feeling low, providing you pick the right ones. Aunty is always cheerful and usually funny and on this occasion lives up to her reputation, entertaining us for a couple of hours while sipping lemon and mint.

We had planned to go back to the marathon party in the evening but neither of us is keen now so we go straight home, meeting Munjad in the camp. He stops and speaks to us and it seems he is forgiven as Echlas asks him to buy some cigarettes for her. Ida comes to help lift Echlas into bed and we spend a quiet evening, with Echlas sleeping at midnight.

Saturday

Echlas sleeps until 11am. Yesterday was such a long day she must have been exhausted. I am busy all day, doing household tasks and looking after Echlas so the time passes quickly. Now that the volunteer room is empty Echlas has the idea of letting it, for two reasons: one, to earn some money; two, to have someone else in the house who may be able to help out occasionally. By chance Deanna and her friend Veronica are looking to move from their expensive room in Beit Sahour to Bethlehem. When she first mentions this, I have to tell Echlas about the terrible mattress with the protruding springs and that I feel she cannot let the room in that condition. The other 'bed' is a pile of mattresses on the floor. She decides to buy at least one new bed.

When Julian comes for a lesson I go out for essential shopping and call in to see Mohsin. He did the half marathon yesterday with no training and then was out partying until 3am and is complaining of feeling tired today!

Later on Mohammed and his sister come for a meeting with Echlas for advice on how to save money for their school outings. They both have to pay 50IS, about £10 – little to us but unaffordable for their mother, so it is up to them to save up their one or two shekels. I know Echlas will make up the balance if they are short and I offer some money too but Echlas says it is good for them to save and nearer the time we will make up the shortfall. Meanwhile

Echlas continues to give Mohammed a few shekels each time he goes shopping for her.

Tomorrow is Palm Sunday and I am excited about the prospect of going in the procession into Jerusalem but not absolutely sure where I am starting from. Luckily Sister Lucille calls to enquire if I know how to get to the Mount of Olives and gives me directions. How kind of her to think of me.

The CL wrong-foots me by banging on the door at 8.30am. Having had a disturbed night, I am still asleep and I am sure I notice a look of triumph on her face when I open the door, looking dishevelled and bleary eyed. She helps me get Echlas in the wheelchair and is generally very helpful, making coffee and washing up. I leave at 10.30am to go to the checkpoint. As expected, being Palm Sunday it is crowded and I am glad for the people lucky enough to be issued a permit to travel to Jerusalem for this holy day. They are distinguishable by their smart clothes and slicked hair (the boys and men). I do have a sense of guilt though, that I, as a foreigner, can go to Jerusalem whenever I choose but the citizens of the land are denied that freedom. Perhaps I should not be going and remain in solidarity with the Christians here but on the other hand, this may be the opportunity of a lifetime that may not come again for me.

The queue moves slowly and after about forty-five minutes I am through. I am glad I had left early to allow for this hold-up. With time to spare I go to the educational bookshop for coffee and a piece of their delicious cake and I see Susan sitting outside. We sit and chat for a while and watch the passers-by. Ambling down Salah ah-Din Street, looking at the shops, my eye is caught by an art shop up a flight of stairs so up I go and cannot resist buying a pair of prints by a Palestinian artist.

I find the bus going to the Mount of Olives and examine my fellow passengers for indications that they are going on the procession so that I can follow them, as I have no idea where to go when we get off. A pair of nuns is an obvious choice so I keep them in my sight as we join the throngs of people but need not have worried as it was evident that everyone is making for the same place. Joining the crowd, I walk about two miles to the church, clearly the starting point. Groups of soldiers lounge around looking bored, food stalls are doing a good trade and families and friends wander about or sit where they can and eat. I lean against a wall and eat my sandwich, then go down the steps into the church grounds and make my way behind the church where it is all happening. A band composed of priests, playing drums, guitars, saxophone and trombone and a singer are really getting the crowd dancing and it is so unexpected to see such joyful expressions of faith with groups of nuns and priests alike waving palm branches in the air and singing with gusto. Adjacent to the band is a raised dais covered with a canopy, where the Cardinal and a bishop or two sit, flanked by a cohort of priests. Standing in the front is one of the traditionally dressed guards I had seen at the Church of the Holy Sepulchre, wearing his extraordinary costume of blue and gold, a red fez on his head, a large silver sword at his side, leaning on a long pole which he bangs on the ground to announce the progression of the procession.

Keen to capture this occasion on film, I go up the slope to an area where all the scouts and guides are gathered. What a wonderful sight! Hundreds of young men and women, girls and boys in their smart uniforms, holding the flags that represent their particular troop, some wearing long capes from their shoulders, mingle and wait. I see some capes emblazoned on the back with 'The Papal Scout Troop, Beit Jala, Est 1950' and others with the Jerusalem cross. Christians from all over Palestine have travelled here, but I surmise this is only a small proportion of those who would have been here had they been issued permits. It all looks chaotic but beginning to know the Palestinian way of organisation, I have faith it will all come together somehow. I see Sister Lucille and we stay together at first, so many people saying hello to her. Groups from Yafa, Israel, Bethlehem, Nablus and Beit Jala I see, including a man I recognise from the one Mass I went to. The procession moves off, large palm branches waving in the air, and I think this is how it was on the first Palm Sunday when Jesus walked this very path into Jerusalem. There is an air of expectation, of festivity, joy and to see Palestinians expressing this, despite how they are forced to live, brings a lump to my throat.

Large groups of internationals, singing their own songs, pass by: a Filipino group singing in Tagalog, followed by a group of Africans with their rhythmic music and then some Germans singing hymns and so it goes on, an endless stream of people from all over the world. I join in with whomever I happen to be walking with to get a taste of this multicultural stream of humanity, all here for the same purpose: to walk with Christ to his Passion. Moslem families watch and wave from their balconies and windows and rooftops and young boys, always ready for a retail opportunity, try to sell bottles of water and olive branches at the roadside. It is hot and the walk is long and undulating but at certain points there are wonderful views of Jerusalem. Trying to soak up the atmosphere so that I can always remember this day is not difficult, but what is making the most impact on me now is the unity of all the diverse nationalities and the evident enjoyment of the Moslem spectators. The presence of the soldiers reminds me that Roman soldiers would have been present on that journey 2,000 years ago, watching and ready for any sign of insurrection against their cruel occupation. So even the IOF have their part to play and the irony of this strikes me.

At last we begin the ascent into the Old City and entering through the Lion Gate I can almost see Jesus on the donkey, his apostles behind him, entering under this very arch, treading on this very stone. I can only describe this as a transcendental moment when the man Jesus becomes real to me.

The procession ends in St Anne's church grounds, a large, unexpectedly green oasis in this old city of tightly packed buildings. Singing has already begun but I cannot stay to enjoy the festivities as I have to get back for Echlas and it is already 4.30pm. Knowing my way fairly well now around the Old City I rush back to Damascus Gate and the bus station and bump into Eugene who has just got off the Bethlehem bus. I cannot stay any longer and manage to get back by 5.30pm.

Echlas is already in bed as she needed a bedpan so enlisted the help of Mohammed's sister. The CL has made good use of the day: the volunteer room bedless, the wardrobe moved and everything clean. How she moved the wardrobe into the garden shed I could not imagine but there it is when I look the next day, with a feral cat already ensconced, not believing its luck. The door will not shut completely so I cannot stop the cats getting in. I just hope they do not start producing kittens in there.

The Spanish lady and her friend come for a visit at 7pm, livening up our evening with tales of their Palestinian experiences. The CL had prepared food, for which I am grateful, but unfortunately it is far too salty, even for Echlas, so we abandon it and have strawberries, bananas and yogurt instead.

I must have been tired after all the walking yesterday as, for the first time, Echlas has to wake me at 9am. Layan comes to help put Echlas into the wheelchair and I carry on with washing and dressing her. We have two missions today: one, to find a bed; two, to give out flyers in Bethlehem. The weather is warm and sunny, a little windy but pleasant to be out in. We take the lower route, along Star Street. I drop in at the Holy Land Trust to ask if they could advertise for a volunteer for Echlas. A very helpful man insists on coming down the steps to see Echlas as he knows her and wants to say hello. He says he will do his best regarding the advertising.

Bed shops are not common in the centre of Bethlehem; they are generally to be found on the outskirts but there is one small furniture shop that I have passed numerous times without giving it much attention. This shop is Echlas' hope for a bed, secondhand, if possible. Outside the shop is a single, metal-framed bed, so we will not be bewildered by too much choice, the only one being whether or not to have this bed. Echlas thinks the bed looks short so I lay down on it and judge it to be the usual six-foot length. The mattress, displayed separately, looks too big for the bed so I ask the man to put it on the frame and have another lie down to test for comfort. By now we have an audience looking on with anticipation for the next display of odd foreign behaviour. Disappointed when I sit down on an old office chair to sip at the coffee the shop owner insists I have, they drift away. Meanwhile Echlas and shopkeeper enter into some lengthy negotiations, Echlas having decided to have the bed if the price is acceptable. The outcome is Echlas will buy two beds for 1,000IS and can pay in instalments, a reasonable deal. I am glad she is buying two beds as I wonder which would have been discarded: the lumpy mattress bed or the pile of mattresses on the floor? She gives the man 250IS and asks for a receipt. This is obviously a first for him as he goes across the street to ask a young man in charge of a clothes shop to write it out for him. Arrangements are made for delivery tomorrow with me directing the delivery man to Echlas' house. We leave the shop, both feeling satisfied with the purchase and I wishing that shopping was that easy at home!

There is a new office building at the end of the road, a sort of Citizens Advice centre, so Echlas thinks it is worth asking if they have any contact with foreign volunteers. Miraculously there is a wheelchair ramp so Echlas is able to go right into the rather plush, new reception area where all the staff are most helpful. A smartly dressed woman shows us into an inner sanctum to meet a suited man sitting behind a large desk, a picture of Mahmoud Abbas above his head, the walls lined with glass-fronted bookcases. He and Echlas talk and it transpires that he was the ambulance man who was present when Echlas was run down and took her to hospital. He says he has never forgotten her as it was such a horrific 'accident' and often wondered how she had got on. Now here they are meeting again like an episode of *Surprise Surprise*.

Still reeling from the coincidence I have just witnessed, we stop at Mike's shop to give him a leaflet. He is a red-headed Palestinian and owns a souvenir shop with his mother. The first time I saw him I was confused by the red hair but later discovered it is due to a gene persisting from the Crusades and red hair is not that unusual here. Next stop is Visit Palestine, a new centre and shop, where I had seen Mark Thomas all that time ago. Echlas waits while I climb the hundred stone steps, arriving panting at the top to ask the assistant if she could put a flyer on her noticeboard.

We stop at our usual Bankat Stores to stock up on essentials. The owner appears to be opening up a bit and attempts a smile. Sister Lucille comes for a visit later and brings us a pot of homemade strawberry jam and a card for Easter. Echlas gives her some hand cream and a card in return. I love the way that Moslems and Christians here respect and acknowledge each other's religious feasts. Sister Lucille brought me the Mass times for the church here in Bethlehem and I hope I can get to one Mass but do not want to ask too much of Echlas as I know how difficult it is for her to arrange cover for me. Echlas spends the evening Skyping and watching her favourite Egyptian soap, while I make the dinner and a quantity of tomato juice for Echlas' breakfasts.

She eventually goes to sleep at 3.40am! I doze fitfully, disturbed by the Arabic version of *EastEnders*, judging by the amount of shouting and histrionics, and then have to get up to lay her down to sleep. It seems it is only a few minutes later that the call to prayer rouses me to wakefulness again but then I sleep until 10am and Echlas wakes shortly afterwards. She has her stomach pain again so is not in good spirits. Today is a bed day, so while Eugene has his lesson, the older Mohammed and I go to the bed shop. I assume Echlas thought I should have a male escort as 1) I cannot speak Arabic and 2) a female foreigner in a truck with a delivery man would be unseemly. We hop on a bus and travel to Manger Square for 2IS. I wish I had known before that you can stop a bus anywhere and pay 2IS for wherever you want to go.

The bed man is ready for us but the delivery man has not yet appeared so I am pressed to sit down and drink coffee while he attempts to make conversation in halting English. He asks me first if I am married, then if I have children and then how old I am. This takes me aback but I answer politely, wondering if this is a chat-up line, but when he proceeds to tell me about his family I am relieved. Relaying this later to Echlas she reassures me that this is the usual line of enquiry when meeting someone new and is often followed by the question, "How much is your salary?"

Saved from further probing questions by the delivery man, whose revving engine announces his skilful reversing up the narrow one-way street, Mohammed and I squash ourselves into the already packed truck. He sits in the back behind a large mirror, next to the young assistant, while I am given the 'best' seat in the front (no seat belt). The truck is ancient, judging by its bodywork, and the engine is noisy but functioning. The beds have to be collected from a store up an extremely steep hill and the poor old truck coughs and splutters and strains as we crawl up the bumpy road and arrive severely jolted about in the springless seats. Once the beds are on board the rest of the journey is exhilarating – speeding along, windows open, loud music playing – so that I am sorry when we arrive at the camp.

Eugene helps to bring in the beds and mattresses and stays to help Mohammed assemble them, while I run back and forth between them and Echlas, who, I have the feeling, does not appreciate me giving my attention to them and not her. The room is transformed with proper beds and I cannot wait to make them up. Simple pleasures?

A fifty-year-old woman has died in the camp this morning from a gynaecological cancer. Echlas had heard the announcement from the mosque and is tearful. She phones her sisters to tell them so I wonder if they will pay a visit to the bereaved family, as is customary. When Layan comes to bath Echlas, I take the opportunity to go out while she is doing her hair, for some chocolate. Echlas tells me to go the other way out of the camp as there will be a lot of men in the street between the mosque and the community centre at the end of our street. They will be gathering for the funeral this afternoon and she will be buried in the graveyard in Aida camp. It seems very quick but this is the custom.

While out shopping I am thinking about BDS (Boycott, Divestment, Sanctions). I am very aware now of not buying Israeli goods as I know Echlas avoids them and made sure the beds were not from Israel. I go to Shadi market, a large greengrocer, where much of the produce is Israeli but find oranges and tomatoes and some olives which Echlas has been looking for, and also buy a jar of honey and black cumin – delicious on toast.

Boycott, Divestment and Sanctions (BDS)

In 2005 the Palestinian people put out a call to international civil society organisations and people of conscience all over the world to support the boycott of illegal Israeli settlement goods, the divestment from Israeli companies operating in the settlements, and to put pressure on governments to apply trade sanctions, especially in arms sales. Since then the movement has grown world wide and major organisations and companies have divested, causing the Israeli economy to feel the effect. The cultural and academic boycott of musicians, singers, artists and academic institutions has a major impact on Israel's perceived image of itself. Sport is included, especially football, as Israel sees itself as part of Europe in this regard. It is through public pressure that BDS is so successful and continues to be so despite attempts by Israel and the USA to thwart its effects. Governments have to listen if enough public pressure forces them to take notice so although individual boycott of settlement goods is vital, so is the mass lobbying of our MPs, peaceful demonstrations, petitions and other non-violent activities to draw attention to the unjust, racist Israeli regime.

CHAPTER NINE

POLITICAL CAMP

Wednesday 1 April

Echlas has been to considerable trouble to enable me to go to the political camp this week and arranged for various people to be with her from 7.30am until the evening so I am very grateful to her for this.

On the first day I wait outside the Souk al Shab in Beit Sahour, as instructed, looking out for anyone who I think looks like a tour candidate. I am early as I would hate to miss the bus after all these arrangements, so stand for a while until a young foreign man comes across the road towards the shop and loiters with me until I break the ice and ask him if he is with the tour. Luckily he is. A few minutes later, two girls and a young man, who I recognise from AIC, join us and turn out to be our leaders – Italian and Spanish – and have come to collect us. We walk along a wide empty back road to the guesthouse where the German group are staying and from where the minibus will pick us up.

Altogether we are twelve on this first day, a mix of nationalities but only one English – but fortunately all communication is in English. It is strange being the only English person and considerably older than the rest but they are all very friendly, introducing themselves and speaking in English for my benefit as we board the bus for Ramallah. It is about an hour's drive, along the bypass road, now familiar to me.

On the way our guide gives us interesting information, most of which I have not heard before, so already I think it is worthwhile coming on this tour. Evidently there is a large Chinese labour force in Israel who each pay 8,000USD for a work permit. Palestinians only pay 2,300USD to work in Israel so it is more economic for Israeli companies to import their workforce. Filipinos also pay 8,000USD but when they arrive in Israel they are treated like slaves and due to the strong ties between the companies and the government they have no redress.

As we drive on the outskirts of Jerusalem, Maria explains about the E1 project – the expansion of Male Adamin settlement to divide the West Bank into two halves, thus having complete control of the movement of Palestinians between the North and the South. This huge settlement looms above us on the hillside, like a malevolent presence, gobbling up the land. Much of the Palestinian land through which we are now passing is polluted by raw sewage from Jerusalem and the settlements, running down to the Dead Sea. The stench on some days is hideous. The PA wanted to build a water treatment plant to save their land from this pollution but Israel would not allow it. However, they are now building their own in order to divert water to Israeli agricultural land.

Maria goes on to talk about the displacement of the Bedouins in the Negev as someone brings up the topic. The Prawar Plan has been simmering in the background since 2013, after strong world opinion forced the Israelis to abandon the plan, but only in the short term. Since 1946 the Bedouin population of the Negev has been diminishing, expelled by Israeli troops or forced to flee to Gaza, the West Bank or Sinai. Now there are estimated to be approximately 80,000 Bedouin in the land around Beersheba, living in unrecognised villages without water, electricity, roads, telephone lines, schools or health centres. They are Israeli citizens but discriminated against with the aim of forcing them from their ancestral lands, into seven overcrowded and impoverished towns, to make way for Jewish settlements. Two thirds of their original land, where they used to roam freely with their livestock, is now designated as military training grounds and firing ranges.

One particular community of Negev Bedouin, the Jahalin, is the largest refugee Bedouin tribe in the West Bank. They were violently driven out of their homeland in 1949 and now live in several communities east of Jerusalem, 300 metres away from the Jerusalem municipal dump. I had been to visit these Bedouin with Angela Godfrey Goldstein, a British Jew, who works for the Bedouin, on a previous visit. The families live in makeshift shelters made of corrugated metal, tarpaulins and concrete blocks with their sheep, goats and camels on a hillside, watched from above by an Israeli military outpost. They have very few material possessions and their way of life seems primitive by our standards but their standard of living has been eroded by loss of livestock, constant demolitions of their homes and inaccessibility to Jerusalem markets, the main outlet for their produce. The only support they get from UNWRA is a sack of flour, milk powder and a litre of oil per family twice a year. They have no access to medical facilities, being forbidden to cross the checkpoints. Their lives are unstable as they never know when they are going to be moved on or where to as their 'illegal' homes now have eviction orders on them. The children walk up to 5km to school and if they are very lucky they travel on a donkey.

The communities live in the shadow of Male Adamin, the rapidly expanding settlement, along with its road for Jews only to enable them to reach Jerusalem in seven minutes. The settlement homes can clearly be seen from the encampment and the contrast is astounding. The Bedouin live with no running water and electricity from a generator while the settlement has hospitals, schools, shopping malls, fountains and swimming pools.

The tragedy is that the Bedouin way of life is being destroyed. They have for centuries grazed their animals and know no other way of life and there is no employment for them anyway. Their encampments are in E1, an area between Jerusalem and Male Adamin, earmarked for settlement expansion so the whole community will be displaced again. Abu Emad the spokesperson for the Jahalin has said, "Bedouin are to the land what fish are to the sea": either let them return to the Negev or let them stay here."

The expansion of settlements, as well as being political, i.e. a land grab, is also economic, many companies collapsing without the constant building programmes, including banks.

Our first stop in Ramallah is Addameer, an NGO for political prisoners. A very articulate young Palestinian woman gives us a *comprehensive presentation of the work that Addameer does. Their work is divided into three units: Advocacy for Human Rights, Documentation and Legal. Prisoners can be interrogated for up to sixty days without a lawyer. They are tortured and put in stress positions. Child prisoners are refused food until they sign a statement in Hebrew, which they do not understand. Prisoners are transferred to Israeli territories to sixteen different prisons – against international law. There are only two prisons in Palestinian territory. The conviction rate is 99.7% in a military court where all Palestinians are tried. As well as torture, lack of a lawyer and transfers, they are denied family visits.*

There has been an increase in arrests of human rights defenders in recent years. From 2003 to 2009 292 arrests were made, most under administrative detention which means there is no charge, no trial and a secret file, seen only by the judge and prosecutor, and the prosecuted is held for six months at a time. This is one area that Addameer advocates for. In February 2015 approximately 6,000 prisoners were held, of which 454 are under administrative detention. Nine are Palestinian Legislative Council members, 160 children and 26 women, and 376 are Gaza residents who very rarely get family visits. Even traffic violations are taken to the military court.

Funding for Addameer comes from international organisations and NGOs, Christian Aid being a major funder. In 2012 the offices were raided and laptops confiscated. The Legal Unit coordinator was arrested under administrative detention.

Under Israeli law any gathering of more than ten people is prohibited.

Sexual assault on women prisoners has decreased but whether this is due to pressure by Addameer or other prisoner rights NGOs cannot be ascertained.

The UN stance on administrative detention is not clear since statements against its use have been issued but not followed up. Approximately 700 children a year are arrested and detained, the most common offence being stone throwing, punishable by up to twenty years in prison. Most are arrested at night and taken away for interrogation, many reporting ill treatment, i.e. slapping, beating, kicking, violently pushing and verbal abuse, before they are forced to confess. This treatment results in traumatised children who often drop out of school. Those most at risk are in Jerusalem or near settlements. UNICEF is trying to stop overnight raids and arrests of children.

After a sobering hour and a half, we move swiftly onto Al Haq, another human rights NGO founded in 1979, which documents violations of Palestinian human rights. This includes house demolitions and land grab for settlement expansion and the Gaza blockade. They undertake studies and research, and provide reports for the UN and the EU. Christian Aid is again a major fund provider for their work. Al Hak has a specialised library on international law for the use of students here and abroad. Some of their current work includes an accountability project: exploitation of the environment, pursuing companies and individuals, i.e. they took a Dutch company to the European Court for their complicity in building the illegal 'wall' but unfortunately they were not prosecuted.

Ahawa Dead Sea products, sold in over thirty countries, are produced illegally in two settlements in the West Bank, using natural resources which do not belong to Israel. This is just one example of illegal settlement goods being exported, stating that they are produced in Israel and allowing Israel to benefit economically from the Dead Sea, therefore perpetrating the war crime of pillage.

Al Haq focuses on international law and they have to be unbiased to maintain credibility, therefore they cannot advocate demonstrations or any activities that have the potential to become violent. One of the main obstacles to lawful dealings with Israel is that it does not admit to being an occupying power, neither is it a signatory of the Geneva Convention. However, since it is totally illegal, neither would make any difference.

On that dismal note we leave the Al Haq office, hungry for the lunch awaiting us in a nearby restaurant. The meeting with the political representatives, scheduled for the afternoon and to which I have been particularly looking forward, has been cancelled but we are given the opportunity to meet with Khalida Jarrar, the deputy leader of the PFLP (Popular Front for the Liberation of Palestine) or to look around the town. Five of us choose to meet her, so have to quickly eat our huge lunch of rice and vegetables and chicken, salad and yogurt then hurry through the busy streets to the PFLP HQ.

We are invited to sit in comfy armchairs in a rather small office and drink coffee while Khalida tells us something of her party, the Popular Front.

It is left wing, opposes the Oslo Accords and believes in resistance to colonialism and occupation. In the past it was known for its violent resistance but now opposes violence. Khalida is standing in for the General Secretary of the party, a political prisoner, sentenced to thirty years of which he has done twelve. He spent four years in jail in Jericho under the PA and in 2006 was taken to an Israeli jail when Israeli forces invaded the Jericho prison and removed the prisoners. He has 450 'comrades' in prison. Khalida herself has been arrested and jailed for one month and lives with the insecurity of being arrested again at any time. Twenty four of her colleagues are in Israeli administrative detention.

There are growing PFLP youth and women's movements gaining them nine seats in university elections. Khalida says it is dangerous to continue the internal division between Fatah, Hamas and the Islamic movement and they need to unify the left-wing parties to oppose the right-wing religious and nationalistic parties.

Their social policies oppose the free market which denies local producers the means to compete with large companies. They concentrate on agriculture and BDS, encouraging the organisation of farmers' committees into cooperatives enabling the export of goods like olive oil. Likewise, women's co-ops are set up to produce and sell pickles, soap and cheese. High unemployment and poor wages conspire to restrict development but through small initiatives progress can be made. They also work in health and education, human rights that should be accessible to all.

Khalida speaks about security coordination between the PA and Israel which the PFLP opposes, resulting in the arrests of a number of comrades. The coordination gives Israel more opportunities to arrest

Palestinians through information given by 'spies', putting more pressure on the resistance as they do not know who will inform on them. Soldiers frequently come into homes and arrest party members. She tells us that Hamas was established as a reaction to the global weakening of the left and communism.

We thank her very much for giving us her time and I am so glad I met her and learned first-hand what her party stands for.

My impression of Khalida is that she is a very unassuming woman, very brave to do what she does and totally dedicated to her people's cause. That night soldiers broke into her house and arrested her and today, 6 June 2016, she was released, so spent eighteen months in prison.

Returning to Beit Sahour, overloaded with information, we are given a supper of delicious toasted tuna and mozzarella sandwiches in the Singer Café. The young Germans are very interested in what I am doing in Bethlehem and also, being a Catholic, my views on the religious aspects of the conflict. They are very polite and if one of them lapses into German then another will remind him that I cannot understand so they resume in English.

The day is not yet over and our next talk is by a political activist, a middle-aged man who, despite all the setbacks over the years, still continues his fight against the occupation. For once, this speaker only speaks in German so one of the Italians kindly translates for me and this is what he said:

I have been involved in resistance since the First Intifada in 1987, leading to the Oslo Accords of 1995, a deliberate ploy by Israel and America to slow the 'peace process'.

The Second Intifada in 2000 yielded no results but created deep divisions within the Palestinian community. In 1995 the first elections were held, Arafat giving the illusion of democracy and progress. In 2005 the second elections were held giving the left a very low result, so were unable to influence politics at all. Mahmoud Abbas became the leader in the absence of any real will from the people. It was the best result for Israel as they have a governor of Palestine who works for them and they do not have to pay for the occupation. The PA are happy to keep their privileged positions so the status quo is maintained, serving the best interests of the leaders of both sides. Unfortunately there is no real interest for national unity between Fatah and Hamas, the two main opposition parties.

After Arafat died, Abbas was put into the position of leader by the West, not by a fair election of the people. The successors of Abbas have already been chosen; unsurprisingly they are very right wing so nothing will change. The current political figures do not have the experience of the First Intifada so they lack the ability to co-ordinate. In that uprising the entire Palestinian society joined together to take part, responding to the orders of the unified command of the Intifada or to the calls of the Islamic Resistance Movement. Israel most fears a united Palestinian society so employs measures to divide it.

The population over sixty is only 5% and they have no say in political matters.

In 1996 America and Israel planned to dispose of Arafat and Saddam Hussein and bring outside forces in to infiltrate Syria in order to take control of a large part of the Middle East. Bill Clinton refused to cooperate but G.W. Bush took it on when he came to power and we now see the result.

Until 1996 Palestinians believed they would have their own state but once the promises of the Oslo Accords proved false they began to realise that this was not the plan of Israel and the US. Abbas was also involved in this betrayal.

The Oslo Accords were built on corruption. Papers passed between Israel and the US were not given to Arafat so he was duped into signing away any hopes the Palestinians had of forming their own state. Seventy per cent of Palestinians are under thirty so there is potential for a revolution.

The First Intifada began in December 1987. A settler crashed his car into four Palestinians, killing them, and at the same time the uprising in Gaza started. These incidents lit the tinderbox that was the culmination of years of repression, deportation, land confiscation, *settlements, humiliation and imprisonment. Many young Palestinians were trained to be activists and felt themselves to be politicised. The prisons and universities were the centres of these activities. Massive demonstrations in the West Bank became a movement against occupation. They organised themselves very quickly into communities which spread and connected in the West Bank and Gaza with young people risking their lives passing paper communiqués (before mobile phones) and organising general strikes and marches.*

Israel retaliated by arresting and imprisoning 600,000 people between 1987 and 1991. The prisoners became heroes and the prisons were part of the political movement, centres of planning and co-ordination. Every punishment the Israelis used had no effect. The will of the people was so strong they could not be crushed. Leaders were imprisoned but new highly trained ones took their place. Towns and villages got rid of collaborators, usually by violent means.

In 1997 Beit Sahour invited thirty Israeli families to their town to prove they were not anti-Semites'. The IOF told the visitors to leave as they could not guarantee to protect their lives but they said they felt safe and they could not travel anyway as it was Shabbat.

Beit Sahour led the civil disobedience movement, influenced by Gandhi's non-violent resistance. They refused to pay taxes from 1988 to 89, resulting in imprisonment for the leaders of this action, houses demolished or ransacked and possessions stolen. The IOF took everything moveable from the people and they were put under twenty-four days' curfew. The movement grew and became stronger. The French, Italian, Belgian and Spanish Embassies in Ramallah were attacked and damaged. People came from all over the West Bank to Beit Sahour to demonstrate solidarity, including foreign ambassadors, but the American ambassador was not invited. On 5 November 1989 Israel lifted the curfew and ended the punishment.

It is important that these stories of the Intifadas are passed on to the children to keep their history alive.

All this was translated from German into English by an Italian and I was very impressed by her linguistic skills. She wants to become a translator so this was good practice for her and I expressed my admiration and thanks.

To end a very full day we now have a Skype connection with the director of a human rights organisation in Gaza: Khalil. This is seven months after the bombardment by Israel, the worst since 1967 and the Six-Day War. Palestine has just joined the Rome Protocol enabling it to bring Israel to the International Criminal Court for the crimes committed in this bombardment. Twenty thousand homes destroyed, 44,000 families affected, thousands homeless and not a single home has been rebuilt. Public services, i.e. water, health, education, are limited and electricity is limited to six hours on and twelve off.

The majority of applications to send patients to the West Bank for treatment are refused, even cancer patients; the reason given: security. Imports are restricted, especially building materials. A hundred thousand homes need to be built and it is estimated it will take fifteen years to rebuild. There is a lack of donations by the international community. Money was promised but so far only 420 million USD has been received. There is a shortage of basic needs and 600 people are still living in UNWRA shelters. The future looks bleak. They are hoping that the ICC will start investigating the conflict. Four hundred thousand children are suffering from trauma and need psycho-social support. They are suffering the worst shortages for five years, especially medicines and other hospital supplies.

Ninety-five per cent of their water is imported and if the water supply is not improved there will be no water at all in two years.

1.2 million are dependent on UNWRA.

Only 5% of goods produced in Gaza are allowed to be exported. The cut-flower fields have been turned over to grazing for cattle. Two thirds of their daily needs are denied. This collective punishment is totally against the Fourth Geneva Convention, and the closing of the Rafa crossing, effectively imprisoning them, is illegal and dangerous as isolation produces extremism. All the Gazans want is their human rights, justice and peace.

Hamas is a political movement for the liberation of Palestine, not a terrorist organisation. The director of Khalil absolutely disagrees with targeting civilians, which Hamas is accused of, but the Israelis have committed a massive violation by deliberately targeting densely populated civilian areas. He believes Hamas is losing support as they have failed to gain any benefit for the Gazans during the last eight years and the people want change. Israeli reprisals for taking them to the ICC were taken into account but the Palestinians have nothing left to lose and they are pursuing the legal path to justice for the victims of the Israeli war crimes.

This very moving account of Gaza has left all of us feeling drained but we are very grateful to our speaker for taking the time to speak to us, a bunch of foreigners who so far are being pretty ineffective in changing anything for the better.

As well as trying to absorb all the information we have received today and making sense of it all and listening to Arabic, German, Italian and Spanish all around me it has been an exhausting day but very worthwhile.

I get back to the house at 9pm and Melena and her friend are there creating a fun atmosphere which Echlas loves. The street is still full of men spilling out from the community centre where the wake goes on but I walk through them and no one blinks an eye.

As Melena is sleeping with Echlas I manage to get to bed early as I have to be up for 7am for tomorrow's visit to Hebron.

HEBRON

Hebron is the largest city in the West Bank and of major importance to both the Moslem and Jewish faiths. King David was supposedly anointed here and four biblical couples are said to be buried here: Adam and Eve, Abraham and Sarah, Isaac and Rebecca, Jacob and Leah. A holy shrine to the three patriarchs, Abraham, Isaac and Jacob, venerated by Jews and Moslems, stands in the centre of the old city — half mosque, half synagogue. It has had a stormy past and continues to be a beleaguered city.

In 1968 a group of right-wing Israeli Zionists rented a hotel in the centre of the city and refused to leave in protest at the Israeli government's reluctance to authorise a settlement in Hebron for fear of an uprising. In 1970 the government approved the first settlement on the outskirts of Hebron.

In 1979 a group of women and children took over an abandoned hospital in the city centre and obtained permission for a permanent settlement. Now 1,000 settlers live in unconnected buildings in the city centre, most in Shuhada Street, once the most important commercial street for the Palestinian residents. Five hundred and twenty Palestinian shops were closed down, walls built and checkpoints established to restrict movement. Shuhada Street was the hub of the city, with a market, buses, taxis, but restrictions are increasing and now Palestinians are not allowed to walk on the street. Israelis have free access but anyone else has to show their passport to enter the ghost town of shuttered, abandoned shops and empty pavements. During my last visit to Hebron in February 2016 the situation was worse and the street was occupied by armed settlers and IOF, and barred to everyone else, including us. There was also a shooting of a young woman by the IOF for supposedly trying to stab a soldier, during our visit, and she was left on the ground to bleed to death, paramedics prevented from going to her aid.

In 1994, during Ramadan, Dr Baruch Goldstein, a settler, burst into the mosque and opened fire with an automatic rifle, killing twenty-nine men and young boys, mostly shot in the back, and wounding 200. Demonstrations broke out all over the West Bank and Gaza. The IOF killed twelve more Palestinians gathered near the Hebron hospital and wounded others there and in other towns in the West Bank. A curfew was immediately enforced for thirty-five days, while Israelis were allowed complete freedom of movement. For nine months Palestinians were not allowed to go to the mosque. Barricades were set up and neighbourhoods around the mosque closed down and declared 'security zones'. Another 700 shops closed due to harassment by the IOF of potential customers.

After this, part of the mosque was closed off to make a synagogue. IOF soldiers guard the entrance and ask what religion you are and can refuse entry.

In 1997 the city was divided into two sectors: H1 of which 80% is under the PA and H2 of which 20% is under Israeli control. In H2, which includes the mosque and the Tomb of the Patriarchs, live 40,000 Palestinians and 500 settlers, mostly from the US. Four thousand soldiers are deployed to protect the armed settlers.

The Hebron Defence Committee is an NGO set up to counteract the activities of the settlers and to campaign for the re-opening of Shuhada Street. They mark the anniversary of the mosque massacre every year, organise children's fun days and plant olive trees, to replace those frequently uprooted by the settlers.

They also host groups like ours and organise tours of Hebron to show people the harassment and restrictions that the people live under and also the progress that they are making to bring some of the streets back to life. They put pressure on the PA to help people to stay here, and lobby political parties and NGOs.

One of their successes, as a result of their Right to Movement demonstrations, has been to get a barrier lifted and a gate installed which is now always open and makes the difference between driving 4km and 14km. They continue moving other barricades and the army move them back. Since the recent uprisings against the occupation this situation may well have reverted back.

Moslems and Jews lived together in the same community for 800 years but in 1929 violence broke out. Zionist groups raised the Israeli flag at the Al-Aqsa Mosque in Jerusalem causing riots to break out. The violence spread and an Arab mob from the district around Hebron descended on the town and killed sixty-seven Jews, fifty-eight of them Zionists and not local Jews, but 435 Jews were given refuge in twenty-eight Arab homes. The British police stood back and did nothing to defend the Jewish population due in part to lack of manpower, causing them to recruit any British citizens they could find, including students, tourists and clergymen. At this moment, in 1929, there was a division between the Arabs and the Jews when it was realised that the Zionist immigrants were there for reasons other than simply to increase their population.

Walking in Hebron, along Shuhada Street, around the mosque and in what is left of the souk, the military presence is oppressive. Soldiers are everywhere, watching, and the atmosphere is tense, yet the Palestinians carry on their daily business as best they can. We see homes where the owners have to use ladders to get in and out through the windows since their front doors have been welded shut.

Wire netting protects the souk customers from debris thrown down by settlers occupying property above and military cameras are everywhere, looking down on us from every vantage point.

Children, particularly, have a stressful childhood in Hebron. There are daily detentions of children, and tear gas attacks occur three to four days a week. To go to school, they pass at least one checkpoint and whenever the children throw stones the soldiers use excessive force. A continual international presence helps to avert the worst excesses of violence by the IOF and settlers, as although they have no compunction about their behaviour toward Palestinians, it is all documented by NGOs, i.e. International Solidarity Movement, Christian Peacemakers, Ecumenical Accompaniers, and reported to the UN. The Red Cross and Medicine Sans Frontieres work with the children providing psychological support. Under international law the occupying power has a duty to protect the occupied but Israel does the exact opposite. Sometimes the IOF chase the children into their schools, even into their classrooms, some as young as six, violating their one place of safety. They are also provoked daily by settler children throwing stones at them and all the time see adult men and women settlers in their neighbourhoods carrying guns.

Palestinians living close to settlers are forced to secure their windows with metal shutters, so blocking out light, to prevent attacks, taunts and abuse from their Zionist neighbours. Some are even unable to leave their homes unattended for fear that the Zionists will break in and claim their home in their absence, as has happened to some families.

Hebron is a city that stirs the emotions, as much as Jerusalem does, when observing the intolerable conditions that people are forced to endure, day after day, and seeing no end to it. The sheer injustice that they suffer, the humiliation, the restrictions, the fear, the uncertainty is unimaginable for us. The Palestinians 'exist to resist' and they excel in standing their ground and showing the authorities that they will not *be forced out. As I mentioned earlier, the Hebron Defence Committee gives hope through their proactive resilience, seeking to better the lives of the people, perhaps in small ways, like painting a regenerated street in bright colours, reclaiming it for its rightful owners now that it is accessible again thanks to their efforts.*

At the end of a gruelling day, a barbeque in the desert is on the schedule but as it is very likely to be a late finish, involving alcohol, I have to decline and get back to relieve Echlas' minder.

LYDD, YAFFA and TEL AVIV

Today I am really excited about our trip as we are visiting three places I have not been to before: Lydd (Lod), Yafa and Tel Aviv. The bus is fuller today with some new people joining us, including an English girl with her baby and Palestinian husband who I had seen at AIC. Amazingly she comes from Brighton and has been living in Palestine for two years. The baby, about eight months old, provides a distraction on the bus but she is very placid and seems to enjoy all the attention. The journey to Lydd is the longest so far and takes an hour and a half. It lies between Ramallah and Tel Aviv.

This is the first mixed town I have encountered so am looking forward to seeing how Jews and Palestinians live together. There are about 70% Jews to 30% Palestinians. In 1948 almost 18,000 of Lydd's entirely Palestinian population of 19,000 were exiled and Israelis gradually moved in, including many Russians claiming to be Jews but who were in fact Christians and worship at the Christian Orthodox Church. When the settlements in Gaza were evacuated many of those Jews were resettled here.

The bus stops near a piece of waste ground so first impression is of a neglected, flat, nondescript town with little to recommend it, reminding me of a small mid-western desert town in the US, tumbleweed blowing down the main street. There is no life to be seen, except for a Jewish family, some distance away, gathered around an open fire under a tree on the wasteland, a result, we are told by our female guide, of home demolitions. The town had gone bankrupt with the influx of Russian 'Jews' and is struggling to recover. As usual there are different rules and levels of service for each community so where Jews have permission to build on agricultural land, 1,500 Palestinian homes on the same land have a demolition order on them.

Lydd's only claim to historical fame is probably the Church of St George where he was supposedly born and his bones returned there after his martyrdom. The church is locked and we cannot rouse the Greek priest with the key so we take a look at the outside where iron rungs can be seen in the walls, used to chain the insane in hope of a cure!

Illustrating the tolerance and respect of Islam and Christianity here, the mosque stands beside the church, also dedicated to St George. Lydd used to be an important trading centre in the Islamic period (638–1516 AD) and two caravanserais (inns serving camel caravans) can be seen nearby but unfortunately upkeep of these as important historical buildings has been completely neglected by the Israeli municipality.

I notice that unlike towns in the West Bank, all the signs here are in Hebrew, so Palestinians have to have some knowledge of the language.

Having exhausted the sightseeing possibilities of this area we move on to the railway station, built during the British Mandate (one thing we were good at is building railways). The land in this area is very expensive so the authorities tried to move the Palestinians out to cheaper areas. Some did go but found the new homes were too small and there was no privacy so the remainder stayed put. We note the proliferation of security cameras.

Driving through a suburban area of pleasant detached homes of differing sizes and styles we learn that this is a Palestinian area but many homes have demolition orders on them and many collaborators are housed here.

At the time of the Oslo Accords in 1993-95 collaborators were recruited through the Israeli secret service using blackmail. By intercepting phone calls and emails and finding a weak spot in an individual they would blackmail the person, forcing them to spy for them. For instance, if a family member was ill they would threaten to deny medical treatment unless the individual complied. In return the victim was promised a safe haven and houses for their family but the price they paid is continued stigmatisation by their own people. Some headway has been made with the passing of time and at least now the children, the descendants of the victims, go to ordinary schools.

In an adjoining area, where the land is wanted to build a road, homes have been demolished, the owners receiving no compensation or rehousing, forcing them to live in tents and caravans, also destroyed by the Israelis. These people are now dependent on their neighbours, camping out on their land. We are unable to access the site as the way is closed, a new development, according to our guide.

At the edge of the suburban area a wall separates the homes from the wide green space where the children used to go and play. Some distance away, behind some trees we can just see houses, belonging to a Jewish community. They requested the Israeli municipality build the wall as they did not like their children playing with the Palestinian children in the field.

Housing is obviously a major problem here as the Palestinians are being squeezed out of the town through demolitions and building prohibition. Social housing is also being sold off to Jews. There is no law to say that a Palestinian cannot rent or buy property in an Israeli neighbourhood, proven in a recent court case, but no one will sell or let to Palestinians, another example of the apartheid policy, of which there are 200 different laws catalogued by human rights NGOs. Urban planning used to declare homes illegal, i.e. designated agricultural land, but was only enforced for Palestinians not for Jewish immigrants.

Hospitality, as always with Palestinians, is not lacking and we eat a delicious meal of rice, chicken and salads in someone's garden, at a long table, relaxing in the shade from the midday sun. As usual, the women cook, the boys and men serve and the children look on shyly at first but their curiosity winning, they examine cameras and iPhones. The baby, Louise, gropes her way among the chairs, exercising her chubby legs, cooing at anyone who pays her attention. It is all very pleasant but I cannot help comparing the lives of the people living here to those in Hebron and wondering which is worse or are they on a par? On one level they are coping with the same discrimination, the same threats to their homes, the same insecurity and limited access to resources but in different ways.

If this is what a one-state solution would look like with Palestinians and Israelis living side by side, it would never work unless all are treated equally and each side learns to trust the other, a scenario as likely as the second coming, all the time Zionists rule Israel.

I am not sorry to leave Lydd and its atmosphere of desolation and distrust as we speed away towards Yaffa and the sea and the expectation of a livelier town. As soon as we enter the town and are put down in the old city, I smell the sea air and feel energised and excited by the prospect of seeing the sea. Our guide is a good-looking, muscular young Palestinian. Where we are standing is surrounded by attractive old buildings, some of the few left of old Yaffa, most having been destroyed by the British in 1936. At this point I wish I was not English. The day is hot and sunny so hugging the shade as much as possible, we follow our guide to an attractive park of green spaces and flower beds, and finding some steps to sit on we listen while he outlines the history of Yaffa.

Yaffa is the second oldest city in Palestine, the first historical reference being recorded in 1468 BC. Since then it has been under Egyptian, Philistine, Assyrian, Greek, Roman, Arab, Marmaluke, Ottoman, British and now Israeli control. Being a natural port it was a very important city, serving Jerusalem with pilgrims, but with the development of Tel Aviv it declined. Up until 1936 it was one of the most densely populated areas but the British destroyed a large area of it in reprisal for Palestinian resistance to their Jewish immigration policy. I feel ashamed again of the deeply regrettable part Britain has played here in attempting to destroy Palestine.

At the beginning of the twentieth century, two German engineers brought the steam railway to Yafa, encouraging agricultural regeneration and causing Yafa to expand too fast, becoming a dynamic urban, industrial, cultural and political centre. Evidently Ben-Gurion was so jealous of the city he would not stay there for even one night.

Tel Aviv developed on the back of the Palestinian city, the first Jewish neighbourhood growing its economy through the success of its neighbour Yaffa. Where Tel Aviv is now, thirty Arab villages used to occupy the land but this was requisitioned by the Jewish National Fund and became the principal place of arrival for many new Jewish immigrants.

In 1947 when the UN partition plan was announced, the 'cleansing' of Yaffa began with Zionist groups Hagana and Irgun terrorising the inhabitants by bombing and looting, causing the mass exodus of Palestinians leaving just 4,000. Those that escaped went to Gaza and Lebanon. Now 20,000 Palestinians, one third of whom are Greek Orthodox Christians, make up half the population of Yafa.

Having a brief overview of the history of Yaffa in our minds, we climb the steps and then – what joy – the sea, the azure blue of the sea, sparkling in the sun. I just want to jump in and swim. At this moment, I think the sea makes up for any amount of deprivation, just to have it there to look at every day, to listen to the sound of the waves, watch its changing moods, would certainly lift my spirits. I am surprised at my reaction, as I live fairly close to the sea and tend to take it for granted but having been deprived of its proximity for nearly three months my response reveals to me my life-long affinity to the sea. Some boats are bobbing about in the harbour and people are strolling along the seafront; it could be any Mediterranean holiday resort.

Mesmerised by the colour and movement of the sea and taking deep breaths of its invigorating ozone air, I struggle to concentrate on what we are being told. The gentrified old city we have just passed through was the result of Israeli requisitioning to turn the attractive but now sterile narrow alleys and steps into an artists' community to attract tourists. A few expensive boutiques reveal that this is no longer an authentic neighbourhood and apart from the visitors, we saw no inhabitants. Our guide tells us that most of the homes are empty.

One of our party asks our guide about the Druze, a group of people in Palestine who do not fit into a category and are therefore confusing us. He replies that Druze is a branch of Islam and that there are two types, each loyal to the country in which they live, i.e. the ones who live in Golan support Assad of Syria and those in the State of Israel do not see themselves as Arabs. They serve in the IOF and last year a Druze soldier shot thirty-five Palestinians in a school. I am still not 100% sure about their identity; in fact, I may be a little more confused.

The guide points out the large houses and flats tiered up into the hillside facing the sea. These are the most expensive properties in Yaffa and mostly belong to Israeli businessmen who bought them from Palestinians and then made huge profits selling or renting them to Jews.

In front of us is an undulating greensward, stretching for miles, and looks to be a wonderful facility for citizens to relax in. Our guide tells us it is developed over a rubbish dump, where toxic waste was dumped for years and was the local hangout for drug dealers and gun traders, a notoriously lawless area. Israel at last decided to make a park and asked the Palestinians for their input as to what they would like to see there. They requested a basketball and football area and a place to have barbeques but none of these were provided. Ball games are prohibited so it is just a green area for people to walk and run, however, I can see several families ignoring the rules and having barbeques on the grass. There are two large playgrounds for younger children and the whole space is very pleasant and relaxing and the best recreational area I have yet seen in Palestine, with the bonus of being next to the sea.

Going back to the subject of the sea, our guide tells us that the Israelis over-fish the area, fishing all year around, whereas the Palestinian professional fishermen, with their heritage of sea fishing, would have three months' rest to preserve the stock – yet another example of Israeli disregard for the environment. When asked his personal feelings about the future our guide replies that he does not believe in coexistence as there are huge cultural divides, i.e. Jews complain about Arabs sitting outside as they do to smoke *shisha* and gossip or drink coffee or play backgammon, all part of their culture. He says that reality needs to be acknowledged, that the Palestinian struggle is not a social one but a national one. He believes in socialism but says that capitalism is not black and white and he has no faith in the PA. Some Palestinian behaviour is detrimental to the cause, i.e. one Arab man he knows does not rent homes to Palestinians as Jews pay more.

Reluctantly we leave Yaffa, the sea, and our lovely guide, who risks his freedom every time he takes a group on a political tour.

The last stop of the day is Tel Aviv, the hedonistic capital city of Israel, and the contrast between this modern city and the towns I have been used to seeing is startling. It is like entering a different country, a wealthy European city dumped in the Middle East, with its boulevards, high rises, pristine streets and European shops. We stop outside a new-looking office block, architecturally elegant with an abundance of glass and steel, in a quiet street with seats and trees on the other side of the road. Inside the building is luxurious, spacious, air conditioned, making me slightly suspicious of the organisation we are going to hear about.

Probably for the first time in my life I am linguistically in a minority of one. The speaker is German and speaks in German; since most of the audience are German this makes sense. Very kindly one of the German students translates for me and the gist of what is relayed to me is as follows:

The foundation he represents is linked to the left in Germany. He grew up in Jerusalem, then went to Germany. In 2001 he came back to the Middle East. He has been in Tel Aviv for two months and has a good life here (yes, I can imagine that). His work is about political awareness and is divided into internal and external work. There are seventy offices around the world. His office is responsible for Israel and he has a regional office in Ramallah. The organisation also works in Jordan with grassroots NGOs, i.e. working with Bedouin in the Negev. The aim is to make people aware of their rights. Being a left-wing organisation in Germany, they have connections to leftists all over the world but their 'think tank' is based in Germany. This enables them to make decisions, as working here is very difficult due to the backwardness of the thinking in Israel. The Communists used to be stronger but now there are only 2% in the Knesset. They work on peace issues. In the 70s there was greater socialism but now there is a big difference between the rich and the poor, more than anywhere in the world. Because of the right-wing Israeli government he is not free to do what he wants to do here. Every three years he can decide who to support. Israel is a small country so he knows many people and Palestinian Israelis make up the leftist parties.

He interprets political statistics in a different way from the Israeli government and concentrates on the occupation, i.e. the cost to Palestine. Asking the question, 'Does Israel profit from the occupation?', his department collects data and statistics to try to find out.

They provide courses for internet bloggers and train people to think critically, particularly Russians who are victims of brainwashing by Leiberman, the notorious right-wing extremist. They also work in feminist organisations in Arab countries and with Iraqi refugees to help them integrate into society, and they teach Hebrew.

The political system in Israel is like the US, i.e. the 'rednecks' and certain ethnic groups vote for a certain party just because that is tradition, not because they agree with their policies.

He is antinationalistic but believes in solidarity between people who experience the same struggles.

Some of what he said may have been lost in translation and I would have liked clarification on some points. I can see how teaching critical thinking and integration would be helpful, but wonder where the results of his research go and does it actually change anything. Having a left-wing presence in Tel Aviv to undermine the hard right could only be beneficial but I wonder how much he can accomplish without drawing attention to the seemingly subversive nature of his organisation. Also, I cannot help wondering about the cost of all this and how it is funded and how results are assessed. So many questions leave me feeling rather frustrated after a very mixed day and I need time to think about and digest what I have seen and heard.

It is dark when we go outside and into the bus but the drive back is much quicker than I expected. I still forget that this is a small country and distances between places are relatively short.

THE JORDAN VALLEY

The last day of the political camp and again one I am looking forward to, knowing virtually nothing about the area we are visiting: the Jordan Valley. The valley is extremely fertile and driving along we see large plantations of date palms, banana trees and orchards on the hillsides. Unfortunately, they are now owned by Israeli settlers and the produce exported to Europe.

Jericho is in Area A but all access to it is in Area C, including the main road, which in the Second Intifada was closed off. We stop at a roadside café to wait for our guide. I am grateful for the Arabic coffee to which I have become accustomed and enjoy relaxing in the sun on the rickety, dusty sofa admiring the recycled tyre plant pots, painted in bright colours, adorning the café entrance. Eventually when all the local photo opportunities have been exhausted and I feel we are wasting time, a car pulls up in a cloud of dust and a middle-aged man jumps out, apologising for being late.

Once on the bus again our man talks as we go along. He tells us that in his village most have left the land and found other jobs due to land confiscation, lack of water and export restrictions all of which make farming unprofitable. Their large banana plantations are no more, since water is restricted in Area A and siphoned off for settlements. Large amounts of land are empty where there used to be flourishing farms. Some communities have no electricity and have no access to mains water, even though they can hear water flowing underneath their houses. In the 70s there were eighty-five wells; now only seventeen are viable.

By this time, we have stopped in a beautiful valley, where wild flowers are growing and water is running freely in a narrow gully by the side of the road. The water comes from a spring and used to be abundant all year round, even enough for swimming in, but in summer it now dries up as the Israelis take it. Palestinians have to buy water. It costs approximately 700IS a month for a household but Israelis use sixteen times as much water. Their aim is to drive Palestinians off the land by making it impossible for them to make a living. At the same time, they are also destroying the natural environment for plants and wildlife.

We can see caves in the hillside and our man tells us that sometimes families will live in them when their homes are demolished.

Apart from us, there is a pick-up truck parked up and a man filling up some water containers while his young son is having a great time wading out in the water. The only other vehicle is a car, driving slowly up and down, playing an ice cream van tune from the open window. He is actually selling ice creams which seems a bit odd to me as this is not by any means a busy area or a tourist attraction. Our man tells us that he could very well be a collaborator spying for the IOF as this sort of countryside is ideal for resistance training. I will now always be suspicious every time I hear an ice cream van.

The police work with the settlements and the IOF to 'protect' the settlers and harass Palestinians, i.e. stopping water trucks. Segregation of the two communities is enforced by the threatening red signs at the entrances to Area A, of which we have seen plenty.

Back on the bus again we pass a huge date plantation, stretching for miles, followed by miles of grape vines, all now belonging to settlers. The Israelis keep their cows in air-conditioned buildings while Palestinians suffer frequent power cuts especially in the summer.

Fourteen kilometres north west of Jericho we stop at the village of Fasayel, comprising a few spreadout dwellings. The bus bumps along a rough track until we reach a two-storey building seemingly in the middle of nowhere. This is the HQ of the Jordan Valley Solidarity (JVS) Campaign and here we meet Rashed, the coordinator of the project. Various children of differing ages form an entourage as he comes to greet us and welcome us to his home. We climb up a practically vertical flight of wooden stairs into a light airy room with a large verandah on one side where mattresses and sun loungers are spread about. I see a stone sink and drainer but no evidence of plumbing and this is next to a very basic toilet. The kitchen is a small room off the main room and I can see, hear and smell the frenzied activity as our lunch is prepared. A woman, presumably Rashed's wife and mother of the assorted children, brings out two jugs of lemon and mint, followed by a girl carrying a trayful of cups and glasses. We find seats around the room and Rashed explains something about the village and the campaign.

This area is extremely vulnerable to land confiscation and since 1967 Israel has been gradually attempting to annex the area which forms 28% of the West Bank. It uses home demolitions, restriction of water and movement, curfews, arrests and detentions, denial of access to electricity, health and education. There is no infrastructure for the people who live here.

In 2003 Jordan Valley Solidarity was born from a few communities banding together to try to defend the indigenous population's right to be here. The campaign continues to grow and now includes the whole of the Jordan valley. They have no funding, only what people donate, and rely on members to donate their time and resources. One month ago they planted a hundred trees on a piece of land to try to protect it. Other activities include building roads and schools and education about using hay and mud bricks.

The other arm of the project is raising awareness about the plight of the Jordan Valley Palestinians and the urgency of protecting this area through preparing materials for use by advocates, attracting media attention, persuading international agencies to operate here to monitor Israeli activity and to provide the services most needed by the community. Part of this awareness-raising includes eyewitness tours for visitors to Palestine and ten-day stays in the house, assisting with projects.

Four years ago they built a school here out of mud bricks and Rashed invites us to join him outside to see the machine that has revolutionised the making of these bricks. Before, they were all made by hand, a long, painstaking process, but now this machine makes the process far more efficient. The bricks are sustainable, cheap and environmentally sound, ideal for the Jordan Valley where demolitions are common and frequent. A building made of these bricks can easily be rebuilt by recycling the damaged bricks through the machine. To earn our lunch Rashed asks us to move a hundred bricks from the pile on the ground to the adjacent lorry, to use in building another school. Happy to do something practical, we quickly form a team: young strong men on the lorry and we 'girls' picking up the bricks and handing them up to the boys. They are extremely heavy, large and dusty and some take two of us to carry and hoist onto the lorry. It is tiring work and we are certainly working up an appetite. Finally we lift the last of the bricks, now covered in dust.

As we walk back to the house, anticipating lunch, I notice a sign on a small outbuilding, saying that the well inside has been donated by UK aid through the UN. This is the first time I have seen anything donated by the UK to Palestine.

The lunch, consisting of fried fish, salads and homemade flat bread, is abundant, delicious and a miracle considering it has been produced in such a small space, under extremely basic conditions and for so many of us. The worthy cooks, Rashed's wife and two young male volunteers, emerge hot and sweaty from the kitchen, to a round of applause.

Rashed continues his very informative talk, now that we can concentrate with renewed energy.

Before 1967, and later, 'the wall', Jordan Valley had been the breadbasket of the West Bank and sold its produce all over the Middle East, through Jordan, itself importing 60%. Now 57% of the Jordan Valley is a closed military zone on the usual pretext of 'security' but in reality is a strategy to take land and boost Israel's economy. Since 1994 Israel has prohibited sale of produce to Jordan. Two hundred and sixty thousand people lived in the Jordan Valley but hundreds of villages were destroyed and the people transferred to Jordan's refugee camp. Now only 64,000 still live here. Ninety-three per cent of the area is in Area C and only 6.6% in A and B. Many people live in Area C in tents. They are not Bedouin but have a similar lifestyle except they do not move around and have owned their land for at least a hundred years. There are five checkpoints to control and block the Jordan Valley, enabling the IOF to ruin the livelihoods of many farmers in the Second Intifada by prohibiting the unloading of their produce, causing it to rot. The Israeli plan is to divide the Jordan Valley from the West Bank, part of their divide and rule policy. There are thirty-seven settlements in the Jordan Valley, meaning 6,500 people control the land and take the water. They sell dates, wine, flowers, vegetables and grapes to Europe, all grown on land stolen from the Palestinians, so Rashed encourages us to boycott everything Israeli.

He has lived with the constant harassment and domination of the army since he was five years old and continues to suffer but will remain steadfast.

He goes on to talk about NGOs, which I gather he has little time for. According to him NGOs take 60% of money raised for salaries and achieve nothing. They spend the money on expensive hotels and cars and I am inclined to agree with him as I have seen evidence of this. Very wealthy NGOs have come to the Jordan Valley to try to solve the problem of water but so far, have found no solution.

NGOs came, unasked, and built five community centres without consultation with the locals and only one is still used. One fell down and was never used and the other three are no longer in use. He thinks the NGOs like the occupation as it gives them a 'cause' and makes them feel needed but they make no difference and are not needed. I have not heard anyone here express such a scathing attack on NGOs but he probably has a point, although I am sure this is not the opinion of all Palestinians. I have often wondered though what the Palestinians think of all these foreign do-gooders' in their country. He does not seem to have a problem with volunteers as such, more with the organisations themselves.

Since there are few employment opportunities now in the Jordan Valley, many are forced to work for the settlers, working on land that was theirs, receiving half the basic rate of pay, in poor and dangerous conditions and with no insurance. Ten thousand Palestinians work in the settlements, including children, and of course there are no health and safety rules so they are exposed to toxic chemicals without any protective clothing.

Rashed's sister was arrested in 2013 and spent two months in prison followed by two months' home arrest and had to pay 7,000IS fine. Her crime was teaching someone how to use Facebook and because she has friends in Gaza and around the world she is considered a threat. Rashed has had his computer and camera confiscated on several occasions and the IOF come to the centre regularly to try to scare him and his family and the volunteers. The Israelis are trying to destroy hope but the Palestinians continue to resist, just by existing. The symbol of the JVS is the thistle, chosen due to its tenacity, being able to exist without water.

During a break, I talk to Dan, one of the two volunteers who made our lunch. He is a French/Irish activist with an astonishing story. He was a chef for seven years working in Michelin-starred restaurants (no wonder lunch was so good) but then decided he wanted to do something more meaningful with his life, so gave up cheffing and went to Ireland to do a building course with an Irish uncle. Having completed that he is now an activist in France, helping Romanies, immigrants and refugees. His aim is to get a building degree and some agricultural training and set up environmental and sustainable building projects all over the world. He says he loves being here in the Jordan Valley and being part of a project that embraces the very values that he believes in.

I try to communicate with two little girls aged seven and eight and despite our lack of a common language manage to build a rapport. First they want to explore the contents of my bag, examining my phone, glasses, purse and other odds and ends with great curiosity. I find some paper and a pen and they write their names for me in Arabic and I write mine in English and then Arabic, which they find very amusing.

Now it is Dan and his colleagues' turn to tell us what they are doing here. Apart from brick making they have been helping farmers plant trees, attempting to stop house demolitions and have been making a film on the brick production machine with the aim of encouraging more people to use this sustainable way of home building. Where Palestinians are given a permit for a well, they are only allowed to sink to a certain depth, so the water is often salty, so another project they have been involved in is running water pipes and making pumps for farmers in Area C.

The latest plan is to build a factory to make cheese. This will be done by a women's group who will sell to major Palestinian towns, also helping to promote knowledge of Area C outside the Jordan Valley. At present farmers have a problem with marketing cheese but by forming a co-op they will have the advantage of cheaper animal feed and efficient marketing. The aim is to teach young farmers, with expert French support, how to make different types of cheese and grow a sustainable cheese-producing centre.

This seems a marvellous initiative as there is an obvious gap in the market for this. I am always looking for cheese but can only find Dutch Edam in two shops in Bethlehem. Apart from this the choice is limited to' Puck' spread or the cubes in salted water.

Reluctantly we have to leave Rashed and his family to visit another village, in the northernmost part of our journey. We promise to take their story back to our various countries, feeling inspired to support these courageous people in their fight for existence.

At the next village we sit outside on carpets under the trees, drinking tea and eating biscuits. The boys of the family offer these round and although I have barely recovered from lunch it seems impolite to refuse. This is a farm of 14,000 *dunams* (one *dunam* = 1,000 square metres), but after 1967, 12,000 *dunams* were confiscated and the population reduced from 6,000 to 1,200 people. The Israelis took the land and the water and conducted army training inside the village to intimidate the occupants into moving out. As this is Area C, no building is permitted so young people move away, having no future here. The stolen land is farmed by the settlers who sell the best produce to the EU and the poor produce to the West Bank, the people there having no choice but to buy it or go without. They have only three wells left. The other three were destroyed by Israelis and they are forbidden to dig a new one.

The farmer explains this is not a business any more as water is too expensive to make any money from growing fruit but he does grow cucumbers and tomatoes and can make a bit of money from them. He keeps going just to hold onto the land; having been in his family for generations he is reluctant to let it go. He said JVS has provided him with support and by working together with the whole Jordan Valley he is stronger. They meet up with the Popular Resistance and with farmers from Ramallah, Tulkaram and Hebron, so providing connections between the different communities.

A recurring message is reiterated by the farmer who says that Palestinians want to live in peace with their families but the Israelis have no interest in peace. This is so obvious to those who observe the situation and listen to the Israeli rhetoric. He wants us to take the message home that Palestinians are not terrorists, they are educated people who only want respect and a just peace. The Geneva Convention must be followed. He still has hope; without that he would not be able to carry on.

Our last stop for the day is in another village, consisting of just three homes on a small hill, surrounded by pleasant countryside with fruit trees in blossom. A pen of sheep and their lambs give off a ripe smell, a few cows graze on the scrubby ground and a donkey gazes at us over a fence.

Sitting in the late afternoon sun, listening to the call to prayer in the distance and the birds singing, with a view over to the Golan Heights, it is idyllic and so peaceful. Forcing myself to take sips of the sickly-sweet tea, I listen to the spokesperson for this village, inhabited by three brothers and their families. Although today it is peaceful, he tells us that they suffer repeated incursions by the IOF to intimidate them off the land, frightening the children, killing some of the animals on which they depend for their livelihood, destroying crops and generally making life untenable. They have nowhere else to go so have no option but to stay put and resist.

As usual, the children, full of curiosity, overcome their shyness and lead us to the sheep pen, where they climb over the gate to get among the lambs and lift up the smallest ones for us to pet. Although they have no possessions, just a few broken toys, they always offer what they can, in this case, lambs. The natural generous hospitality of the Palestinians always shines through; even the most impoverished children want to give us something and despite their grubbiness, the smiling faces of these children is humbling to me, a 'materialistic Westerner'. I really wish I had something to give them but then on reflection realise that sometimes 'receiving' teaches the lesson of humility, and it is not my turn to give but theirs.

My camera has run out of battery, much to my dismay, but the Italian guy who is taking lots of pictures says he will send them to me. He never did. Sitting on the bus, waving goodbye to all the families gathered to see us off, I see a tiny girl and boy about two or three years old, standing, holding hands, dirty faces, like little angels watching us, amazed at our bus in their village.

With their image in my head I reflect on what we have seen and heard today and the sheer injustice of it all makes me determined to continue doing, in whatever way I can, my bit for the human rights of Palestinians. This intolerable situation cannot continue and those of us who have witnessed this brutal occupation are morally obliged, I believe, to speak out on behalf of its victims. To ignore our human duty makes us complicit in this crime against humanity and in all conscience, I cannot live with myself if I do not actively seek to bring about justice for the Palestinians. I am amazed that Palestinians welcome British people in view of our heinous past with them. Of course, they remember Balfour and what he did to them, but generously they do not blame us for the sins of our forefathers. I am not sure I could be so forgiving to a nation that, having been a major instigator of the occupation, continues to support its criminal acts and is a major arms supplier, along with the US, to its brutal regime. Surely one day justice will prevail.

CHAPTER TEN

EASTER, SURPRISES AND LAST DAYS

Easter Sunday

I wake up at 10am today, tired from four days of intensive information overload and realise this is the first Easter I have been away from home, not cooked a roast dinner for my family or been to the Vigil Mass on Saturday night. My plan had been to go to Jerusalem for that but with the political camp it was not possible.

With Ida's help I get Echlas into the wheelchair and off we go to Aida camp for coffee and chocolates with some of the family. It is so warm we can sit outside and I am quite content to sit and listen to the babble of Arabic around me but we have shopping to do for Easter. Kimberley is expected around five to tell Echlas why she is suddenly leaving Palestine. We have been speculating as to the reason and our imaginations have run amok so she could be pregnant, have a serious illness, lost her job – anything is possible.

The *souk* is hellish as usual, with cars trying to get through the crowds of shoppers and causing mayhem. We do the necessary shopping, pay the bed man another instalment then sit in Manger Square and eat falafel to fortify ourselves for the trip home. Kimberley is already there when we get back, having been let in by Ida. Not able to wait a minute longer to know her mysterious reason for leaving she tells us it is because she wants to work with children and has to go home to do a course first so nothing dramatic, thankfully. I wonder if I will have to move out of my room but Kimberley offers to sleep with Echlas so that gives me a break. I have developed a cough today and my voice is gradually disappearing. Perhaps that is why I have felt so tired. We go to the station restaurant for a meal

205

and on the way back buy two large bags of miniature chocolate eggs for tomorrow's Easter egg hunt. At home, I boil up some eggs with red onion skins but they turn out a dirty yellow colour.

Veronica and Deanna are getting up at 5am in the morning to walk to Jerusalem and see the sunrise.

Monday

My chest is sore and I feel a bit rough but I soldier on and do the washing and ironing, hoover and make a quantity of tomato juice for Echlas so have no time to examine how ill I feel. Later Kimberley and I go out to the copy shop to get birthday cards that Echlas ordered and buy some food for tonight. It feels really hot out. My voice is now just a croak or a whisper.

We get Echlas up at 4pm and then prepare for the 'party', hiding eggs all over the garden and house and wrapping the little presents we had bought in the *souk*. When the girls arrive (Mohammed is still busy with his mates) we sit them down at the table with Echlas' paints and the hard-boiled eggs and show them how to decorate the egg with patterns or faces. They soon get absorbed but I notice they are covering the egg with a dark-coloured paint and then trying to paint over this with another colour so not altogether the desired result but they are having fun. Mohammed arrives and soon gets just as absorbed as his sisters and has very good concentration. Deanna and Veronica join in as well so it is quite a party. When the eggs run out we leave them to dry as I explain the egg hunt. They are off with great excitement and a competitive spirit, all aiming to get the most eggs. It is fun for us too, watching them running about and willing them to find the most discreetly hidden ones. I did find eggs scattered about the place for some days to come but they all gathered a good bagful each.

The last activity is the egg and spoon race which we have to do in pairs owing to the limited space, but they all enter into the spirit of it with enthusiasm. Kimberley and I go last, but shamefully set a bad example to the kids; Kimberley jogs my elbow, causing my egg to fall and we end up collapsed in laughter, me accusing Kimberley and she vehemently denying it but all in good humour.

For the final surprise of the day we give out their presents and although they are all cheap things from the *souk* – fancy hair clips for the younger girls, a baseball cap for Mohammed and a scarf for the older sister – they are all so delighted and keep saying '*shukran*'.

Echlas is tired and wants to go back to bed so we pack them off with all their goodies and once she is comfortable, Kimberley and I start preparing stuffed courgettes which take ages to prepare so we eventually eat at 8.30pm. I go to bed at 10.30pm, not feeling well. I get an email from Hannah saying she is fine and is in Tel Aviv.

Tuesday

It is only two weeks until I leave – difficult to believe. I am still feeling rough and wake up coughing at 8am but my voice is coming back. When I go out into the garden I discover it is really hot and I have the luxury of lying out on one of the 'beds' there while Echlas and Kimberley go out. Eugene is still talking about what lies he will tell on the way out at the airport when he comes for his lesson. I plant out the rest of my seedlings and some mint that I bought in the *souk*. I hope my successor will water them when I have gone.

Wednesday

Hebron sister pays a flying visit on her way to a funeral and brings us some *freekeh*, pumpkin and tomato sauce and some homemade bread so that saves cooking tonight.

Kimberley goes out to say goodbye to her boyfriend and Echlas has her nephew with her so I go to Majde's shop to get a skirt for Echlas to give Kimberley.

In the afternoon Kimberley and I go over to Aida camp leaving Echlas with George and a new student, so that she can buy a scarf from Rosha's mum but there is some misunderstanding and we sit in Afaf's home for about half an hour with Layan, Afaf, aunty and Nizreen, making polite conversation. Eventually we get to see Rosha's mum, when the reason for our visit dawns on them, and I cannot resist buying a bag and a scarf.

On our return we get Echlas into her wheelchair and set off down to the bus station restaurant for a farewell drink. It is so warm and the town is buzzing. It seems all the youth are out: lots of young men driving about in their flash cars, playing loud music. I see a row of about eight of them sitting on some steps eating ice creams and thought that in England they would be drinking pints of beer and getting rowdy. Everyone seems to be so happy; amazing how weather can change one's mood. We had already eaten *freekeh* so just have a bottle of wine and some nibbles and sit outside on the terrace admiring the lights of Bethlehem.

Thursday

Kimberley is leaving today so I am feeling both sad and a little apprehensive as I will be on my own with Echlas. It was so warm last night I slept with just a sheet over me and both windows in my room open but it is cooler today. Kimberley helps me get Echlas into the wheelchair before she goes. There are hugs and tears when the taxi arrives to pick her up but she will be back.

For distraction, we go out to pay the phone bill and up to pay the bed man. It seems many people like to have the personal contact when paying a bill so there is always a queue but we never have to wait long as it is efficiently run. What a contrast in the weather today – very cold and windy – so we are glad to get indoors to relative warmth.

Echlas has lessons for two hours so I have a rest, then go out again to get some shopping. There is a wedding going on and numbers of young men, smartly dressed, are hanging about in the street by a car decorated with flowers.

Veronica and Deanna are moving out. They informed Echlas of their plans yesterday when she was forced to ask them for rent. They should have paid a month in advance when they moved in last Thursday but only gave her two weeks so should go next Thursday. They made an excuse about having a rent-free flat offered to them but Echlas thinks they just do not like living here. My view is that they are not being very fair to Echlas, although I know they have to think of themselves and have very little money to live on, but she spent 1,000IS on new beds so she is making a loss. It has been a change for Echlas as well, having other people living in the house, and I get the impression that Echlas is not really comfortable with it. She had expected they might be of some help sometimes but they are out a lot and never offer. My cough is still troublesome so I bought some cough medicine. Echlas goes to bed relatively early – midnight – and wakes twice in the night.

Friday

I am woken by my cough again. I just hope it does not develop into anything as I just realise I am no longer covered by health insurance.

The weather is dull and chilly and it has rained a little. It seems as if it will be a quiet day but as I should know by now anything can happen here.

Layan comes to bath Echlas so that takes up a couple of hours and gives Echlas a chance for a gossip. Then Echlas reads a terrible thing on Facebook. A young man from Hebron was imprisoned and injected with something which gave him muscle weakness. After he was released from prison the PA and NGOs promised to send him for specialist treatment but he died today. Later we found out that he had been given an insulin overdose. Of course, no one has been held accountable for this crime. To compound this atrocity, one of the mourners was shot dead by the IOF at his funeral.

Our first unexpected visitor is Sister Lucille bringing Easter gifts, a little tray of Easter eggs and cakes, so she stays and chats for a while. Shortly after she leaves, another knock on the door reveals Hebron sister and daughter flying in with food for us: *maqluba* with some chicken for me. As Echlas is hungry we eat this around 5pm. Our day of surprise visitors is not yet over. Later on in the evening I open the door to find a group of people: aunty, sister and three other people who turn out to be two nephews, one married to a Belgian visiting with their baby daughter and their mother.

They all crowd into Echlas' room and I scurry around finding chairs and making coffee and trying to get the gist of the conversation. This is the first time aunty has been to Echlas' house since her mother died and she sheds a few tears but cheers up after a while and joins in the laughter. Echlas is delighted that her aunt has been persuaded to visit her house so it is something of a celebration.

When they leave after two hours, I feel exhausted and doze on my bed until Echlas goes to sleep at 2am.

*

Today I feel worse. I think it is a combination of lack of sleep and the virus. Mohammed's sister comes to help me get Echlas into the wheelchair and then we go to Aida camp to see the baby. Echlas loves children and makes a fuss of the baby, riding around with her outside in the garden in her wheelchair. I could go to sleep in the chair. Fortunately, a German friend is coming to stay the night so she can take over. Sara arrives at 5pm, then Maria, the Spanish friend, comes so I go to bed and sleep till 8pm, get up for something to eat and go back to bed, leaving them to drink wine and eat nuts.

I sleep through until 8.30am, get up and put the water heater on and have a shower, then return to my warm bed as it is so cold and pouring with rain. Sara and Echlas get up at 11am and then she leaves. It was a shame I missed all the Easter celebrations yesterday and the music night at AIC but just did not feel well enough. This week I need to get organised for going home. Echlas has arranged with Majde that I go to his shop with all the stuff I need to send home, to pack it up, and I have emailed my boarding pass to Echlas so she can get the copy shop to print it. The day passes quietly, reading, eating, looking after Echlas. It has rained all day and now I want to go home. I have one week left and there is nothing I really want to see or do and the anxiety around leaving is beginning. People say that leaving is worse than arriving regarding border control and you can be asked some difficult questions so it is best to have a plan in mind of what you are going to say to explain what you have been doing for the last three months. My strategy is to be vague and forgetful. I can truthfully say I have been to Jerusalem, Tel Aviv and Jaffa (Yafa), even though only very briefly. If they ask me where I stayed then I will be stumped. I consider making up a fake itinerary, using my guidebook to Israel and the Occupied Territories but would never be able to remember it, so decide to look innocent and hope for the best and not carry any incriminating evidence with me. That means I have to send all the political material – my diaries, T-shirts, photos, books and anything Palestinian – back in a box to England.

The cleaning lady comes the next day to give me a day off. I am awoken by a terrifically loud banging on the door which, in my half-asleep state, I fear can only be the IOF as it is only 8am but it is the CL who seems to have no sense of time or perhaps she does not have a watch. Echlas had asked her to come at 9am, allowing me to go to Majdes', so now I am in plenty of time. Laden with bags I walk over to the shop where Majde at once finds a box, cuts it to the right size, packs it and seals it securely in a matter of minutes, then drives me around the corner to the shipper's office. I would have had no idea where to send a parcel from so am very grateful to him as it is so quick and easy.

With the rest of the day free I decide to phone Eugene as he is always asking me to meet up, to see if he is available. He is giving an English lesson at Alrowwad Centre in Aida camp so I walk over there, enjoying the warm sunshine and feeling much better, and find him in the library giving a lesson by asking a young woman about her life and experience living in the camp. I can see this is a very good way for Eugene to converse with Moslem women and find out about them. He has a number of male friends and it is easy for him, as a man, to mix with the male community but not so easy to talk to Moslem women.

I have not been in this centre before so Eugene shows me round and I am most impressed with the facilities. As well as the large library for adults and children, there is a recording studio, a large hall for theatre productions, a museum, a shop, a computer lab, sewing machines and a programme of classes and events to cater for all ages, covering health education, music, *dabka* dancing, women's empowerment and much more.

We walk through the camp and stop at the antique shop, a place I have passed by many times but never had the opportunity to stop and look. It is full of amazing objects like 1950s record players and radios, all working, old embroideries, jewellery, old household items – an Aladdin's cave to someone like me who cannot resist 'junk'. Bearing in mind the limited capacity of my suitcase, I restrain my purchases to small items of jewellery.

The owner of the shop tells us he used to be a civil engineer but then had back surgery and was no longer able to work. To support his family of nine he opened the shop and just about makes a living. He makes jewellery from recycled items and also some of the embroidered things he upcycles. He collects antiques, the radios, record players, typewriters, restoring them to working order. Next to the shop he has a museum which he opens onto the street in summer.

After that interesting interlude we walk along the wall looking for spent bullets and tear gas canisters to give to the man to recycle but only find two. The graveyard is looking attractive with wild flowers growing among the graves so we pick our way through, admiring the flowers and wondering how many of these graves belong to martyrs of the occupation and how many more will lie here.

Opposite the entrance to the camp is Divanos restaurant so as it is lunchtime we decide to treat ourselves as it will be the last time we meet. I order prawns fried in batter with hot sauce and chips and Eugene has a Greek salad, saying his stomach is a bit upset, then orders a bottle of red wine as a cure! We enjoy a leisurely lunch, a rare occurrence, then dare to go back to Eugene's place, despite Echlas' orders, but as this is my last week I am living dangerously.

From the outside the building is nondescript, a concrete block with nothing attractive about it, but inside is a different picture . The ground floor, a large open space, is used for wakes and weddings and today lots of children are running around and playing here. On the next floor is a custom-built children's centre with units for books and toys, bright colours, small-size toilets and washroom and a full-size drum kit. Going up to the second floor we arrive at the guesthouse, Eugene's abode, and I am pleasantly surprised. From what he has told me I imagined it to be very basic and perhaps rather shabby but this is a large, open-plan sitting room, light and airy with fantastic views across Bethlehem. The kitchen is modern and well equipped but lacking a washing machine, and the furniture modern and clean. All the soft furnishings look new.

The bedrooms have bunk beds and accommodate eight people; the bathroom is modern and clean. Very impressed with what I am seeing we go up to the top floor and find another excellent facility: a fully equipped gym with eight pieces of equipment plus mats for yoga, weights, table football, but sadly, all rarely used. We cannot access the roof but Eugene says the views are amazing and should be used for something, a roof garden maybe?

The building was funded by Fatah and that apparently is why it is underused as those who support Hamas or any other political party will not use it. It is such a waste of a badly needed centre.

I have to return as it is 4pm and time for the CL to leave. I find she has been busy and sorted out all Echlas' clothes and packed her bag ready to go to Hebron next week. Luckily she also cooked lunch for Echlas so now we have both eaten we only need a snack for supper.

Tuesday

Echlas did not sleep at all last night. I went to sleep at about 11.30pm, telling Echlas to wake me up when she wanted to lie down to sleep. At 4am I woke up, astonished to see Echlas still on her computer and told her the time but she was totally engrossed so I tried to sleep again with the noise of the TV soap making it impossible. An hour later *salah* started but I must have dozed off again as it is 9am when I finally wake. Echlas has watched seventeen episodes of the soap but seems none the worse for it.

Rosha comes a bit later to cut Echlas' toe nails and Eugene comes for his lesson and to use my iPad, so making the most of the opportunity to go out I take the unwanted skirt back to Majde's shop. A young Spanish man is sitting with Majde drinking coffee so I join them, enthralled by his strong Northern Irish accent, incongruous with his Spanish looks, but he tells me his father was Irish and he grew up in both places. He is here with his Spanish wife, volunteering at the Bible College, teaching Spanish. Majde leaves us chatting and after a while the young man has to go so I am left minding the shop. Luckily there are no customers. Majde eventually returns and I am able to get back before Eugene leaves. He is travelling tomorrow so this is our last meeting. I wish him good travels and hope he has a wonderful time when his daughter arrives.

Wednesday

Now I am counting down the days until I leave. As the date looms ever nearer I am impatient to go. I think I am nervous about the journey, getting to the airport on time, the flight, but also about getting through border control unscathed. It feels like time to leave now. Everyone I know has gone or is going and to be honest I am bored at times.

Echlas has another bath today when Layan comes and later we go out but she is not feeling well again. There seems to be no reason for it, except that she did drink some red wine last night but she slept well, from 11pm to 10.15am. Now she is feeling cold, although the day is warm and even hot at times, but she is fully dressed, wrapped in blankets, with wheat bags and two heaters.

While we were out I bought some Arabic coffee, spice mix and crystallised ginger that I eat like sweets and two Arabic music CDS to take home.

During the evening, Echlas suffers from an uncomfortable abdomen and needs to be moved frequently to try and relieve the discomfort. We sleep at twelve but are awoken by a tremendous thunderstorm which lasts about three hours as it keeps coming back. The rain is so heavy I imagine the lesson room being flooded again.

Thursday

Echlas slept well apart from the storm disturbance and she feels slightly better today. While she gives a lesson I go out to the Bible College library to return my books and say goodbye to the librarian. As I am here I decide to go into the college to see what volunteering opportunities they may have. Apart from teaching, they need a home manager but it sounds like hard work and too tying as it is full time. I just have time to walk to Alrowwad to buy a few small items from their excellent shop, made by local people in the camp, at the same time worrying about how it will all fit into my suitcase. It is very wet underfoot but not too cold and the sun is shining and it feels good to get some air. We have no water again today so no washing – bodies or clothes.

Friday

Today we have water so I can have a shower and do a load of washing. I will never take water for granted again. In the afternoon we go down Star Street to Manger Square and have bread and hummus and a lemon and mint drink as it is warm today. Then back up to Aida camp to collect some food from sister. It is Prisoners' Day and I am keen to see how it is commemorated in the camp, knowing that there are many political prisoners from Aida in administrative detention or serving long prison sentences. A large crowd of people are assembled outside Largee Centre in the road leading to the metal gates, where the soldiers enter. Men stand on one side and the women on the other with the children running about in between. After some speeches a huge bunch of balloons is released, one for every prisoner from the camp, and they are supposed to float away into the sky but unfortunately get entangled in the wires overhead so the effect is lost. That seems to be it so we go home for forty-five minutes, then it is off out again for a night at the theatre. So exciting!

I had no idea *The Siege* was on in Bethlehem and it was only this morning that Veronica told me. Fortunately Echlas is able to access the venue as it is in the place we go to, to sit in the garden sometimes. We go with Deanna and Veronica and are then joined by some other friends while we are waiting to be let into the theatre. It is a real social event and I see several people I know: Maria from the political tour, Loren from Jerusalem and some of Echlas' students and from AIC. One of the front-of-house from the Freedom Theatre recognises me and we say hello, making me feel like I really belong.

While we are sitting at a table, chatting, a strange man comes and sits with us. He says he is a tour guide for the Church of the Nativity and asks us questions about Jesus and the story of his birth. We think he is some kind of eccentric as he makes his way round to other groups, telling them about the church but when the play starts there he is on stage, playing... a tour guide. Very clever.

We are lucky to get seats near the front due to Echlas' wheelchair and the place is packed out, with some people standing. It is all in Arabic but I know the story of the siege, having read *Imm Mathilda* by Alison Jones Nassar and Fred Strickert, so I get the gist but miss some of the humour. Echlas tells me that the VIPs in the front row are relatives of some of the men exiled or killed in the siege and I can see so many people are moved as the play unfolds. It is a powerful piece of theatre and even without understanding the language I am completely absorbed in the actors and the horror of the event. To see *The Siege* in Bethlehem is a truly special experience and one I will never forget.

Saturday

I feel restless but do not really want to do anything or go anywhere in particular. The new American student does not turn up for her lesson at 10am, after we have got up specially, and I am all ready to go out and get milk and cigarettes for Echlas. I keep fiddling with my case, packing then discarding more clothes. I should have brought the minimum with me but easy to say with hindsight. Echlas calls Mohammed to allow me to go to Majde's shop again to change a skirt and while I am there I buy three pairs of 'crazy' trousers (the Aladdin type). I must be crazy when I am discarding clothes and worrying about case capacity.

We go out at 2pm to Bethlehem University market and it is so warm, almost hot for me. There are lots of stalls selling different sorts of food, homewares, gifts, books, toys both inside and out in the grounds. Loud music is playing, encouraging a carnival atmosphere and there are so many people. We have an ice cream and I buy four doughnuts for later. The American girl is supposed to come at 5pm, rearranged from the morning but again she lets Echlas down. We talk with Veronica for a while, then Amia comes and the gas runs out and we have no spare cylinder. Veronica and I leave Amia and Echlas to sort out the gas and go to AIC. The talk is given by a young man, who I remember sharing a taxi with on that awful night. His name is Ghassan Al Azza, so a relative of Echlas', and he lives in the camp. He was a political prisoner for eighteen months, imprisoned at sixteen. While he was there he made wonderful pictures of revolutionaries, using brown paper, sugar sacks or X-ray folders employing a technique involving a smoking candle which he demonstrates to us. When I discover they are for sale I just have to buy one – another thing to fit in my case. Munjad and Ahmed are there so we talk to them afterwards and Munjad is telling me who all the portraits are of; most of them I have never heard of but all are well known to Palestinians.

Thank goodness the gas is on when we get back. In desperation Amia had to go to Aida camp to fetch her car and borrow a gas cylinder from a relative as the gas company was not answering its phone. Having had no dinner, I make two pieces of toast with cheese, followed by a Twirl as I could not face stuffed aubergines at 11pm.

Sunday

My last full day here. It does not seem possible that I am going home tomorrow. I have no idea what we are doing today and Echlas is still uncertain about her plan to go to Hebron tomorrow. I feel anxious about the timing of everything as it is essential that I am outside the Jerusalem Hotel by 11.30am, by my estimation, to get the *sherut* I have yet to book, to take me to the airport in time for my flight. I know how long it takes to get Echlas into the taxi and she has not arranged for anyone to help yet, except Layan, but we need three people. Layan comes to bath Echlas so she will be clean for her stay in Hebron then we go out to get some sun.

As we negotiate around the deeper holes in the road, a woman from the camp approaches Echlas and says something to her, provoking a startled reaction. Almost immediately we see Mohammed's mum and Echlas stops her and they speak in a conspiratorial and anxious way but of course I cannot understand what they are talking about. Echlas looks worried and I ask her what is the matter but she says she will tell me when we get to the bus station restaurant. We take the shortest but not usually the quickest way through the *souk* but surprisingly it is quieter and easier for Echlas today. The American girl calls and Echlas arranges to meet her outside the bus station to collect the money she owes Echlas. She is not there when we arrive so we go straight up to the restaurant and then try to call her but there is a problem with Echlas' phone so I fiddle about trying to change SIM cards and batteries around and getting confused and slightly irritable as I am hot and thirsty and the waiter is extremely slow. Finally, I go back down to look for the girl but there is no sight of her. Echlas is quiet after this, I think because she needs the money and this girl is always letting her down.

We slowly make our way back home as there is nowhere else to go and it is hot. We sit around for a while indoors in the cool until Echlas decides she wants to go to bed. Luckily Amia arrives so helps me and is a distraction for Echlas, and then Veronica and Deanna come back and are busy in the kitchen. I hope they are making something for us as Echlas has not mentioned food. I try to cram more into my case and rearrange things to make more room but have to give up when even my rucksack is full to bursting.

Deanna has been busy making a Lebanese dessert with cornflour, milk, rosewater and orange – very kind of her but milk puddings are not my favourite thing. I eat as much as I can to avoid offending her. We all sit in Echlas' room and chat and I take some photos, then a friend of Deanna's arrives. She comes straight into Echlas' room, flings herself onto my bed and complains aggressively about the behaviour of the taxi driver, who, in her opinion, had tried to charge her too much. She is very rude and loud but Deanna senses her behaviour is not appropriate and takes her out for a walk to calm down. We carry on talking till about 11pm, when I go to have a shower and when I come out, there is Ramallah sister. What a surprise. My first thought, selfishly, is, *Great, I will be able to sleep in 'my' bed for the last time.* My second is, *Why has she come and at this late hour?*

My question is soon answered. The reason for Echlas' change of mood earlier and which we never did discuss was because the woman who spoke to her told her that her brother is seriously ill and not expected to live. I knew there was another brother somewhere but understood they were estranged as Echlas never spoke about him. Astonishingly he lives upstairs! Well, this is a real shock. Part of Echlas' house has another floor but I had never thought who lived there as the houses in the camp are a jumble of added storeys. I did know that a man lives in the basement as he comes to pay rent to Echlas every month.

I cannot quite comprehend that this brother lives upstairs with his wife and children and yet I had not known in the three months that I have lived here. Echlas explains that his wife refuses to let him or their children have anything to do with the Al Azza family and they have not spoken for seven years. The brother is not in good health and the last time he was in hospital the wife refused to let any of the sisters see him. Now he is seriously ill in Beit Jala hospital and expected to die at any time hence Ramallah sister's visit. She always appears at times of death. The custom is for mourners to gather after the death, females in the house and males elsewhere, but as the wife will not let the family into her house Echlas and her sister are thinking they will have to open up this house for female mourners, so Echlas should not go to Hebron, or at least not yet.

I wonder where this leaves Veronica and Deanna as they have been informed, rather at the last minute, that they cannot stay in the house while Echlas is away. Now it appears she is staying so can they stay? Nothing is decided so I still do not know what the morning arrangements are and even whether Echlas has called Mohammed to take her to Hebron. After several anxious phone calls to the *sherut* company they tell me I have to be outside the Jerusalem hotel at 10.45am, earlier than I had anticipated.

I go to bed and sleep fitfully, worrying about tomorrow, and get up early at 7.15am so I can at least get myself ready before helping to dress Echlas and get her up. I am surprised to see her already sitting up, helped by sister, and relieved to hear that she has decided not to go to Hebron this morning, so I can leave knowing she has Ramallah sister to sort out any future plans. Layan is coming to help get Echlas into the taxi, not yet informed of the change of plans, but Mohammed comes to take me to the checkpoint before she arrives so I cannot say goodbye to her. I give Echlas a card and 300IS towards her German trip and after hugs and kisses and tears, I load my luggage into the car and I am off on the first stage of my journey home.

*

Three months seemed a long time when I was at the beginning of it but looking back it has gone so quickly. Being home again took a period of assimilation but I had given myself the summer before making any definite plans for my 'retirement'. As it happened, I had no need to make any plans. My life has been taken over by Palestine and I have never been busier. What with writing this, giving talks about my experience, setting up a local support group, keeping up to date on the situation in Palestine through social media, going on protests and demonstrations, to talks, learning Arabic, reading my library of Palestinian books and becoming more involved with Brighton Palestine Solidarity Campaign, I hardly have time to give to my garden and allotment. I have become much more political thanks to Palestine and my eyes have been opened to the issues that are not reported in the mainstream media.

I feel I owe it to Echlas, her family and all the wonderful people I met during my stay, to fight their cause to the best of my ability, as without international solidarity their voice will not be heard. Sometimes I am so angry about what is happening daily to the Palestinians and feel frustrated that world governments are either oblivious or uncaring about the ongoing ethnic cleansing of a population that has been wronged, principally by the UK, the US and the EU. One day I believe that the ordinary people of the world, who recognise the severe injustice done to the Palestinians, will win against the imperialist, colonialist powers whose strategy it is to eradicate a people for their own ends. I pray that it will not come too late for the survival of Palestine.

RECIPES

These are some of the recipes I used but amounts are not necessarily accurate and a lot was guesswork so they are more for information than to follow to make the dishes. However, you can try but please do not blame me if they do not turn out as expected.

VEGETAGABLE MAKLUBA

This is enough for five people
3 cups of rice
4 ½ cups of water
2 stock cubes
2 carrots
1 large aubergine
1 cauliflower
2 sliced potatoes
8 garlic cloves
Ginger
Makluba spices -2 tablespoons of mixed cumin, turmeric, paprika, cardamom
Soak the rice first in some water. Oil the sides of a large saucepan and fry all the vegetables lightly in some oil in it. Put them aside.
Lightly fry the whole garlic cloves and some ginger, then add the veg and make flat.
Strain the rice and put on top. DO NOT STIR.
Add 2 stock cubes and the spices to the measured water and pour over the rice. DO NOT STIR. Bring to the boil, then simmer gently with the lid on until cooked.
Turn out like a cake onto a plate. This will take two people.
Serve with salads.

LENTIL SOUP

This recipe needs a pressure cooker, although it could be cooked in a saucepan but will take longer.
1 cup of orange lentils washed
A large onion, cut up small
Salt
Ginger
1 sliced carrot
1 sliced courgette
1 or 2 potatoes cut up
Fry the onion with the ginger, add the veg, fry lightly.
Add the lentils, a large spoon of cumin and enough water to cover and cook in pressure cooker for 15 minutes.

Mujudera
2 cups of green lentils
4 cups of rice
1 onion
Salt and pepper
Cumin
1 cup of olive oil
4 onions to caramelise
Cook lentils until soft. Drain and keep water. Add the rice.
Fry the onion in some oil until soft. Mix the lentils and onion, add the rice and lentil water. For each cup of rice add 2 of lentil water or plain water if not enough. Add cumin and seasoning. Leave to simmer.
Slice the 4 onions and fry in oil slowly until dark brown and caramelised and serve on top of rice and lentil mix.
Serve with salads and yoghurt.

BROAD BEANS

This is excellent for using the whole bean but they need to be not too old and tough.

Approximately 1 kilo of broad beans

1 onion

Cumin

Salt and pepper

1 stock cube

Turmeric

½ cup of rice

Laban

Cut up washed beans and fry lightly. Add the chopped onion.

Add spices and fry for a few minutes.

Add the rice then the water to cover

Add the turmeric

When the beans are soft and the rice nearly cooked stir in the Laban.

CAULIFLOWER AND RICE

1 cauliflower broken into florets

1 onion

7 cloves of garlic

2 cups of rice

1 stock cube

Laban

 turmeric

Salt and pepper

Lightly fry the onion and 5 garlic cloves in oil. Add the cauliflower and cook for a bit.

Add 2 cups of Laban, 1 cup of water and the stock cube.

Cook the rice in 3 cups of water with salt, a little turmeric and 2 cloves of garlic.

GREEN BEANS WITH RICE

2 onions
4 cloves garlic
Mixed spices
Large tomato
Tomato puree
Green beans
Fry onion and garlic in saucepan with the spices and salt
Add the green beans.
Put the tomato, puree and stock cube in a liquidizer with water and whizz up.
Add to the green bean mix and simmer until cooked.
Cook the rice.

MAFTOUL WITH CHICKEN

1 whole chicken, cut up into segments.
Maftoul
Onions
Garlic
Courgettes
Tomatoes
Tomato puree
Sumac
Spices
Stock cube
Chick peas
In a saucepan fry the onion and add 3 chopped courgettes and water and boil.
In a blender put 3 large chopped tomatoes, diced onion, garlic cloves, 1 tsp of chill sauce or a fresh chilli, water and a stock cube and the water from the courgettes. Blend. Pour back into the courgettes and simmer.
Fry more onion and garlic in a large pot, add chicken and fry until

brown. Add water to cover and season. Cook chicken and put aside. Steam the Maftoul over the remaining water. After about half an hour add some garlic cloves and chickpeas and stir.

Sprinkle the chicken with sumac, cover and put in oven to reheat. Serve the chicken on the maftoul and pour over the sauce.

SALADS

Red cabbage shredded with mayonnaise
White cabbage and carrots, with white vinegar and oil
Tomatoes with parsley, cucumber, spring onion, diced small with lemon and salt.
Parsley with tahini and lemon juice mixed, Add yogurt and season

BABA GANOUSH

A few aubergines depending how much you want to make.
Garlic cloves
Lemon
Tahini
Olive oil

Preferably grill the aubergines or roast in oven until soft, about 20 mins.
Scoop out the flesh, mix with crushed garlic, lemon juice, tahini, olive.
oil and pepper or whizz the lot in a blender.
Serve with Pitta bread.